T0361899

European Works Councils

European Works Councils were established just over a decade ago as the first transnational industrial relations institutions at company level. They have had a major impact on governments, employers, employees and trade unions as well as being the subject of intense academic scrutiny and debate. This edited collection draws from each of these sources with contributions from leading academics, senior trade unionists and employers.

The book is organised around four distinctive themes. The first introduces European Works Councils and provides overviews that will inform the understanding of both newcomers to the subject and specialists. The second part of the book focuses on an assessment of the European Directive 'in action' with contributions from European employers and trade union representatives. The third part, focuses on the experience of managers and trade unionists in facing the problems and possibilities involved in running a European Works Council. The final section takes us into the future of European Works Councils in a globalised economy. Published at a time of a major review of the European Directive this book provides a unique review of developments from the perspectives of both practitioners and academics.

With case studies, theoretical overviews, data analysis and contrasting opinions, this book will be essential reading for advanced students and researchers of Business and Management Studies, Industrial Relations and Employee Relations.

Ian Fitzgerald is a senior researcher in the Sustainable Cities Research Institute at Northumbria University. His general research interest has been workplace industrial relations. He has published in the areas of quality management, the fire service, European Works Councils and Higher Education.

John Stirling is Director of the Work and Employment Research Centre at Northumbria University. He has research interests in trade unions in general and trade union education in particular. He is co-editor of *Trade Union Education in Europe* (2000) and has published widely on European Works Councils.

Routledge Research in Employment Relations

Series editors: Rick Delbridge and Edmund Heery
Cardiff Business School

Aspects of the employment relationship are central to numerous courses at both undergraduate and postgraduate level.

Drawing from insights from industrial relations, human resource management and industrial sociology, this series provides an alternative source of research-based materials and texts, reviewing key developments in employment research.

Books published in this series are works of high academic merit, drawn from a wide range of academic studies in the social sciences.

Also available from Routledge:

Rethinking Industrial Relations
Mobilisation, collectivism and long waves
John Kelly

Employee Relations in the Public Services
Themes and issues
Edited by Susan Corby and Geoff White

The Insecure Workforce
Edited by Edmund Heery and John Salmon

Public Service Employment Relations in Europe
Transformation, modernisation or inertia?
*Edited by Stephen Bach, Lorenzo Bordogna, Giuseppe Della Rocca
and David Winchester*

Reward Management
A critical text
Edited by Geoff White and Janet Druker

Working for McDonald's in Europe
The unequal struggle?
Tony Royle

Job Insecurity and Work Intensification
Edited by Brendan Burchell, David Ladipo and Frank Wilkinson

Union Organizing
Campaigning for trade union recognition
Edited by Gregor Gall

European Works Councils

Pessimism of the intellect,
optimism of the will?

**Edited by
Ian Fitzgerald and John Stirling**

 Routledge
Taylor & Francis Group

LONDON AND NEW YORK

First published 2004
by Routledge
2 Park Square, Milton Park, Abingdon, Oxon, OX14 4RN

Simultaneously published in the USA and Canada
by Routledge
270 Madison Ave, New York NY 10016

Routledge is an imprint of the Taylor & Francis Group

Transferred to Digital Printing 2008

Typeset in Baskerville by
Newgen Imaging Systems (P) Ltd, Chennai, India

British Library Cataloguing in Publication Data
A catalogue record for this book is available
from the British Library

Library of Congress Cataloging in Publication Data
A catalog record for this book has been requested

ISBN 0–415–30986–7

Contents

Illustrations

Contributors

Rachel Annand was an International Officer from 1989 to 2001 in Britain's largest public sector union, UNISON, She now works part-time as a senior lecturer at Oxford Brookes University. Rachel has an M.Phil in Social Work and an MA in European Industrial Relations and Human Resource Management. Her main research interests lie in the field of European and world-level trade union organisation.

Willy Buschak is Confederal Secretary of the European Trade Union Confederation (ETUC). Before joining the ETUC he worked in the central administration of the German trade union NGG (Food, Beverage and Restaurant workers). He studied history in Bochum and has many publications on the history of the international labour movement.

Ian Fitzgerald is a Senior Researcher in the Sustainable Cities Research Institute at Northumbria University. After returning to academia in later life, his general research interest has been workplace industrial relations. Recently, he has been working on numerous projects that focus on Higher Education including university engagement with the wider economy, student employability and work-related learning. He has published in the areas of quality management, the fire service, European Works Councils and Higher Education.

Mark Gilman is a Lecturer in Industrial Relations and Human Resource Management at the Canterbury Business School, University of Kent at Canterbury. He has researched and published in the areas of the regulation of labour and pay and European industrial relations.

Richard Hume-Rothery is Director of the European Study group of leading multinationals. He specialises in human resource management with a particular emphasis on international personal taxation. He worked for twelve years with de Beers Consolidated Mines in Italy, Thailand, Malaysia, Mauritania, South Africa and Botswana. He launched The International Employer Ltd and its subsidiary TIE Systems Ltd both of which became part of Sedgwick Group plc.

Paul Knutsen is Professor of Contemporary History at Lillehammer University in Norway. He has particular research interests in modern Norwegian history, contemporary European history and problems in the theory of history. His publications include *Korporatisme og klassekamp* (1994) *Pengar, stäl og poitikk* (1998), a problematical introduction to the history of the European Union and *Analytisk narrasjon* (2002), an introduction to theories and fundamental problems of history.

Paul Marginson is Professor of Industrial Relations and Director of the Industrial Relations Research Unit at the University of Warwick. He has researched and published extensively on employment relations in multinational companies and the Europeanisation of industrial relations. His research on European Works Councils includes major studies of the agreements establishing them and their impact in practice.

Miguel Martinez Lucio is Reader in Industrial Relations at Durham University. He has published extensively on trade union change and new forms of worker representation. He has worked with Syd Weston on union responses to new forms of organisational change. More recently he has researched partnership and the emergence of micro-corporatism within industrial relations. He has also published on the State's new role within the regulation of economic relations.

Antonia S. McAlindin is a Barrister and Employment Law Adviser to Scottish and Newcastle. She is a companion of the CIPD, a member of its employment relations panel and also a member of the CBI employment law and employee resourcing panels as well as an Employment Tribunal member. She has extensive practical experience of employee relations and lectures regularly on employment law to a range of organisations including universities and professional bodies.

Doug Miller is on secondment to the International Textile, Garment and Leather Workers Federation from Northumbria University where he is a Senior Lecturer. He is currently multinationals co-ordinator with the Federation and has previously published widely on international trade unionism and European Works Councils. He has been a trainer and consultant for the TUC in the UK and for other trade union organisations in Europe and beyond.

Satoshi Nakano is Associate Professor in the Department of Management and Information Science at Toyohashi Sozo College where he teaches modern European economic and social history. He has written extensively about industrial relations and corporatism in Europe and his recent publications include *EU Shakai eisaku to Shijo keizai* (Sodosha, Tokyo): social policy and the market economy – information, consultation and participation in European companies.

John Stirling is Director of the Work and Employment Research Centre at Northumbria University. He has research interests in trade unions in general and trade union education in particular. He is the editor (with Jeff Bridgford) of a study of *Trade Union Education in Europe* (2000) and has published widely on

European Works Councils as well as running training programmes in Europe, Africa and the USA.

Sjef Stoop is an Advisor and Trainer for the European Works Council service of FNV Formaat in the Netherlands. Since completing his doctoral thesis he has had a longstanding research interest in European Works Councils. He has worked with the Deutscher Gewerkschaftsbund, International Labour Organisation, European Trade Union Institute and the European Trade Union College and was responsible for the FNV project on European Works Councils published as *The European Works Council: One Step Forward*.

Barbara Tully is Principal Lecturer at the English Language Centre at Northumbria University. For the last ten years she has taught English as an international language both in the UK and Europe. She has worked extensively as a consultant and trainer for European Works Councils and for the European Trade Union College. She has published teaching material and journal articles and is currently researching issues of language and intercultural communications.

Syd Weston is Reader in Industrial Relations at Sunderland University Business School. His research interests encompass European integration, multinational company strategy and cross-border trade union activities. His current research is concerned with the rise of large logistic organisations, their contractual relationships with companies and how they impact on the employment relationship. He is particularly interested in the growth of labour supply companies and their relationship with trade unions.

Jane Wills is Reader in Geography at Queen Mary, University of London. She is co-editor of *Antipode*, and a convenor of the London Union Research Network. Her publications include *Union Retreat and the Regions* (with Ron Martin and Peter Sunley 1996), *Geographies of Economies* (edited with Roger Lee 1997) *Dissident Geographies* (with Alison Blunt 2000), *Place, Space and the New Labour Internationalism* (edited with Peter Waterman 2001) and *Union Futures* (Fabian Society 2002).

Acknowledgements

The following chapters have been published before and we would like to thank the authors and publishers concerned for allowing us to use them again in this edited text.

Chapter 2 – Paul Knutsen is a revised and updated version of the 1997 article 'Corporatist Tendencies in the Euro-Polity', which first appeared in *Economic and Industrial Democracy*, 18(2): 289–323, published by Sage Publication Ltd.

Chapter 6 – Richard Hume-Rothery, 'Implementing the Directive: a view from UK business', appears here with kind permission of European Study Group Limited, © European Study Group Limited.

Chapter 7 – Mark Gilman and Paul Marginson first appeared in 2002 as 'Negotiating European Works Councils: Contours of Constrained Choice', in the *Industrial Relations Journal*, 33(1): 36–51, and appears here with kind permission of Blackwell Publishing Ltd.

Chapter 9 – Satoshi Nakano is a substantially modified version of 'EWCs and the Multinational Companies', which appeared in Satoshi Nakano (2002) *EU Social Policy and the Market Economy*, pp. 276–300. Published by Soudosha Publishing Company Ltd.

Chapter 14 – Jane Wills appeared as 'Bargaining for the Space to Organize in the Global Economy: A Review of the Accor–IUF Trade Union Rights Agreement', in the *Review of International Political Economy*, 9(4): 675–700. Published by the Taylor and Francis Group and is reproduced here with permission, journal details can be found at http://www.tandf.co.uk/

1 Introduction

Employee participation in Europe

Ian Fitzgerald

Employee participation at a European level became a reality with the introduction of the European Works Council Directive (94/45/EC); with the potential to expand in scope with the proposals for employee involvement contained in the Supplement (2001/86/EC) to the European Company Statute (2157/2001/EC); and develop at a national level with the universal introduction of national structures of information and consultation (Information and Consultation Directive 2002/14/EC; see EIRR 339/2002 and TUC 2002 for further details). Given this, the current book offers a timely collection of essays on the first European level attempt at employee participation, the European Works Council (EWC).

It has been estimated that the EWC Directive covers 1,865 companies who provide around 10 per cent (17.1 million) of the European economic areas (EEA) employees, of which: approximately five million are in Germany; four million in the UK; and three million in France (Kerckhofs 2002: 34). Of these companies only around 639 have so far reached agreement on the establishment of a total of 739 EWCs, and Kerckhofs (2002) argues that at the current rate of progress 'it will be another 20 years before all covered companies have European worker representation bodies' (ibid.: 46). Nevertheless, drawing on our title this book concerns itself with the 'optimism of the will' rather than the 'pessimism of the intellect', however well informed. Following this introduction the book is divided into four main parts; the first has three chapters that provide a series of approaches to understanding the historical development of the Directive, the shape and structure of EWCs and the changing nature of solidarity within an EWC context. Part II's first two chapters are concerned with the proposed review of the EWC Directive, offering contrasting trade union/employer views of what a review should contain, with the third moving from a discussion of the Directive to a consideration of the main factors that influence the choice of management and employee representatives when negotiating EWC agreements. Part III has four chapters on the EWC experience, including three case studies, providing management and trade union perspectives. The final part has three chapters, which in many ways are optimistic in their focus on extending EWCs beyond Europe. Particularly at a time when some are concerned that they are struggling to engage with national structures (see Chapter 3 by Miguel Martinez Lucio and Syd Weston). The remainder of this introduction gives a brief account of the prior attempts at European-level employee participation and concludes with a summary of the EWC Directive.

Employee participation at a European level

Prior to the EWC Directive there were three main attempts to 'harmonise' employee participation at a European level through drafts of the Fifth Directive, the Vredeling Directive, and the European Company Statute (ECS) Directive. The debate around these drafts can be identified within two periods of European Community/Union policy (Müller and Hoffmann 2001: 12). The first is the 1970s to early 1980s and includes the early drafts of all the above directives. It was a period of 'rigid' employee participation proposals, offering little employer choice in the type of representative structures or the information and consultation that was to be provided. When it is considered that this was combined with the then Member State veto it is perhaps not surprising that early drafts of employee participation failed not only because of business interests but also because of Member States' defence of their national industrial relations systems. The second period begins in 1983 and is characterised by choice in both representative systems and the type of information and consultation that was to be provided. Significantly, it also covers the period of the Social Protocol agreed at Maastricht with the issue of veto being circumvented by the newly adopted route of subsidiarity. This allowed the British Government to opt-out of the Maastricht Social Chapter and consequently the EWC Directive. Member States had been given an increased flexibility over European labour law to allow the social side of the single market to begin to come into force.

The Fifth Directive

The Fifth Directive on the Structure of Public Limited Companies (1972/1983/ 1990/1991) is part of a series of company law based Directives whose aim was to harmonise the national company law of Member States. The drafts after 1972 included proposals for employee participation in public limited companies of over 1,000 employees, similar to the EWC Directive. It was proposed that this would occur through employee representatives receiving information and consultation on such matters as: 'the closure or transfer of all or part of the company; substantial extension or reduction in the activities of the company; important organisational changes; and the establishment of long-term cooperation with other firms' (Europa 2001a).

Representatives were to participate in one of four main types of structure; (1) on the supervisory board of a two-tier board system (2) as supervisory non-executive members on a one-tier board (3) on an employee only works council (4) through an appropriate representative collective agreement structure. Proposals (1) and (2) contained one-third to a half employee representatives at a board level, whilst in (3) and (4) representatives had information and consultation rights equivalent to those available at a board level.

The main changes in the proposals after 1972 were a rise in the company threshold for activation of the Directive from 500 to 1,000 employees and an increased choice of participation systems from the original two-tier board system. Although, even after these and a number of other amendments it still reached an impasse in the European Parliament. The European Union (EU) views the failure of the Fifth Directive as a difficultly in reconciling the 'fundamental differences between Member States' traditions in the company law field' (Europa 2001b). It goes on to state that the legislation itself 'leads to the adoption of extremely detailed and stringent rules' (ibid.) and that with growing world competition there is a need to impose minimum constraints on European firms. Focusing on these issues from a different perspective Streeck (1997) views the main reason for rejection as being the Directives' 'linkage to the issue of industrial citizenship'. He goes on to argue that 'the political costs of changing...national systems of corporate governance in a German direction loomed ever larger [whilst employers were opposed] to any Community social policy that went beyond non-binding general principles'.

The Vredeling Directive

The Vredeling Directive (1980/1983), championed by the Dutch socialist Henk Vredeling, dealt exclusively with employee participation and signalled a shift away from company to labour law. It was encouraged by the increasing momentum of the 1974 Social Action Programme, which had assisted the passage of two Directives increasing employee information and consultation (the Collective Redundancies Directive adopted in 1975 and the Transfer of Undertakings Directive adopted in 1977). The 1983 version of the Vredeling Directive covered all firms with at least 1,000 employees in the EU. This was a wide-ranging proposal covering companies with employees in a single Member State and, as with the EWC Directive, making 'provisions for companies controlled from outside the EU' (EIRR 207/1991: 23). It proposed that existing employee representatives (not those on company boards) should receive annual information on a company's activity in the areas of: 'structure; economic and financial situation; probable development of business, production and sales; employment situation and probable trends; and investment prospects' (ibid.: 26). As well as consultation on proposals that were likely to have 'serious consequences' for employees. The areas covered ranged from restructuring at the workplace through to closures and transfers.

The main changes in the 1983 version of the Vredeling Directive compared to its 1980 original were a substantial rise in the company threshold level from 100 to 1,000 employees and a reduction in the content and regularity of information. The Directive met with what Streeck (1997) describes as 'unprecedented hostility from business', which came from both European and foreign firms (DeVos 1989; Shackleton 1996). The British Conservative government of the time was also strongly opposed, arguing amongst other things that it would 'disrupt existing good industrial relations practices' (quoted in Shackleton 1996: 16) and be inappropriate because of 'the UK's relatively high share of Community inward investment' (ibid.: 16).

With Member State veto and strong business opposition the Directive stalled in Council.

The European Company Statute

The European Company Statute (1970/1975/1989/1991/adopted 2157/ 2001/EC) was proposed in parallel with the moves towards national company law harmonisation. It provides a non-compulsory opportunity for EU-based companies to create a European company (Societas Europea (SE)) that is recognised as incorporated in law by all Member States. In common with the other Directives discussed earlier it contains employee participation proposals that were adopted via a second supplementary Directive (2002/86/EC), which the SE must follow. The creation of two separate but interrelated Directives followed amendments in 1989 to circumvent unanimous voting by splitting the original Directive into two. Although this tactic was not initially successful with concerted opposition from Member States, particularly over the issue of employee participation (Europa 2001b).

   There are four types of SE (2157/2001/EC), the first three are formed through either, *merger* or formation of a *holding* or *subsidiary* company by two companies from different Member States. The fourth is formed through a *transformation* of a single Member State company that has had a subsidiary governed by another Member State's law for at least two years (Article 2 para. 1–4).

   This combined with existing Member States 'rules and practices', and the Directives negotiated progress leads to detailed and complex supplementary Directive rules (see EIRR 336/2002). Although, the spirit of the supplementary Directive is that 'information and consultation procedures at transnational level should nevertheless be ensured in all cases of creation of an SE' (Whereas para. 6). The main routes for employee involvement are through either a newly established representative body or information and consultation procedures. There is also scope for board-level participation depending on negotiations and/or if this is applied in participant companies prior to SE formation. The Annex to the Directive lays out the main areas of information and consultation for the representative body. It is proposed that this body should meet with 'the competent organ of the SE' (Annex part 2b) on at least an annual basis, as does the Annex (para. 2) to the EWC Directive. The issues proposed for discussion in the Annex (part 2b and c) range from the state of the business financially, through its likely business development and changes in production processes, to probable mergers or cutbacks and closures of plants. There is also provision for special circumstance meetings: for example in the case of closures, relocations, etc. The terms and conditions of involvement are negotiated for employees through a proportionally elected special negotiating body (SNB), again found in the EWC Directive. Although, Article 3 para. 6 states that the SNB can decide 'not to open negotiations or to terminate negotiations … and to rely on the rules on information and consultation of employees in force in the Member States where the SE has employees'.

This final supplementary Directive differs in a number of ways from its 1975 and 1989 predecessors. The 1975 draft proposed a far-reaching process of co-determination through an EWC and employee representatives acting as full board Members. By 1989, the emphasis had moved from co-determination through an EWC to information and consultation through four main routes, including board Membership or an employee only company-level representative body (EIRR 207/1991). Streeck (1997) argues that the 1975 draft Directive was the closest 'the community came to a wholesale adoption of the "German model"' and notes Eser's (1994) supposition that the 1989 version of employee participation was 'an instrument of stable labor relations contributing to the success of the firm' (Streeck 1997). Keller (2002: 442) positions the ECS firmly within the national principle of subsidiarity, arguing that it will only make a minor contribution to 'co-operative' rather than 'adversarial' or 'conflictual' industrial relations. In sum, he argues that 'the power relationship that has led to the existence of "management prerogatives" in national contexts will not be seriously challenged by SEs. In other words, strict new models for social partnership and "co-decision-making" or "joint regulation" of strategically important company affairs are not provided' (ibid.: 442). As with the EWC Directive only time will tell its real contribution to greater employee influence through information and consultation.

The European Works Council Directive

The EWC Directive was adopted as part of the Social Chapter but was seen by some as a 'watered-down' or 'toothless' Vredeling (reported in EIRR 207/1991: 27) that was 'extremely modest in its ambitions' (Streeck 1997) compared to earlier employee participation directives. However, aside from these arguments that separate it from the more robust attempts at European employee participation it still displays a number of general similarities to them and perhaps not surprisingly, particularly to those draft Directives from 1983 onwards. For example, with regard to the Directives' general rather than specific information and consultation requirements.

In fact, the Directive comes closest to the 1983 draft Vredeling Directive with its emphasis: on firms of 1,000 employees and over; the fall-back minimum requirements for existing representatives to be informed and consulted; the emphasis on annual information and consultation; and the subject areas to be informed and consulted on. Although, the recently adopted ECS Directive does have similarities, it is more notable for its differences that 'may provide a pointer towards the changes which the Commission is planning to propose to the EWCs Directive' (EIRR 336/2002: 21). For example, it explicitly allows Member States to transpose into law a right for trade union representatives, who do not have to be employed by the SE, to be members of the negotiating body (the SNB). It further offers an opportunity for peak union organisations (e.g. the ETUC) to be present as 'experts' when negotiations take place. It also defines the term 'information' and places a stronger emphasis on 'consultation' such that 'employees' representatives ... opinion on measures ... may be taken into account in the decision-making process'

(EIRR 336/2002: 22; see Chapter 5 by Willy Buschak for an ETUC view on the Directive's weak information and consultation procedures). Finally, it provides for greater scope for representative bodies to negotiate with SEs at times of 'exceptional circumstances' (i.e. closures etc.).

Interestingly, the ECS takes priority over the EWC Directive when companies opt for SE status, Weiss (2001, quoted in Keller 2002: 437) has suggested that this 'may lead in the long run to a significant reduction of the scope of application of the Directive on European Works Councils' (ibid.: 9). Although he goes on to note that this 'will not mean a reduction of information and consultation in functional terms' (ibid.: 9).

The following provides a brief summary of the EWC Directive, adopted in 1994 and then transposed into Member State national law, it covers these and other countries within the EEA, such as Norway. It contains three sections of 16 Articles and an Annex (full text of the Directive is available online at Europa – Europa 1994).

Section 1 – general

Section 1 contains three Articles covering the Directive's objectives and definitions. Article 1 states that the objective of the Directive is 'to improve the right to information and to consultation' (para.1) for employees in Community-scale undertakings. This is to be achieved through either an EWC or a procedure for informing and consulting (where appropriate the Directive uses these joint terms throughout but for ease of reference only EWC is used here) which is established at group level (subject to Article 6). The scope of an EWC is 'all the establishments (or a Community-scale group of undertakings) located within the Member States' (subject to Article 6 wider participation) (para. 4).

Articles 2 and 3 detail the Directives' definitions, which start with an identification of the 'triggers' necessary to activate negotiations for an EWC. Article 2 (para.1a) states that a community undertaking, or groups of undertakings (controlled by a controlling undertaking) must have 'at least 1000 employees within Member States and . . . 150 employees in each of . . . two Member States' (para.1a) for the Directive to apply.

The main parties conducting negotiations are employees' representatives 'provided for by national law and/or practice' (para.1d) and central management 'in the Community-scale undertaking or . . . the controlling undertaking' of a group of undertakings (para.1e). The body convened to conduct these negotiations for employees is an SNB established 'in accordance with Article 5 (para. 2)' (para. 1h).

Article 3 concerns itself with defining a 'controlling undertaking' that is 'an undertaking which can exercise a dominant influence over another undertaking' (para. 1). It lists a number of criteria for this including: holding a majority of subscribed capital (para. 2a); controlling a majority of issued share capital votes (para. 2b); appointing more than half the members of an 'undertaking's administrative, management or supervisory body' (para. 1c). It also notes in para. 6 and 7 that the law applicable to determining whether an undertaking is a 'controlling undertaking' is the Member State law in which it resides.

Section 2 – establishment of a European Works Council or an employee information and consultation procedure

This section contains Articles 4–7 detailing the responsibilities of central management, Member States and employees' representatives. Article 4 lays the responsibility of creating 'the conditions and means necessary for the setting up of an EWC...' on an undertakings central management (para. 1), or its representative in a Member State (para. 2).

Article 5 lays out the procedures regarding an SNB; it opens by stating that the responsibility for initiating EWC negotiations is either central managements' 'or at the written request of at least 100 employees or their representatives in at least two undertakings or establishments in at least two different Member States' (para. 1). Membership of the SNB should be a minimum of three and maximum of 17 (para. 2b – increased to 18 because of the UK opt-in in 1997), with representatives elected in accordance with an appropriate method determined by Member States. Each undertaking in a Member State must be represented by a member of the SNB with 'supplementary members' for those undertakings with higher numbers of employees (para. 2c).

The Article further states that an SNB can be assisted by experts of their choice (para. 4). But the SNB can also decide by at least a two-thirds vote either 'not to open negotiations in accordance with para. 4 or terminate the negotiations already opened'. Where this occurs all procedures to conclude an agreement are stopped and a re-convention of the SNB will be 'at the earliest two years after the above mentioned decision unless the parties concerned lay down a shorter period' (para. 5).

The Article also states that 'any expenses relating to the negotiations referred to in para. 3 and 4 shall be borne by central management' (para. 6), although, it allows Member Sates to 'lay down budgetary rules' for the SNB which 'may in particular limit the funding to cover one expert only' (para. 6).

Article 6 lays down that an agreement reached under the Directive should determine:

- the undertakings covered by the agreement (para. 2a);
- the EWCs allocation of seats, number of members and their term of office (para. 2b);
- the functions and procedure for information and consultation of the EWC (para. 2c);
- the frequency, duration and venue of EWC meetings (para. 2d);
- the financial and material resources allocated to the EWC (para. 2e);
- the duration of the agreement and the procedure for its renegotiation (para. 2f).

The Article also states that central management and the SNB can agree 'to establish one or more information and consultation procedures instead of a European Works Council' (para. 3). Any agreement made under the terms of para. 2 or 3 is not subject to the subsidiary requirements of the Annex, unless it states otherwise. The final para. 5 requires that when concluding an agreement the SNB acts by a majority vote of its members.

Article 7 lays down that the subsidiary requirements for an agreement based on the provisions in the Annexe are laid down in legislation of the Member State in which the central management is situated (para.1). These requirements come into force if:

- central management and the SNB decide that they should;
- central management refuses to commence negotiations within six months of the request referred to in Article 5 (para.1);
- an Article 6 agreement is not reached after three years from the date of the request and the SNB has not taken a decision as provided for in Article 5 (para. 5).

Section 3 – miscellaneous provisions

This section begins with Article 8, which deals with confidential information. It makes it the responsibility of Member States to 'provide' that members of SNBs or EWCs and any experts 'are not authorised to reveal any information which has expressly been provided to them in confidence' (para.1). Central management are also given the right not to pass on information that 'according to objective criteria … would seriously harm the functioning of the undertaking'.

Article 9 emphasises that central management and employee representatives should work together 'in a spirit of cooperation'. It follows this in Article 10 by stating that protection for employees' representatives, whilst undertaking their duties at SNBs or EWC, should be the same as that 'provided for employees' representatives by the national legislation and/or practice in force in their country of employment' (sub-para.1).

Article 11 specifies that Member States are responsible for ensuring that the management of an undertaking covered by the Directive and its employees' representatives or employees 'abide by the obligations laid down by this Directive' (para. 1); that if requested undertakings provide information on the number of employees employed at undertakings (para. 2); that Member States 'shall provide appropriate measures' (para. 3) so that the Directive can be enforced; and that where Member States apply Article 8 (confidential information) there should be provision for 'administrative or judicial appeal procedures'.

Article 12 states that the 'Directive shall apply without prejudice to measures taken pursuant' (para. 1) to Council Directives 75/129/EEC (collective redundancies) and 77/187/EEC (safeguarding employees' rights in the event of transfers of undertakings, businesses or parts of businesses), and to 'employees' existing rights to information and consultation under national law' (para. 2).

Article 13 states that the Directive shall not apply to agreements before 22 September 1996 (Article 14 para. 1), or the date it is transposed into the national law of the Member State concerned if this is earlier and it covers 'the entire workforce, providing for the transnational information and consultation of employees' (para.1). It also specifies that when these agreements expire, the parties can either renew them or have the provisions of the Directive applied.

Article 14 was probably one of the most important at the time as it laid down the final date (22 September 1996) by which Member States had to transpose the Directive into national laws. Article 15 states that by 22 September 1999 the Commission shall conduct a review of the Directive, in conjunction with Member States and management and labour at a European level. It notes in particular that workforce size thresholds will be reviewed. Article 16 simply states that the 'Directive is addressed to the Member States'.

Annex – subsidiary requirements: referred to in Article 7

The Annex specifies the rules that govern an EWC constituted under an Article 7 (subsidiary requirements) agreement. A number of these have already been covered in the Directives' main requirements and relate to an EWCs scope; procedures; and financial expenses. The others state that:

- The EWC shall have a minimum of three members and a maximum of 30 (para.1c). Where size so warrants, it shall elect a select committee of a maximum of three members.
- After four years, the EWC must 'examine whether to open negotiations for the conclusion of the agreement referred to in Article 6 . . . or continue to apply the subsidiary requirements' (para. 1f).
- The EWC shall have the right to meet once a year and be informed and consulted on a report drawn up by central management on the progress of the business. The meeting 'shall relate in particular to the structure, economic and financial situation, the probable development of the business and of production and sales, the situation and probable trend of employment, investments, and substantial changes concerning organisation, introduction of new working methods or production processes, transfers of production, mergers, cut-backs or closures of undertakings, establishments or important parts thereof, and collective redundancies' (para. 2).
- Where there are exceptional circumstances affecting employees (relocations, closures etc.), the select committee or EWC has the right to be informed. It shall have the right to meet with central management or any appropriate level of management to be informed and consulted on these matters. Any members of the EWC directly concerned with any matters have a right to participate in any such meeting. This meeting shall occur as soon as possible on the basis of a report drawn up by central management 'on which an opinion may be delivered at the end of the meeting or within a reasonable time . . . . This meeting shall not affect the prerogatives of the central management' (para. 3).
- The EWC or select committee 'shall be entitled to meet without the management concerned being present' (para. 4).
- The EWC members shall inform the employees' representatives or in their absence the workforce concerned of EWC information and consultation (para. 5).

- The operating costs of the EWC, borne by central management, shall in particular cover '...the costs of organising meetings and arranging for interpretation facilities and accommodation and travelling expenses of members of the EWC and its select committee...unless otherwise agreed' (para. 7).

Conclusion

This chapter has provided a brief introduction to the main attempts at employee participation at a European level, ending with a summary of the successfully adopted EWC Directive. It has detailed the most important issues in each proposal but not dwelt on the debate surrounding these. The opinion here is that each offers only a framework that might, or might not, succeed depending on a complex network of factors, including power, influence and control, and of course one's definition of success. For example, what power will a European Directive have after transposition into national law and submersion in national industrial relations culture? What influence will this have on a multinational company and more importantly its employees and their representatives? How will that alter or influence control at a transnational level?

The remainder of this book begins to explore these questions in the only way possible, through a consideration of the Directive in practice, as EWC agreements are signed and their communication bodies begin to function. In it a number of authors chart the factors that fuse with the EWC Directives' framework influencing the negotiation of agreements and their practice, whilst others question the Directives framework itself. The reader is introduced to the study of the EWC and the discussion surrounding its composition, influence and possible expansion beyond the boundary of Europe.

The chapters in this book each contain within them, either explicitly or implicitly, reference to a continuing debate that can be loosely described as that between the 'optimists' and 'pessimists'. Employers, politicians, trade unions, workers and even academic commentators will offer differing views depending on their own perspectives and, most particularly, their expectations of EWCs. If not much is expected then, perhaps, not much will be achieved and pessimistic commentators on EWCs will be right to judge them as marginal at best and irrelevant at worst. Such a conclusion would confound those who fought for decades to see their vision turned into reality via the European Commission and it is not the conclusion of the authors of the chapters contained here. We present a range of views from employer representatives and individual employers, through 'insiders' dealing with the daily reality of EWCs to 'outside' commentators offering objective appraisals. The chapters in this book share a common view in, now that they are here, at least making EWCs work. That places them in a more optimistic tradition. It is clear that EWCs face major challenges in organisation and practice, that they are challenged in one direction from the pressures of nationalism and in the other by the demands of globalism and that the existence of structure cannot be equated with the practice of action. Nevertheless, as the institution is barely yet a decade old, EWCs are beginning to find a role and develop their particular strengths in ways that will ensure their continued growth and their emergence from what were once described as global outposts representing workers on the periphery (Fitzgerald *et al.* 1999; Stirling and Fitzgerald 2001) to core institutions in an international labour movement.

The following chapters offer a starting point and signpost further reading but hopefully more than this they provide a sustainable collection of essays that can be referenced in the future as EWC history unfolds.

References

DeVos, T. (1989) *Multinational Corporations in Democratic Host Countries: U.S. Multinationals and the Vredeling Proposal*, Aldershot: Dartmouth.

Europa (1994) *Council Directive 94/45/EC*, 22 September 1994, European Union, online. Available HTTP: http://europa.eu.int/comm/employment_social/soc-dial/labour/directive9445/index_en.htm (accessed 30 December 2002).

Europa (2001a) *Structure of Public Limited Companies: Proposal for a Fifth Directive*, European Union, online. Available HTTP: http://europa.eu.int/scadplus/printversion/en/lvb/l26005.htm (accessed 30 December 2002).

Europa (2001b) *Company Law: Introduction*, European Union, online. Available HTTP: http://europa.eu.int/scadplus/leg/en/lvb/l26002.htm (accessed 30 December 2002).

Fitzgerald, I., Miller, D. and Stirling, J. (1999) 'Representing the Global Outpost: European Works Councils in the North East', *Northern Economic Review*, 29: 46–62.

Keller, B. (2002) 'The European Company Statute: Employee Involvement – and Beyond', *Industrial Relations Journal*, 33(5): 424–445.

Kerckhofs, P. (2002) *European Works Councils Facts and Figures*, Brussels: ETUI.

Müller, T. and Hoffmann, A. (2001) *EWC Research: A Review of the Literature*, Warwick Papers in Industrial Relations 65, Industrial Relations Research Unit, University of Warwick.

Shackleton, K. (1996) *The Social Policy of the European Community: Reporting Information to Employees, a UK Perspective, Historical Analysis and Prognosis*, Economic Working paper No. 5, Universidade de Coimbra, Portugal. Online. Available HTTP: http://www4.fe.uc.pt/gemf/estudos/pdf/1996/gemf96_5.pdf (accessed 30 December 2002).

Streeck, W. (1997) *Under Regime Competition: The Case of the European Works Councils*, Working Paper 97/3 MPIfG. Online. Available HTTP: http://www.mpi-fg-koeln.mpg.de/pu/workpap/wp97-3/wp97-3.html (accessed 30 December 2002).

Stirling, J. and Fitzgerald, I. (2001) 'European Works Councils: Representing Workers on the Periphery', *Employee Relations*, 23(1&2): 13–25.

TUC (2002) *EU Directive on Information and Consultation*, discussion document, July 2002. Online. Available HTTP: http://www.tuc.org.uk/law/tuc-5229-f0.cfm (accessed 30 December 2002).

Weiss, M. (2001) *Workers' Involvement in the European Company*, MS. Frankfurt.

Part I

Understanding European Works Councils

European Works Councils (EWCs) are junction boxes with loose connections. They wire together a collection of political cross-currents and produce uncertain outcomes and some very evident blown fuses. These are all represented in the chapters that follow and in this part we seek to contextualise EWCs and locate them within their political and industrial corporate frameworks. In doing so three diverse questions provide the theme for the opening chapters and the book as a whole and they represent three contrasting views (presented here as extremes and ignoring the infinite range of responses). First, it might be said, mainly by employers, that EWCs are a major problem for European businesses seeking to compete in a global economy (this argument is detailed in Chapter 2 by Paul Knutsen and later in Chapter 6 by Richard Hume-Rothery). EWCs are a cost, imposed by Brussels bureaucrats at the expense of flexibility, that re-empower trade unions and will lead to wholly inappropriate attempts to Europeanise industrial relations and collective bargaining. The Directive had to be resisted at all costs and its implementation undermined by a continuous guerrilla war against worker interventions in management's prerogative. Second, it might be argued by trade unionists that the legislation is ineffective (see Chapter 5 by Willy Buschak for arguments for change), that EWCs fuel the development of a labour elite (see Chapter 3 by Miguel Martinez Lucio and Syd Weston) and that they are of highly limited relevance in a global economy (see the chapters in the final part for discussion of this). Third, there are more prosaic and practical questions reflected in the views of workers and their representatives: what is an EWC anyway and what is it supposed to do? When we find out what it is supposed to do, what are the limits and possibilities in my company (see Chapter 4 by Sief Stoop in this part and the part covering the lived experiences of EWCs)? Whilst the contrasting views of employers and trade unions might at least equally reside in a similar expectation of EWCs as potentially powerful bodies, the reality for EWC members shows a much more confusing picture, as they seek to develop and provide a role for this organisation within an organisation.

Corporatism and European Works Councils

Corporatism is the key political concept in contextualising the development of EWCs in the European Community. They are seen as both an outcome of a corporatist process and a potential contributor to its development. The key historical developments in ideas of employee participation were channelled into the European Union (EU) through national social democratic parties and their corporatist relationships with their own trade union movements. The uneven development of the legislative process in the Community (see our introduction and Paul Knutsen's chapter) reflect both the strength and weaknesses of national social democracy and the influence of EU Commissioners, with strong social democratic backgrounds such as Henk Vredeling and Jacques Delors. It is this social democratic corporatism and its inevitable interventionism that Knutsen suggests is as much at the heart of employer opposition to EWCs as the Directive itself. However, Knutsen seeks to re-evaluate concepts of corporatism in the light of the EWC Directive and its historical passage into law. He argues that the Commission has now become an important initiating body, that employers have become 'enmeshed' in a social dialogue however much they may resist and that trade unions are bound to use a process that brings them clear benefits. Knutsen describes the transposition of the EWC Directive into law as the outcome of a 'legal–democratic corporatism' that reinforces trends that were evident but less embedded beforehand. In effect, the Directive is both the outcome of and a contributor to the corporatist process. Martinez Lucio and Weston raise this latter point directly in their reflection on the potential development of a European industrial relations framework in which the EU might play a key role as legislator. In such circumstances, trade union delegates to EWCs become part of a complex network of connections that support 'flexible regulation' through new relationships with employers and EU institutions and their potential role as a focal point in the implementation of European legislation. However, there remains considerable debate about the Europeanisation of industrial relations and there are considerable countervailing pressures. Moreover, as Stoop argues, the question of 'convergence' in this area is often clouded by failure to indicate 'the convergence of what'? He suggests that organisational studies which distinguish between structure, conduct and performance provide a useful starting point for a more sophisticated analysis and that EWCs can have a significant role in each of those areas.

Corporations and European Works Councils

The industrial relations actor most opposed to the Eurocorporatist venture into EWCs has been the employers although their approach has been differentiated and there is evidence of a small number initiating action even before the Directive had been shaped into its final form. The reasons for employers opposition in principle is outlined by Paul Knutsen whereas the chapters by Martinez Lucio and Weston and, particularly, Stoop seek to develop their analysis as much in relation to differences as similarities between multinational corporations and the EWCs that go with them. This has become a critical point following the introduction of the Directive and the implementation of agreements as corporate structures shape EWCs and delimit the expectations that participants might have of outcomes. For Martinez Lucio and Weston, EWCs are characterised by a dynamic that 'pushes' and 'pulls' them between the agendas of capital (employers) and labour (trade unions). As MNCs are shaped by their internal and external environments and develop different organisational structures and strategies to cope with them, so must EWCs respond. For the authors of this chapter, EWCs 'are at the interface of *internal* transnational corporate dynamics and *external* social and political relations with labour' (their emphasis). Both Martinez Lucio and Weston, and Stoop use the Lecher *et al.* (2001) typology of EWCs as one starting point for differentiating between them and Stoop reviews the latest evidence from a range of surveys. His own approach focuses on two sets of relationships between companies and their EWCs: the first relates to organisational structures and the second to management strategies.

The categories developed by Stoop (see Tables 4.1 and 4.2 in his chapter for brief summaries) are critical for understanding and evaluating EWCs, particularly given the constraints they impose on their operational effectiveness. To take the most straightforward example from Stoop's argument, we are more likely to find effective EWCs in smaller companies with undifferentiated products, a high level of integration and clear international strategies. However, as Martinez Lucio and Weston point out, even in such a company, employer policies based on competition between plants will reinforce national identities and reduce the potential for cross-border alliances within an EWC. It is clear from these arguments that, whilst Eurocorporatism might have created a *framework* for the development of EWCs as entities, the form they take within organisations can be very different even where there are similarities in the agreements that are concluded or where European Trade Union Confederations are seeking similar 'best practice' outcomes for EWCs in their sectors (see Chapter 7 by Mark Gilman and Paul Marginson).

Trade unions and European Works Councils

As Knutsen's historical analysis suggests, it is the trade unions that have been the key actors in moving forward the EWC Directive. Following on from Levinson's (1972) 1970s arguments about the need for labour to develop a countervailing power to global capital it has been suggested that EWCs provide a structure for doing so. However, there are strong countervailing arguments that are a recurrent theme of the book.

Both the chapters by Knutsen and Martinez Lucio, and Weston draw attention to the dynamics in trade unions that leads them to both co-operation with capital to secure jobs and employment through business success, and confrontation with capital over the distribution of rewards. They have argued that that this is a complex, dynamic and changing relationship shaped and constrained by a context in which the labour movement is, itself, a significant actor. But what sort of actor? It is clear from Knutsen's historical analysis (and from much of the rest of this book) that trade unions at the European-level have been tenacious supporters of the Commission's uneven but long-term project on worker participation. The expansion of the European State via a tripartite corporatism gives European-level trade union groupings a reason to exist and the opportunity to expand their role.

National trade union confederations have also been supporters of EWC legislation as a 'good' in itself although they are bound by the continuing dominance of national industrial relations systems and the organisational and workplace focus of their memberships. These memberships may have little interest in Europe or EWCs and may even be hostile to institutions that appear to offer little by way of concrete outcome and potentially challenge their own interests during periods of company restructuring where jobs are threatened. As Weston and Lucio suggest, there is an ever-present problem of the dislocation of EWCs from union members and the creation of a Euro elite divorced from workplaces and seeking to preserve a core Europe at the expense of a peripheral developing world (this is further developed in our final section).

Stoop suggests an alternative in which EWCs, rather than perpetuating an elite, are rather 'hollow' organisations that are abandoned by trade unions as an irrelevance to their daily business. His argument stems from the varied structures of corporate capitalist organisation and the strategies of those management that see no 'added value' in EWCs and seek to marginalise them. However, leaving aside the twin dangers of elitism and abandonment there is a clear, mainstream, argument that EWCs offer an opportunity for trade unions to influence corporate decision-making and forge cross-national links. Whether this opportunity is taken or whether EWCs remain on the industrial relations periphery is, as historian Paul Knutsen would argue, a matter that we will only be able to judge in retrospect. However, their current importance is self-evident and beyond debate.

References

Lecher, W., Platzer, H., Rub, S. and Weiner, K. (2001) *European Works Councils: Developments, Types and Networking*, Aldershot: Gower.

Levinson, C. (1972) *International Trade Unionism*, London: Ruskin House Series in Trade Union Studies.

2 European Works Councils and the development of a Euro-corporatist model[1]

Paul Knutsen

The importance of historical time-consciousness

The main aim of this chapter is to analyse the historical preconditions of the European Works Council (EWC) Directive in the light of corporatist theory. Being a historian, I want to emphasise the temporal dimension, that is, a historicity embracing everything and everybody, including political scientists.

One difference between political scientists and historians is that the former (or at least some of them) make predictions about the future (*ex ante*), whereas the latter normally limit theirs to the past and make what we can call predictions *ex post*. Historians' post-dictions therefore amount to what is normally labelled historical explanations. Even if there is a radical difference between explanations modelled on the natural sciences, that is, a scientism advocated by logical positivists, and the hermeneutically oriented understanding presented in a narrative mode (Ricoeur 1984; Knutsen 2002), a historical explanation is always an explanation of something that has already happened and therefore belongs to the past (*res gestae*). Thus, in an article published in 1997 on corporatist tendencies in the Euro-polity, my main aim was to discuss the adoption of the EWC Directive of September 1994 in a historical perspective. As far as the future was concerned, I restricted myself to mentioning the possibility of (1) further development of a peculiar Euro-corporatism, the existence of which was the topic of my article, and (2) the possibility that the EWC Directive would turn out to be an expression of a corporatist 'over-stretch' – carefully leaving the conclusions to 'historians of future generations' (Knutsen 1997: 316). This self-imposed modesty on behalf of the future is part and parcel of the historian's craft, and the study of history presents continual reminders why this is so. During my research in 1995–6 on the background of the EWC Directive, I came across another reminder of this kind: the prediction, published in spring 1994, to the effect that the adoption of such a Directive was extremely unlikely (Streeck 1994), a prediction which was falsified by Clio in autumn of the same year. I was able to register this for the simple reason that what once was the future, had become the past. The future had passed into the past, and thus, in this capacity of *Vergangene Zukunft*, had presented itself as a possible object of historical study.

Now, writing in 2002, seven years have passed since I sought out relevant source material and interviewed a central UNICE legal adviser and EWC expert in Brussels (see Knutsen 1997: 301). This seven-year privilege provides me with an opportunity to evaluate the relevance of the two diverging predictions which were merely mentioned in my 1997 article. Important developments in the issue areas of information and consultation – with a potential spill-over to 'participation' – point clearly in the direction of giving the first-mentioned prediction the best credentials, that is, a further development of Euro-corporatism. First, in October 2001, the EU Council of Ministers adopted the longstanding (since 1970, in fact) controversial proposal on a European Company Statute, which contains information and consultation provisions defined more strongly than in the EWC Directive, in addition to board-level employee participation in some circumstances (see EWCB, 36, November/December 2001). Second, in February 2002, final approval was given to the EU Directive on national information and consultation rules, characterised by the EWCB as another 'major landmark' in EU social policy, bringing to an end a protracted debate over the desirability of 'an EU-wide framework for national-level information and consultation rules' (EWCB 38, March/April 2002). Third, there is pressure from both the ETUC and from the European Parliament for a revision of the original EWC Directive, with a view to strengthening rules, procedures and sanctions in favour of labour. The outcome of this is not yet known. However, in the light of these recent developments, there is substantial justification for giving the adoption of the EWC Directive in 1994 a more prominent place in the historical development of a Euro-corporatism than it was possible to defend on empirical grounds six or seven years ago. Instead of representing the culmination of a project (which was 'neither European nor works councils', and obviously doomed to failure anyway, according to Streeck 1997: 328), this Directive has probably and in several ways served as a trigger for new departures in social policy within a tripartite, corporatist institutional structure. However, the aim of this chapter is not a closer look at these more recent developments (see the Chapters 5 and 6 by Willy Buschak and Richard Hume-Rothery, respectively), but the EWC Directive itself and its historical preconditions. First, some clarification is needed on the concept of corporatism.

What is corporatism?

In the vast literature on corporatism in the social sciences, proliferating especially during the 1970s and 1980s, there is no agreement on the precise meaning of the concept. The actual usage of this ism, it seems, continues to be aptly summed up by the characterisation given in Philippe Schmitter's seminal article: 'nominalistic anarchy' (Schmitter 1974: 93). On the other hand, there has also been an opposite tendency, that is, to delineate the concept by linking it exclusively to the organisational practice in fascist regimes. For my purpose here, it is neither necessary nor desirable to seek a degree of precision which is counter-productive to historical understanding. Some historians have underlined the flexibility of the concept of corporatism as an advantage, promoting a preoccupation with historical process, that is, the diachronically dynamic play of opposing tendencies, rather than the synchronically static system (see e.g. Middlemas 1979: 243). I shall limit myself to indicate what I consider the most central and fruitful dimensions of the concept of corporatism with a view to its application in a historical and materialist analysis of the EU in general and the road to the EWC Directive in particular (Knutsen 1998).

For this purpose, we can single out three problem areas of central concern, and thereby characteristic of the corporatist approach. First, the relations between organised class interests, in particular relations between labour and capital. Fundamentally, corporatism is characterised by a transformation process from antagonistic to collaborative class relations. Second, the structure and function of these organised interests, especially with regard to social representativity, internal hierarchisation, the authority of the leadership to commit their members, etc. (Schmitter 1974). Here, attention has been directed towards the crucial position of the leadership in organisations in their intermediate role between demands from the rank and file below on the one hand, and demands from above (e.g. state authorities) on the other. Schmitter's ideal-typical (and now classical) definition of corporatism as a system of interest representation has therefore been replaced by interest intermediation (Schmitter 1979: 63; see also Crouch 1983: 452).

The third central problem area of the corporatist approach concerns the role of public authorities, and in particular the power of the state at national level. In our context, the growth of state-like competences in supra-national institutions like the EU Commission constitutes a vital precondition for corporatism at EU level, as does the existence of peak organisations of labour (ETUC) and of capital (UNICE) in Brussels. It is probably correct to say that a majority of theorists of corporatism consider the participation of the state as a necessary precondition for corporatism (Cawson 1986: 38). This participation may partly consist in direct state presence in bodies with interest representation, or it may be of a more indirect nature, justified by *à priori* suppositions (Nordby 1994). In any case, there is ample evidence in relevant literature to say that precisely the tripartite relationship state–labour–capital constitutes 'a corporatist core area' (Nordby 1994: 135). An important aspect of this tripartite constellation is the possibility of coalition between two of the parties against the third in a given context.

Focusing on the corporatist core area in its historical evolution, the challenges posed and the various responses given, corporatism can be seen as a fairly specific political strategy for stability and consensus-building. Likewise, a differentiation proposed by Crouch (1993) is obviously informed by historical insight and there-fore valuable for further historical research. He has worked out a scale comprising 'contestation' – 'pluralist bargaining' – 'bargained corporatism' – 'authoritarian corporatism'. As we shall see later, in the tripartite relationship between the peak organisations of labour and capital at European level and the Commission in Brussels, attempts within the paradigm of bargained corporatism broke down at a certain juncture in the Social Dialogue. However, this did not represent a break-down of corporatism at EU level, but a shift within corporatism to what I characterise as a legal–democratic corporatism. In order to analyse this devel-opment, a suitable point of departure is the EWC Directive of 22 September 1994 itself.

Main aims and central premises of the European Works Council Directive

The general goal of the Directive is discussed in the introduction and its Euro-corporatist intention is consistently confirmed in its phrasing which, for example, refers to its eventual evaluation being undertaken as a co-operative effort with the member states 'and with management and labour at European level' (Article 15).

The central premises of the Directive are laid down in the introductory remarks, which help to amplify an understanding of it politically and ideologically. First, it is emphasised that since The Single Market promotes the development of big, transnational companies – a desirable development, not least in order to meet competition from the US and Japan – the dialogue between management and employees in these companies should be improved if this development is to take place 'in a harmonious fashion'. This dream of harmony is also laid down explicitly in the text of the Directive, for example in Article 9, which gives the following instruction: 'The central management and the European Works Council shall work in a spirit of cooperation...'. Second, it is pointed out that existing procedures of information are often inadequate in the sense that they are directed more towards the national than the transnational level, the consequence of which may be unequal treatment of employees in different countries, in addition to the fact that the development of big companies at European level carries implications of a power-political nature in favour of these companies. A consideration of this description of the state of affairs, together with the specific provisions in the Directive, gives reason to conclude that the Commission has been aiming at influencing the power relations between capital and labour in favour of the latter. Third, the principle of the autonomy of the parties is underlined when it comes to specification of what procedures of information and consultation are deemed suitable and expedient. The practical flexibility thus implied is strengthened by explicit reference to the principle of subsidiarity, for example, when it comes to deciding who is to represent various categories of employees. Decisions of this nature are to be taken, then, with due regard to established local practices, which normally means – in this connection – established national practices. There is, then, a dualism between the encouragement of transnational organisational networks crowned by Euro-institutions like ETUC and UNICE on the one hand, and stressing the autonomy of the parties (the social partners), based on national traditions, on the other. This dualism can be interpreted in the light of the Commission's position in a field of tension between (partly) contradictory interests. When the Commission, led by Jacques Delors, inaugurated a new, dynamic period in the mid-1980s under the banner of 'The Single Market' and with '1992' as the seductive symbol, this was rightly perceived as unambiguous support for efforts in the direction of extending markets and at the same time developing more powerful units in Western European capitalism. For employer interests, in particular for those among them with extensive transnational ambitions, this was good news. Delors, however, in his capacity of mainstream social democrat, wanted the active participation of the trade union movement in this project by extending to labour more real influence on the modernisation of industry. Thus, when he presented the action programme of the new Commission in the European Parliament in January, 1985, he underlined the connection between The Single Market and the social dimension (Olsen 1994: 39). And at the Congress of the ETUC in May, 1988, he suggested that the social dimension of the EU should be anchored in a declaration of principle. An important stage in this work was the adoption of the Community Charter of Fundamental Social Rights at the Strasbourg summit in December 1989. This Social Charter or Social Pact, which was adopted by the eleven except UK, called for extension of information, consultation and participation by employees, especially in transnational enterprises in the member states.

Fundamental position of UNICE

Both prior to the adoption of this declaration of principle, and during the tug of war up to the EWC Directive of 22 September 1994, UNICE adopted a critical position, bordering on refusal in principle. It argued that the fundamental social rights of employees had already been guaranteed in the separate Member States, by law or by agreement, in accordance with the different historical background and the level of development in the individual countries. Further provisions at European level were therefore rejected as unrealistic, counter-productive and detrimental to the ability to compete (UNICE 1989). In 1989, the general secretary of UNICE, Zygmunt Tyszkiewicz, demanded that proposals for new statutory regulations with direct consequences for competitive ability should not be made and, at any rate, not be adopted unless an understanding had been reached with those who knew what 'the cold winds of competition' really meant. Ideas about 'statutory procedures for information and consultation' under discussion in political circles both in Brussels and in the European Parliament would according to Tyszkiewicz 'do irreparable damage to Europe's ability to compete' (Tyszkiewicz 1989: 3).

For UNICE, then, the central concerns would consist in striking the right balance between managements' prerogatives and workers' demands for influence, and between centralising at EU level and decentralising to other levels 'according to the principle of subsidiarity'. Thus, the principle of subsidiarity was stressed in opposition to 'new rigidities and constraints' imposed from Brussels. At the same time, managements' prerogatives must not be undermined. This did not mean that employers were opposed in principle to 'social dialogue' in the sense of giving employees appropriate information, but it would be up to the management to decide on procedures and contents of such information. Among relevant elements here, the ability to compete constituted a central criterion: 'The "right point of balance", for UNICE, is that point at which no harm is done to the ability of Europe's companies to compete successfully in a free, open and global market' (ibid.: 2). Confronted with new initiatives from the Commission, UNICE persisted in its attitude of refusal. A specific draft proposal for a Council directive from the Commission around the turn of the year 1990/1991, for example,

(COM (90) 581 final, Brussels 25 January 1991) was characterised by UNICE as 'harmful, dangerous and therefore totally unacceptable' (UNICE 1991).

In this matter, however, as in many others, employer interests turned out to be complex and partly at odds with themselves. The development in this field in some multinationals from the mid-1980s could thus be seen as favouring the approach to the problem represented by the Commission. Some of these companies were recently nationalised, French-based concerns, partly also with socialist sympathisers in the top management such as Thomson Grand Public and BSN-Gervais Danone. During 1991, however, similar agreements were also concluded in three German-based enterprises. Bayer AG led the way in June 1991 by establishing a 'Europa-Forum' consisting of representatives from management and employees in Germany and in five of the biggest European subsidiaries. Similar arrangements were then established in Continental, and in Hoechst. It is clear that such trends in heavyweight, competition-oriented companies could create problems for a continued intransigent stand on the part of UNICE, even though these arrangements were established on a voluntary basis. In addition, preparations for the Maastricht summit held out prospects that EU measures in this field would no longer be dependent on unanimity in the Council of Ministers, but be decided by majority voting. One important consequence of this was that UNICE could no longer rely on the UK being able to block unwanted proposals in the future. Against this background, a *rapprochement* took place from UNICE towards ETUC, aiming at acceptable agreements as an alternative solution to statutory regulation at European level. The fact that UNICE in October 1991 appeared to be ready for collective negotiations with ETUC indicates that the employers' organisation found itself in a defensive position. As pointed out by Gold and Hall (1994), UNICE was 'a late convert to the cause of such negotiations, having previously resisted any development of "European-level collective bargaining"' (ibid.: 179). The explanation of this change of policy is probably that UNICE feared the intentions of the Commission, and that negotiations with ETUC about voluntary agreements were considered a lesser evil than statutory regulations in the form of a Council directive.

The agreement between UNICE and ETUC of 31 October 1991 – which included also the European interest organisation for public enterprises, CEEP (Centre Européen des Entreprises à Participation Publique) – was reproduced without any essential modifications in the Agreement on social policy annexed to the Maastricht Treaty. In Article 3, the Commission was authorised to promote 'the consultation of management and labour at Community level', and Article 4 allowed for organisational agreements at European level, 'should management and labour so desire'. The organisations were also accorded the status of bodies to be consulted by the Commission, concerning 'possible direction of Community action' as well as 'the content of the envisaged proposal', if the Commission after the first hearing found such action appropriate. During the second hearing, the organisations were empowered to proceed on their own with a view to concluding a voluntary agreement, normally within a period of nine months. The implementation of the agreement could be done either in accordance with previously established practice between the organisations and in the Member States, or as a result of a Council decision initiated by the Commission, conditional upon 'the joint request of the signatory parties'. In the latter case, qualified majority in the Council would normally be sufficient.[2]

UNICE expressed its satisfaction with the strengthening of the position of the organisations implied by this annex to the Maastricht Treaty, stressing at the same time, however, that the central principle of subsidiarity in Article 3b of the Treaty proper ought to apply in questions concerning 'social legislation' (UNICE 1992). The emphasis on 'subsidiarity' and on 'autonomy' for the organisations is characteristic of UNICE's attitude to the Maastricht Treaty, often in a context directed against 'the European legislator' in Brussels. In a comment on European social policy after Maastricht, 'The Point of View of European Employers', general secretary Tyszkiewicz could not see why so much needed to be harmonised: 'In our view, relatively few things needed to be harmonised. There is nothing wrong with doing many things differently in the Member States' (Tyszkiewics 1992: 3). He further underlined the importance of 'strict safeguards' for the organisations, and he continued:

> That is another way of saying we don't want *tripartism*, we don't want *corporatism*. Of course we want the social partners to talk to each other, but only when they want to, on their terms and according to their own rules of procedure. We do not want a kind of *Commission-imposed*, tripartite dialogue.
> (ibid., emphasis added)

The same year of 1992, however, gave warnings of a new drive on the part of the Commission in support of preparations for setting up EWCs on a firmer and more permanent basis. With reference to The Single European Act, which (in Article 118b) empowered the Commission to further 'the dialogue between management and labour at European level', the Commission had already provided financial support to trade unions to cover expenses for travel, translation, etc. in connection with international meetings. The Commission's 1992 budget meant that this support was increased considerably, since €14m was now earmarked for 'transnational meetings of employee representatives from undertakings operating on a transfrontier basis in the Community...until the entry into force of the Commission's proposal (for the European Works Council Directive)' (EIRR 229/1993: 20). This did not pass unnoticed in UNICE. And when grants for 1993 were further increased up to €17 m, UNICE contrasted this to the provisions in the Maastricht Treaty that committed the Commission to ensure 'balanced support' to the parties. UNICE also hinted at a 'hidden agenda' behind this, that is, an ideologically motivated co-operation between the Commission and ETUC. UNICE's President, Carlos Ferrer, did not leave his audience in any doubt as to his opinion on the Commission's draft Directive and the financial support which went with it:

> Employers cannot avoid believing that there is a hidden agenda behind all this, more concerned with ideology and the creation of pan-European

unions than with genuine worker involvement. This belief is reinforced by the allocation of €17 million of Community funds to the Unions in the 1993 budget, for the express purpose of training union representatives on European Works Councils – even before the Directive has passed into law. That is more than four times the total UNICE budget, and seems far removed from the Maastricht Treaty, which obliges the Commission to ensure 'balanced support for the parties'

(UNICE 1993)

UNICE's complaints that the Commission was favouring ETUC financially with relatively substantial amounts may give the impression of a bias directly at odds with the Agreement on social policy in the Maastricht Treaty. This type of complaint appears in a different light when combined with information to the effect that UNICE has consistently refused offers of financial support from the Commission. The most obvious consequence to be drawn from UNICE's attitude in this matter, therefore, was not giving UNICE fresh means, but depriving ETUC of theirs. What was at stake here, then, was quite simply to preserve an independence one could afford to preserve.

The Directive is adopted

The critical comments on the draft Directive led to adjustments, during the Danish and Belgian presidencies in 1993. However, UNICE considered these and subsequent adjustments of the text as purely cosmetic, and maintained its fundamental criticism. Moreover, in spite of numerous meetings there was also a political failure to reach agreement on the Commission's proposals. However, from the 1st November 1993 the requirement of unanimity in such matters was formally abolished, as the Maastricht Treaty came into force. The EU Commissioner for Social Affairs Padraig Flynn, made it clear that if UNICE and ETUC showed themselves unable to reach a satisfactory agreement on their own, the EU would decide the matter by means of Directive. Addressing the most influential brake block in UNICE, that is, the Confederation of British Industries (CBI), Mr Flynn stated the following: 'Do not misunderstand me. *If the social partners cannot reach agreement, I am firmly convinced that there will then be legislation.* There is wide agreement between eleven member states on this point' (quoted in Gold and Hall 1994: 180, emphasis in original).

For ETUC, the choice presented itself between a diluted agreement with UNICE and a Directive which would undoubtedly be closer to ETUC ambitions. The opposition between 'the social partners' in this matter would therefore point in the direction of failure. Three days before the deadline for its opinions to the Commission, the CBI published a condemnation of the whole proposal. This was followed up by UNICE, and the ETUC took advantage of this situation to place the responsibility for the breakdown of negotiations with the employers (UNICE 1994a).[3] Pushed on by the Commission, the EU political bodies now saw to it that the case was brought to a close. On 13 April 1994, the Commission decided to present its draft directive to the Council on the basis of Article 2.2 involving qualified majority among the eleven. After the European Parliament had given its opinions, and after final adjustments in COREPER,[4] the Directive passed the Council of Ministers ('first reading'), after which it was finally adopted on 22 September (Blanpain and Windey 1994: 59–62).

Prior to the Council meeting on 22 June 1994, UNICE repeated its main line of argument against the draft Directive. In a letter to the Council, 'freedom for companies to set up arrangements in agreement with their employees' was once again demanded, 'bias' in favour of the trade unions was underlined, together with the threats to the ability to compete (UNICE 1994b). As we have seen, the discrepancy between UNICE's efforts and the results obtained remained considerable.

One might ask why this opposition was so vehement: Is not this strongly debated Directive in reality a rather innocent measure? One might even be tempted to suppose that the Directive in its final version would be in the interest of the employers.[5] The fact is that the Directive deals with information and consultation, the term 'participation' in the Social Charter has thus been excluded. The term 'trade union' likewise is non-existent in the Directive, and the employers' repeated demands for subsidiarity, flexibility and autonomy (for 'the social partners') have, at least to a certain extent, been met. In an interview with Olivier Richard in April 1995 he maintained, however, UNICE's characterisation of the Directive as 'very dangerous and harmful'. In answer to a direct question as to what made this Directive so dangerous, he pointed at two areas. Partly, he emphasised the 'Annex' to the Directive, where minimum standards are laid down. This obviously gives cause for concern in UNICE, and is, no doubt, central to understanding their resistance (Richard 1995). In our context, however, it seems more fruitful to concentrate upon the other area Richard underlined in the course of our interview. He referred to it variously as 'the political setting' and 'the wider implications'. In this connection, he drew a line back to the so-called Vredeling Directive of 1980, which was blocked in the Council because of the unanimity procedure then in force. As we shall now see, this Directive fits nicely into a historical context of considerable interest to our *problématique*.

The European Works Council Directive in historical perspective

Henk Vredeling had his background in the Dutch labour movement. In his capacity as EU Commissioner for Social Affairs he initiated in 1980, a Directive aiming at statutory rights for employees in multinational EU (the then EC) companies, concerning information and consultation. According to Vredeling himself, the draft Directive was partly based on existing voluntary arrangements on models from the International Labour Organisation (ILO) and from the OECD (EIRR, 82/1980: 5). The aim now was to make these arrangements statutory by means of EU-wide legislation. According to an analysis in the European Industrial Relations Review, 'Mr Vredeling, a Dutch Socialist, is particularly keen to demonstrate to the European trade union movement that his tenure in office has contributed towards greater statutory rights for unions'. Prospects were not too bright, however, since UNICE was 'totally opposed'. On the other hand, ETUC was not fully satisfied with the draft Directive either, because it did not go far enough. A revised, more moderate draft Directive from the Commission was presented in 1983, but never had a chance in the Council of Ministers. The importance of Vredeling's draft Directive was given the following assessment by the EIRR: ' "Vredeling" remains, however, a proposal of major significance, since it represents the only attempt to date to introduce an international, legally-binding instrument in this area' (EIRR 115/1983: 7). The initiating role of the Commission in this matter, from Vredeling to Delors and Flynn, can be interpreted as a continuation of reform demands from the international trade union movement dating back to the 1950s and 1960s. The political scientist Udo Rehfeldt is an eloquent advocate of such an interpretation. In a stimulating analysis (Rehfeldt 1993), he makes use of Charles Levinson's International Trade Unionism (1972) as one of his main sources concerning the unions' reform demands.

A central aim for Levinson consisted in advancing the power position of the international trade union movement to a level more adequate compared to the position already conquered by the multinational companies. He identified 'the phenomenal thrust of the multinational corporation' as perhaps the most dynamic and far-reaching structural change in the history of capitalism:

> Impelled by technology and the new mobility of capital and management, the emerging giants are shedding their national identity and are becoming the first, genuinely world institutions with inherently global power and authority. By contrast, the other world institutions are federations of national powers with no real intrinsic authority.
>
> (Levinson 1972: 214)

His central point is the imbalance between the advanced, transnational character of capital on the one hand, and the relative backwardness of the trade union movement on the other. The main task for the trade unions, therefore, would be 'to make *the epochal bargaining leap* from an exclusively national to an international position' (ibid. 1972: 107, emphasis added). Levinson imagined three stages in union efforts to create an 'international, global counterforce'. The first stage was 'company wide support of a single union in one country in a dispute with a foreign subsidiary'. The second stage ('the next quantum jump') consisted in coordinated negotiations with an enterprise in several countries at the same time, in order to mobilise more effective international power 'to counteract the advantages of the multinational company'. The third stage, finally, would mean 'integrated negotiations around common demands' (ibid.: 110–11).

These ideas should be considered against a background where the degree of internationalisation was particularly advanced, for example, the metal and chemical industries. In the car industry, a number of 'world councils' had been established during the 1960s, after preparatory union discussions in the latter part of the 1950s. The first three (Ford, General Motors and Chrysler) were established in Detroit in June 1966. Then came Volkswagen/Mercedes-Benz in autumn 1966, and Fiat-Citroën in 1968. These 'world councils' became according to Levinson 'the vehicles for the concrete co-operation between unions of the companies in the different countries' (Levinson 1972: 123). The European Metalworkers' Federation (EMF) took similar initiatives *vis-à-vis* Philips, the Dutch-based electronics group. Over the years 1967–72, four meetings were held with Philips management, and the representatives of Philips held out prospects for more detailed discussions about demands for 'a permanent labour–management liaison committee, a comprehensive labour policy, and multinational discussions in advance of proposed layoffs and international transfers of employees'. However, such demands, in addition to demands for collective negotiations at European level, were not seriously discussed, and the planned fifth meeting was never held (EIRR, 228/1993: 14).

In the chemical industry, the International Federation of Chemical and General Workers Union (ICF) was aiming at an agreement with the French-based multinational glass combine Saint-Gobain. After extensive, international union action in 1969, certain concessions were obtained, and union members in several countries (France, Italy, Germany and the US) were preparing for a future common strategy (Levinson 1972: 132 and ch. 1). Levinson considered this an important step on the road from the first to the second stage in his development scheme, that is, the beginning of 'true multinational negotiation for all or several branches of a company'. He seems to have had a clear understanding of the considerable obstacles confronting the trade union movement as far as really comprehensive, co-ordinated international action was concerned. He was none the less convinced that his road to the future was the right one, and that it had to be followed: 'But despite such difficulties, progress must be made *if the trade union movement is not to be confronted by serious, even mortal, threat to its power and effectiveness*'. (ibid.: 111, emphasis added). In a summary of 'The trade union answer', he modestly characterised his programme as 'perhaps the single most important task of the international movement as a whole in the immediate future' (ibid.: 141). In his opinion, the 'objective' conditions for such a programme were clearly there, whereas the 'subjective' conditions, that is, the national unions' insight into the need for internationalisation, were far weaker.

The plans for the future presented by Levinson remained, however, more a dream than actual fact. Udo Rehfeldt writes about an idyllic image quickly at odds with reality (Rehfeldt 1993: 72). The establishment of some fifty 'world councils' seemed impressive but, to begin with, this was a small number compared to the number of multinational companies. Second, and more important, these councils did not, on the whole, perform effectively. Rehfeldt characterises their existence as 'transient and fictive'. He also draws attention to the ideological division between the Soviet-dominated union movement in the East and the 'free' union movement in the West, a fact which diminished the possibilities of efficient international union action. An assessment of Levinson's visions also has to take into consideration the fact that he was writing at a time when a protracted boom was approaching its end. In periods of increasing unemployment, unions will normally find themselves in a defensive position, as the strategic balance of power will tend to favour the employers. During the 1970s, an agreement was nonetheless concluded, of some importance partly because it points forward to the future, but partly also because it represents an exception to the prevailing developmental tendency in this field. The agreement in question concerned the French-based enterprise BSN-Gervais Danone, which in some important respects pioneered the development during the 1980s, as we have seen. After the take-over of the Belgian glass firm Glaverbel at the beginning of the 1970s, BSN signed an agreement with Belgian unions which included a provision to the effect that 'a multinational association of unions should be established to meet with management' (EIRR 228/1993: 14). ICF participated in the first meeting in September 1973, but due to disagreement with the BSN management representatives, they were pushed to the side lines, and agreements were concluded directly between BSN and representatives of the unions and other employees in the subsidiaries in Austria, Belgium, France, Germany and the Netherlands. Among the main concerns here were discussions of measures that could contribute to maintaining existing levels of employment. Meetings were held on a regular basis twice yearly between management and employee representatives – but, to be sure, on a national level – in bodies denoted by EIRR as 'permanent employment commissions' (EIRR 228/1993: 14). The driving force behind this, however, seems to have come from management rather than from employees.

At the beginning of the 1980s, then, practically all initiatives for transnational negotiations on the Levinson model had vanished from the political agenda. It is possible to argue that Levinson's strategy was not only premature, but also 'structurally inadequate' (Rehfeldt 1993: 73). For our analytical purposes here, however, it is sufficient to emphasise two main barriers against Levinson's trade union strategy: the economic recession from about 1973, and the strength of the new economic liberalism in the 1980s, with 'Reaganomics' in the US and Thatcherism in Great Britain as towering symbols. The socialist victory in the French elections in 1981, however, contributed in a decisive way to prevent the new liberalism from running freely all the way. It is true that the orthodox-socialist leftist faction under Bérégovoy and Chevènement suffered defeat when Francois Mitterrand from 1983 onwards gave his support to the more moderate, social democratic mainstream, represented, among others, by Jacques Delors. The result of this was partly a break with the idea of 'socialism in one country' in its French variant, partly another 'relaunch' of Europe. This change of direction in French politics from 1983 gave an important impetus to the new dynamism in the history of EU from the mid-1980s (Moravcsik 1991). At the same time, however, the French government confirmed its interest in promoting information and consultation between management/employees in big companies, partly by means of legislation.

Jacques Delors' initiatives in social policy as President of the EU Commission emerge in a meaningful light when considered against this background. One should be aware that the lack of a common framework in labour law at the European level had been an important obstacle to solutions *à la* Levinson. At the same time, references to the variations in the different national labour law regimes have been important for UNICE's demands for subsidiarity and flexibility. The initiatives from the EU Commission to promote a common juridical framework for EWCs therefore easily lend themselves to an interpretation into the dangerous pattern of 'wider implications' that worried UNICE's legal adviser Olivier Richard. Given the historical connection to what we may call the trade union movement's social democratic, transnational project, however, the central problem which presented itself was not whether or not the capitalist system should be maintained, since a defining feature of social democracy is its acceptance of 'the mixed economy'. Instead, the central question to be addressed concerned what kind of capitalism should be predominant, or, to be more precise: to what extent should the competition-oriented economic profit motive be balanced against social and democratic ambitions in the new transnational context? It is not difficult to understand why the initiatives from the Commission were opposed so actively, since these initiatives ran counter to employer efforts to curb the power of the unions.

Conclusion: legal–democratic corporatism

As we have seen, the development towards the adoption of the Directive has taken place in various phases. After the 'Eurosclerosis' of the 1970s, Delors tried from the mid-1980s to stimulate a new drive in 'the social dialogue' by means of a Commission-initiated, bureaucratic corporatism based on voluntary acceptance from the parties. These *Val Duchesse*-talks represented for the ETUC an important stepping stone to 'joint agreements' and to legislation at European level. UNICE, on the other hand, wanted more limited commitments, and stressed the informal character of discussions that might, or might not, lead to the publication of 'joint opinions', as distinct from 'joint agreements' (Olsen 1994: 41). When UNICE, in spite of this, concluded an agreement with ETUC on 31 October 1991, this should be seen in the light of the new dynamism released by – among other factors – Delors' promotion of this kind of meeting. As a result of this, UNICE was forced out on a downward slope: UNICE felt compelled to conclude an agreement in order to avoid legislation, after which this legislation was adopted. The process took place within the corporatist core area in the triangle capital–labour–public authority at European level, and the tendency in the political ideology of the provisional end result is largely in accordance with the social-democratic thinking we have identified behind relevant reform demands from international trade unionism dating from the 1960s. With reference to Colin Crouch's continuum between 'contestation' (i.e. uncontrolled interest in politics) on the one hand, and 'authoritarian corporatism' on the other, we can identify 28 March 1994, as marking a developmental leap: up to this point in time, the Commission, ETUC and UNICE were involved in a process best characterised by the ambition of 'bargained corporatism'. Given the de facto breakdown of negotiations from this date, it is no longer adequate to speak of a bargained corporatism between three parties. Nor is it appropriate to talk of an authoritarian corporatism – which seems to be implied by UNICE's complaints of a 'Commission-imposed dialogue'. Judged by the procedures during April–September 1994, as well as by the essential elements of the end result, it seems more to the point if we characterise this phase as an expression of a legal–democratic corporatism. The legal aspect is evident in the strict adherence to the rules of the game laid down in the Treaties. The democratic element lies primarily in opening the road to more influence in economic and industrial matters for an extended demos, and partly in the active use of qualified majority voting in these matters pursuant to the entry into force of the Maastricht Treaty in November 1993. Compared to a classical analysis by the Norwegian sociologist Stein Rokkan, this legal–democratic corporatism combines elements from his well-known dichotomy 'numerical democracy' and 'corporate pluralism' (Rokkan 1966).[6] In his famous shorthand expression 'Votes Count but Resources Decide' (ibid.: 105), the parliamentary channel of influence ('votes count') is set against the corporatist channel, where the real decisions are taken by the powerful few, the men and organisations of power ('resources decide'). In the legal–democratic corporatism expressed through the EWC Directive, there is a bias in favour of numbers – the millions of rank and file represented by the ETUC – in opposition to the voice of the millions (of euro) in the hands of UNICE. And at the same time, the real decisions were taken in the corporatist channel of influence.

The dialectical development in the period from 1994 to date – that is, the play of oppositions within the corporatist core area – can be seen as conditioned by the EWC Directive itself. Developments and prospects within the three fields of the European Company Statute, the EU-wide framework for national-level information and consultation, and the proposed revision of the EWC Directive, do point in the direction of a more well-established EU corporatism, more embedded in the political structure than the corporatist tendencies detectable seven years ago. On the organisational level, it is also probably reasonable to say, with Justin Greenwood, that UNICE through the Social Dialogue mechanism has been to some extent 'enmeshed within a structure from which it cannot escape' (Greenwood 1997: 107). This is a somewhat paradoxical situation, bearing in mind that when UNICE was established in 1958 it was not primarily in order to promote the customs union, but to seek protection against the Commission (Cowles 1998: 109). We can also observe a tendency in the direction of mandating the leadership more strongly than before when it comes to bargaining. This tendency, even if weak, has been noted by Greenwood (1997) for UNICE, and seems to be stronger on the ETUC side. Viewed from the present point in time, there is sufficient empirical evidence to support a conclusion in the opposite direction of what was thought to be the case some ten years ago, when two highly visible theorists wrote the following in an interesting article in which the main thesis was the absence of corporatism at European level:

> In a nutshell, our point is that in uniting supra-national Europe, it was not only the case that labor was, and continues to be, *underorganized* but there also was never a real possibility of a mutually organising *interaction effect*, a

Wechselwirkung, between labor and the two other major players in the political economy, capital, and the state.

(Streeck and Schmitter 1991: 139, emphasis in original)

These authors are quite right in drawing attention to this interaction effect as characteristic of the corporatist phenomenon in theory. Now, we can see that precisely such an interaction effect was instrumental also in practice, that is, in the run-up to the EWC Directive. As we have seen, the Commission has been an important initiating body in this respect, from Henk Vredeling, whose attempts were premature and unsuccessful, via the Val Duchesse meetings orchestrated by Delors, and to the process resulting in the EWC Directive. I consider it a reasonable working hypothesis that this *Wechselwirkung* has been central and even more important in the period after 1994, including the development leading to extended employee rights exemplified by the European Company Statute. More generally the EU, especially during periods with a politically ambitious Commission, seems to be developing into a regulation regime in this field, distancing itself, in the process, from the unholy alliance characteristic of a Thatcherite ambition: nationalism and neo-liberalism.

Notes

1 A full-text pdf. version of this chapter, with extensive footnotes, can be found, Online. Available HTTP: http://domino2.hil.no/web/forskning.nsf/0/25041B5AA0E50285C 1256C7D00302D75?OpenDocument – 94 2002 Knutsen, Paul: 'Corporatism Revisited' (ISBN 82-7184-271-4) (accessed 30 December 2002).
2 Quotations from The Agreement on Social Policy, Articles 3 and 4 (annexed to the Maastricht Treaty).
3 In spite of certain improvements in the Commission's draft, the attitude of UNICE was still the following: 'Nevertheless, in its present form, the latest text remains unacceptable to companies for two fundamental reasons: (…) Article 5 requires companies to set up a special, centralised structure to negotiate mechanisms for information and consultation. Companies see this as an unwarranted and unnecessary interference in their relationships with their employees. (…) Article 7 and the Annex…will bias the outcome in favour of centralised, rigid and bureaucratic structures of the Works Council type, which most companies consider harmful and unsuitable'. Further, the following bias was underlined again: 'However, UNICE must point to the virtual impossibility of conducting a free and impartial negotiation when the Commission's document has promised in advance, to grant to one side virtually all it has always requested' (UNICE 1994a). To quote the Secretary General of ETUC (meeting of 9 March 1994): 'We cannot give-up what is already in our pocket'. Richard said in my interview with him, UNICE 27 April 1995: 'The ETUC was happy to take the pretext'. Richard also emphasised that ETUC was clever in taking advantage of the situation, and that their people did a good job (Richard 1995).
4 COREPER is abbreviation for Comité des Réprésentantes Permanentes, that is, representatives of the permanent national delegations among the EU countries in Brussels. This body probably wields much more influence on the decision process in the EU than the sparse treatment of it in the literature might indicate. COREPER relates both to the Commission and to the Council, which implies 'a system of bureaucratic intermingling', in which 'the borderline between the initiating institution and the decision-making institution becomes blurred' (See Ludlow 1991: 103).

5 Here, I am not referring to the employers' 'objective' interests, which are normally identical with what they *ought to* think, based on some standard or other, but to their interests as subjectively perceived by themselves and therefore also within the realm of what is possible to verify empirically.
6 The adjective used here, 'corporate', is unfortunate and may be misleading. 'Corporative' would be better, and 'corporatist' the adequate choice, in keeping with my wording in this chapter. The Norwegian translation of Rokkan uses the expression 'korporativ pluralisme'.

References

Blanpain, R. and Windey, P. (1994) *European Works Councils. Information and Consultation of Employees in Multinational Enterprises in Europe*, Leuven: Peeters.

Cawson, A. (1986) *Corporatism and Political Theory*, Oxford: Basil Blackwell.

Council Directive 94/45/EC (1994) Printed in *Official Journal of the European Communities*, No. L 254/64, 30 September.

Cowles, Maria Green (1998) 'The Changing Architecture of Big Business', in Justin Greenwood and Mark Aspinwall (eds) *Collective Action in the European Union*, London/New York: Routledge.

Crouch, C. (1983) 'Pluralism and The New Corporatism: A Rejoinder', *Political Studies*, 31: 452–60.

Crouch, C. (1993) *Industrial Relations and European State Traditions*, Oxford: Clarendon Press.

Gold, M. and Hall, M. (1994) 'Statutory European Works Councils: the final countdown?', *Industrial Relations Journal*, 25(3): 177–86.

Greenwood, J. (1997) *Representing Interests in the European Union*, London: Macmillan.

Knutsen, P. (1997) 'Corporatist Tendencies in the Euro-Polity. The EU Directive of 22 September 1994, on European Works Councils', *Economic and Industrial Democracy. An International Journal*, 18(2): 289–323.

Knutsen, P. (1998) *Penger, stål og politikk. En problemorientert innføring i EUs historie*, Bergen: Fagbokforlaget (*Money, Steel and Politics. A Problem-oriented Introduction to the History of the EU*).

Knutsen, P. (2002) *Analytisk narrasjon. En innføring i historiefagets vitenskapsfilosofi*, Bergen: Fagbokforlaget (*Analytical Narration. An Introduction to Fundamental Problems and Theories of History*).

Levinson, C. (1972) *International Trade Unionism*, London: Ruskin House Series in Trade Union Studies.

Ludlow, P. (1991) 'The European Commission', in R.O. Keohane and S. Hoffmann (eds) *The New European Community. Decisionmaking and Institutional Change*, Boulder, San Francisco, Oxford: Westview Press.

Middlemas, K. (1979) *Politics in Industrial Society. The Experience of the British System Since 1911*, London: Andre Deutsch.

Moravcsik, A. (1991) 'Negotiating the Single European Act', in R.O. Keohane and S. Hoffmann (eds) *The New European Community. Decisionmaking and Institutional Change*, Boulder, San Francisco, Oxford: Westview Press.

Nordby, T. (1994) *Korporatisme på norsk, 1920–90*, Oslo: Universitetsforlaget (*Corporatism in Norwegian*).

Olsen, T. (1994) *Den sosiale dialogen og staten som arbeidsgiver*, Oslo: FAFO-rapport 164 (*The Social Dialogue and the State as Employer*).

Rehfeldt, U. (1993) 'Les syndicats européens face à la transnationalisation des entreprises', *Le Mouvement Social*, No. 162.

Richard, O. (1995) Interview by the author, Brussels, 27 April 1995.

Ricoeur, P. (1984) *Time and Narrative I*, Chicago: Chicago University Press.

Rokkan, S. (1966) 'Norway: Numerical Democracy and Corporate Pluralism', in Robert A. Dahl (ed.) *Political Oppositions in Western Democracies*, New Haven and London: Yale University Press.

Schmitter, P.C. (1974) 'Still the Century of Corporatism?', *The Review of Politics*, 36: 85–131.

Schmitter, P.C. (1979) 'Modes of Interest Intermediation and Models of Societal Change in Western Europe', in P.C. Schmitter and G. Lembruch (eds) *Trends Toward Corporatist Intermediation*, London: Sage Publications.

Streeck, W. (1994) European Social Policy after Maastricht: The 'Social Dialogue' and 'Subsidiarity'. *Economic and Industrial Democracy*, 15(2): 151–77.

Streeck, W. (1997) 'Neither European nor Works Councils: A Reply to Paul Knutsen', *Economic and Industrial Democracy. An International Journal*, 18(2): 325–37.

Streeck, W. and Schmitter, P.C. (1991) 'From National Corporatism to Transnational Pluralism: Organized Interests in the Single European Market', *Politics and Society*, 19(2): 134–64.

Tyszkiewics, Z.J.A. (1989) 'European Social Policy: Striking The Right Balance', UNICE Archive, Brussels.

Tyszkiewics, Z.J.A. (1992) 'European Social Policy After Maastricht', UNICE Archive, Brussels.

UNICE (1989) Communiqué, 22 February 1989, concerning Droits sociaux fontamentaux communautaires.

UNICE (1991) Position paper, 4 March.

UNICE (1992) Position paper on 'The Social Chapter of the Maastricht Treaty', 25 May.

UNICE (1993) Informal meeting of ministers of employment and social affairs, Nyborg, 3 May, opening statement by Mr Carlos Ferrer, president of UNICE.

UNICE (1994a) Letter from UNICE to the Commission, acting director general DG V, Hywel C. Jones, 31 March.

UNICE (1994b) Letter from UNICE to Mr Yiannopolous, president of the Council of Social Affairs Ministers, 7 June.

3 European Works Councils

Structures and strategies in the new
Europe

Miguel Martinez Lucio and Syd Weston

Introduction

The European Works Council (EWC) Directive in 1994 was seen as a significant development within European industrial relations and the outcome of exhaustive political negotiations. The question of worker participation had always been central to the aspirations of the European Union's (EU) social dimension but significant steps had been virtually non-existent since the Treaty of Rome in 1957. The eventual Directive required transnational companies (TNCs) within the EU to develop specific structures and systems of cross-border consultation with their employees (see the introduction to this text). It responded to an ongoing concern within the international labour movement with regard to the regulation of new forms of international capital. The long-term expectations of the trade union movement, and indeed the European Commission, emerging from the EWC Directive are therefore far reaching. Research within this complex area of industrial relations straddles the issues of economic and political convergence in the EU, the changing strategies of TNCs, the declining significance of national sectoral collective bargaining arrangements and the institutional and political complexity of European trade unions. These broad areas of research are now being further explored following the implementation of the EWC Directive and the challenge the new structures pose for the European labour movement. Coming to firm conclusions with regard to these developments is obviously unwise at this early stage.

It is beyond contention that EWCs are subject to interventions from a range of actors. They are subject to influences within the internal environments of their relevant TNCs and a host of external political and regulatory factors. Within these two environments there are dual pressures that both push unions towards managerial agendas and pull them towards autonomous labour ones. These distinct pressures mean that EWCs cannot be viewed as given entities with coherent actors that develop clear and consistent interests. Instead, they will vary according to the way these internal and external environments, and their corresponding actors, influence their development. In this respect EWCs share a historic characteristic of worker representation generally in that they are capable of being both forces for aligning worker and employer interests and, on the other hand, creating new forms of worker dialogue and action. This uncertainty and inconsistency is very much a part of labour politics and representation within a capitalist context (Hyman 1989). The research being conducted into the opera-tion and functioning of EWCs is also more fruitful when it occurs in the context of a greater sensitivity to the new dynamics of labour internationalism in terms of the impact of networking and new forms of 'organic solidarity' (Hyman 1999).

What this chapter suggests is that we are experiencing the emergence of a new form and dynamic of solidarity within industrial relations that is more complex, variable and less hierarchically induced to previous forms of linkages of worker/union representational forms. Because of these developments EWCs require a language and methodology that is capable of locating them within the complex corporate and political environments that envelop them. The chapter also emphasises the significance of political linkages in understanding labour representation and its complex environmental contexts. This is of particular importance in accounting for the intriguing location of EWCs within the new multi-dimensional relations of transnational and, in particular, European industrial relations.

This work emerged from an initial interest in how unions were responding to the challenge of organisational change and the emergence of new management practices within the workplace such as teamworking. Given the significance of 'whipsawing' and the establishment of competition between workplaces by various firms, the focus of that research eventually moved to a broader under-standing of union responses and the transnational dimension. We observed the development of new forms of trade union and worker networking as a key feature of the way these responses unfolded. Alongside these developments, the presence of EWCs was emerging as a salient factor. We began to realise the influence these could have, and indeed were having, on the dynamics of international labour co-ordination. We felt that these institutional dynamics had to be studied with a degree of sensitivity and socio-political understanding that did not hinge on pre-conceptualisations of worker representation and union–management relations. Hence, from wanting to explain how working people and their representatives could influence management changes within their workplace we ended up discussing the way these responses connected with each other across and interfaced with the new dynamics of political regulation and worker representation within Europe.

The 'incorporation' of European Works Councils?

The discussion on EWCs has been laced with many critical interventions. A wide range of concerns have been raised with regard to their functioning and impact which arise primarily from the modern day practices of TNCs themselves. For example, there is growing evidence that many TNCs now practice: (a) regular meetings for production and personnel managers from sites in different countries; (b) rotation of managerial personnel from one site to another; (c) a corporate management task in the compilation of manuals of best practice on a site-by-site basis (Coller 1996). The above practices of TNCs are also said to be complimented by a central system of measuring the performance of employees in sites across Europe and beyond. In turn, such practices are now being used strategically to 'reward' and 'punish' individual units regarding future orders/investment (Mueller and Purcell 1992) and as a means to condition the bargaining behaviour of local management as well as local workforces. The suggestion is that the formation of such institutional arrangements and managerial practices within TNCs is resulting in a form of 'concession bargaining' with employee representatives who become principally the defenders of local interests (Schulten 1996), and that over time undermine the necessary conditions for union solidarity. Accordingly, this will lead towards some form of 'negative convergence' of labour standards throughout the EU based upon a managerial-market agenda. Such a scenario becomes very real if we account for intra-firm competition, which forces local management to pursue constant improvements via the adoption of 'best practice methods' throughout the organisation, hence creating a form of convergence of work organisation, conditions and quality of employment within TNCs (UNCTAD 1994: 270). Consequently, many commentators are seeing the EWC Directive as a managerial tool to consolidate their strategies of control over labour, rather than an effective tool for the trade unions to influence the employment relation for more positive outcomes. Certain commentators have argued that EWCs are unable to override the competitive relations that are established between different sites and workplaces by many TNCs:

> New forms of organisation within workplace regimes, be they continuous improvement or EWC gatherings, can be seen as 'rituals of affirmation' drawing their rationale from a game of 'musical chairs' created by insecurity. Far from bounding shop floor behaviour 'the game of musical chairs' permeates social relations through the company legitimating the rationale of corporate restructuring and the intensification on each of the plants.
>
> (Tuckman and Whitall 2002: 68)

This concern echoes some of the insights by Mueller and Purcell (1992), Martinez Lucio and Weston (1994) and Ferner and Edwards (1995) with regard to the way transnationals govern their organisational politics. However, in the case of Tuckman and Whitall they suggest that EWCs can actually contribute to these competitive relations and become subject, in certain instances, to extensive management utilisation. Thus, as production and organisational processes become decentralised it is likely that the 'centre' of TNCs may actually reinforce the use of competitive relations. This viewpoint further reinforces the argument that EWCs may act as a form of worker representation that undermines national and sectoral bargaining, as employers capture them as a form of business unionism (Streeck 1997). This could lead to 'disconnection' from the dynamics outlined by some of the more positive observers: the corporate identity of EWCs may become paramount and override social and 'solidaristic' considerations (Royle 1999; Wills 2000).

The more negative approaches to the EWCs, therefore, have a certain unity and common logic to them. The overarching concern is one of how EWCs *connect* with other agents, processes and agendas: connections are seen to be unlikely to emerge due to a variety of factors and if they do it will be the connection with employers which will mediate and disconnect EWCs from alternative 'labour-led' and social agendas. The more negative school of thought raises legitimate concerns that need to be addressed because of their emphasis on relations and connections. However, the issue of EWCs must also be understood in the context of the 'limits and possibilities' of organised labour. The following section will synthesise the nature of the 'push' and 'pull' factors that influence EWCs in both their internal and external environments.

European Works Councils in context: 'if only to connect'

Lecher *et al.* (2001) have argued that there are a variety of EWC typologies ranging from the mere 'symbolic', which are dysfunctional and the 'service' oriented, which facilitate management processes through to the more 'project oriented' and 'participative' where autonomous worker voices impact in decision making (further discussed in Stoop's chapter). Symbolic EWCs are merely passive and minimal bodies that satisfy the minimal requirements of the legislation, whilst service EWCs are based on mutual exchanges of information that serve all parties but which do not lead to ongoing negotiations or focused projects within and between each side. However, Lecher *et al.* (2001) also point to EWCs that are more active, such as project-oriented EWCs, where employee representatives establish independent relations and objectives. Here real and effective networks of EWCs representatives co-ordinate in relation to specific issues and developments, exchange information and create stronger relations across national boundaries. Then there is the noticeable emergence of participative EWCs where negotiation and real consultation is apparent. Here, joint working between employee representatives and key tiers of management on a variety of issues – based in some instances on traditional forms of bargaining behaviour – underpin the actions of the EWCs. We are seeing a variety of EWCs emerge which indicate that there is no one singular experience. These are the outcome of a range of sectoral, ownership and regulatory dynamics, amongst others. It is also the outcome of the extent of integration within TNCs in terms of their divisional structures and the nature of their production systems. It is possible to find more interdependence within some TNCs when compared to others in terms of production or service delivery processes and this can influence the basis for employee and management co-ordination. However, from our point of view much of this is conditioned by the way EWCs are caught between distinct pressures in terms of push and pull factors between labour and capital both inside and outside the firm: there are dual pressures within these environments that both push unions towards managerial agendas and pull them towards autonomous labour ones. This internal–external binary, which no doubt has limitations as is the case with all binarisms, will therefore serve as a basis for discussing the dynamics that frame the possibilities and pitfalls of EWCs (see Table 3.1). What we aim to

Table 3.1 The competing pressures and environments of EWCs

	Internal environment	*External environment*
Factors 'pushing' EWCs towards the agendas of employer	Establishment of competitive relations and 'coerced comparisons' lead to productivity coalitions and tensions between sites; Elite based corporate and workplace dimension of 'involvement'	Development of enterprise focus due to trade union 'elites' and sectoral factors; The discourse of 'Euro-centrism' the 'Euro-company' as privileged site of engagement; Political denial of global linkages; Political denial of conflict strategies
Factors 'pulling' EWCs towards alternative social and economic agendas	Increasing interest in autonomous networking brought by management benchmarking and 'new management practices'; Alternative benchmarking of labour response strategies to organisational change; Indeterminate element of social relations between worker representatives started by EWCs	EU project of 'flexible regulation' as institutional context and objective; Impact of connections with diverse regulatory institutional bodies; Impact of independent and union-led education system; Social and political connections in international labour; Alternative information circuits facilitated by Information Technology

do is recast the discussion regarding EWCs by providing it with a degree of sensitivity to these complex internal and external dynamics and contexts.

The internal environment of European Works Councils

In terms of the internal environment, the internal corporate dimension of the firm and how it is governed, will clearly influence developments in the form and content of EWCs. As indicated earlier, TNCs are developing multi-dimensional control strategies as they mature and Ferner and Edwards (1995) argue that they rely on an array of methods as a way of governing their internal organisational spaces, including resource-dependent power relations, authority relations, exchange relations and culture relations. This could suggest, as Tuckman and Whitall (2002) have argued, that competitive relations between sites within TNCs erode the effectiveness and autonomy of EWCs. High profile examples where transnational worker co-ordination did not manage to erode the impact of restructuring are Renault Vilvoorde in Belgium and Fujitsu-Siemens in Finland (EIRO February 2000). Establishing benchmarking and competitive reference points around quality indicators between and within sites of TNCs can undermine cohesive transnational employee representation. Such strategies will be complemented by employee representation and negotiation between management and unions at the local level, along with languages and ideologies that facilitate such competition. However, it does not necessarily follow that competitive relations *between* sites inevitably leads to productivity coalitions being formed between local management and trade union representatives within them (Martinez Lucio and Weston 1994). In fact, if we were to view EWCs as inevitably facilitating this by becoming elite forums, that are minimalist in content and disconnected from the broader dynamics of the labour movement, then there is no need for any proactive management strategy. Yet we see a variety of instances where direct 'political' intervention by management has been required to shape the nature and impact of EWCs along these lines. For example, Pepsi Cola initially attempted to monitor and control the micro-level processes of EWCs in the late 1990s, through direct forms of control over EWC delegates in earlier meetings, such was the level of concern amongst senior directors.

As we previously argued (Martinez Lucio and Weston 1994 and 1995), the constant cross-referencing which is central to coercive comparisons is a contradictory process. It instils interest in employees and their representatives in 'other sites', in the way the workplace is represented and on what basis. Reference points are broadened and therefore the benchmarking process is opened up to diverse interventions. For example, within General Motors the constant referencing to the development of quality indicators and to the development of substantive issues of work organisation, such as teamworking, led to a broad range of information exchanges between groups of workers within each of its plants in Europe (Martinez Lucio and Weston 1994) and this has become common in a number of sectors (Weston and Martinez Lucio 1997). For example, in General Motors there were substantive exchanges amongst trade unionists across national boundaries on the manner in which work reorganisation was introduced. This was also apparent in the cases studied by Hancké (2000) who argued that one of the few positive features that were emerging in car manufacturing were how strategic issues raised in the EWCs were, in the main, shared between different union representatives in a co-operative manner. In the airline industry the impact of restructuring throughout the sector, and constant cross-referencing of the quality practices of different airlines, such as the use of sub-contracting or performance measurement in British Airways, has developed a greater degree of convergence in terms of the sharing of information generally and the discussion of management practices between distinct national constituencies of organised labour (Blyton *et al.* 2001).

This information-oriented activity in and around EWCs can impact upon the prospects for transnational bargaining and the joint regulation of employment relations more generally. Marginson (2000: 30) puts it succinctly:

Are EWCs likely to provide a focal point for the further development of European industrial relations, and with what consequences? For the present, European level agreements on pay and major conditions within TNCs are most unlikely. Instead forms of 'virtual collective bargaining' at Euro company level could emerge... [through] framework agreements or joint opinions on aspects of employment policy... [and] 'arms length bargaining' in which management and employee or union representatives do not negotiate face-to-face at European level, but in which negotiating positions and bargaining outcomes within the different national operations of a Euro company are increasingly coordinated across countries.

This rests on an appreciation of the subtle referencing and benchmarking that underpins industrial relations practices. Industrial relations, in great part, depend on 'going rates', 'acknowledged practice' and 'fair comparisons'. EWCs may act as a filter and mediating point for these in a transnational perspective. Placed alongside the transparency that the Euro currency may generate in terms of comparisons in pay levels, the scenario outlined by Marginson (2000) and Marginson and Sisson (1998) could be facilitated by EWCs. Co-ordinated bargaining could, therefore, be a possible outcome of not solely trade union pressures, but the very nature of benchmarking, isomorphic processes and information management within capital (Sisson and Marginson 2002). This is why worker representation and dynamics must not be seen as a static process but part of a push and pull dynamic across time in terms of relations with various tiers of management. In addition, worker networks that emerge on the basis of such developments may eventually create alternative and politically motivated dynamics and social relations.

Given these likely dynamics, management is constantly modifying and responding to these alternative reference points as well as the impact of the broader dynamics of worker representation on the regulation of employment. In research conducted by the authors in the food, textile and manufacturing sectors, corporate management were responding through quite sophisticated strategies that were not solely based on *contrast, compete and therefore control* (Weston and Martinez Lucio 1997). For example, management utilised the Directive's time limits as a means of finding ways of limiting the remit of EWCs meeting. Second, on various occasions issues of financial and economic information were reconstructed and represented in terms of the requirements of market competition such that common interests between management EWC representatives were referenced in order to limit the political space available for contentious distributive issues. Third, training was developed to ensure that lower tiers of management were not isolated from the EWC process and information exchanges and that representatives became conditioned in terms of their roles within EWCs. This was particularly common in non-union or weak-union contexts. Fourth, specific national constituencies of worker representatives were privileged by companies as a way of forging a strong alliance, which would isolate 'problematic' and 'marginal' representatives who were most likely to present challenges given their weaker and more precarious contexts within the value chain of the firm. Interestingly, TNCs have themselves developed new types of informal networking practices within their own management cadres as they try to cope with the limitations and contradictions of their own governance structures (particularly their communication systems), let alone the impact of EWCs (Edwards *et al.* 1999). TNCs are therefore being forced to deal with tensions and contradictions arising within their own management systems following the implementation of internal competition and benchmarking.

The external dimension of European Works Councils

There are a range of external dynamics that influence the nature and role of EWCs. The first relates to the extent in which EWCs act as a space for the development of a new set of hierarchical international trade union representatives. EWCs, especially the most significant and larger ones, can be prone to being influenced by trade union structures of a more bureaucratic nature. The question of who represents the workforce constituency of each country represented within the EWC is itself the subject of discussion and may include sectoral trade union officials, leading company representatives, workplace representatives or specific 'experts'. Clusters of trade union officials from specific countries may condition the development of EWC agendas and actions and as Streeck (1997) suggested, they may constitute the basis of an enterprise-oriented union structure. The lack of a cohesive model of industrial relations participation within Europe, both collective and individual (see Gill and Krieger 2000), can reinforce this unevenness and reliance on institutional hierarchies. This dynamic can be sustained by a second factor, which is the development of a Euro-centric identity of an elitist nature that fails to raise broader agendas and issues in relation to global and social TNC behaviour. Constructing European-centred forms of regulation within industrial relations may merely further the divide between the developed and the developing world around an organised and privileged European constituency of workers and industrial relations practices that are based on conflict-avoidance and 'partnership' (Turner 1996). Hence, the external environment in the form of, for lack of a better term, bureaucratic and elitist tendencies within Europe may reinforce the 'push' factors within TNCs that draw EWCs closer to the interests of capital.

However, as with the internal environment of EWCs, there are factors that tend to enhance the potential for EWCs as vehicles for independent and labour-oriented networking. First, EWCs form part of an alternative logic of economic regulation that has emerged within the EU. Increasingly the EU has searched for indirect forms of regulating capital given a series of constraints on its direct role. The development of EWCs provides the possibility of developing a more 'flexible' form of regulation, which does not entail financial or extensive political support (Martinez Lucio and Weston 2000). Steadily the emergence of a trade union and employee voice within the confines of the decision-making processes of TNCs will, it is hoped, strengthen the long-term and social orientation of these entities. In effect, such developments will allow the EU to 'call the tune without paying the piper' (Cram 1994: 210). In addition, a Euro-corporatist trajectory could emerge as EWCs and their broad constituency of actors interface with new forms of European legislation such as the Working Time Directive and Information and Consultation Directive thus limiting the isolation of EWCs (Knutsen 1997; Jensen *et al.* 1999). International labour action and regulation is therefore bound up with the broader issue of international state formation in terms of how the EU will develop as a political actor shaping issues of employment (Visser 1998: 233–4). EWCs are likely to form part of a broader dynamic within the EU's industrial relations (Abbott 1998). 'Virtual' and 'arms-length bargaining' within EWCs, combined with greater exchanges of information and co-ordination within and around supra-national institutions such as the European Trade Union Confederation, can lay the basis of a 'thickening network of cross-border activities' (Martin in Visser 1998: 252). EWCs can also become a player within the new relations that constitute the employment politics of the EU. Drawing on Cram (1994), with regard to policy-making processes within the EU more generally, EWCs may act as a 'window of opportunity' for the development of a new set of relationships between unions, employers, EU institutions and others which could underpin what Knutsen (1997 and Chapter 2) considers to be an enhancement of Euro-corporatism. In this respect, EWCs may form part of a complex array of linkages and system of 'flexible regulation' – as opposed to direct state regulation – that in relation to other elements contribute to an intriguing network of actors that condition the behaviour and comportment of capital (Martinez Lucio and Weston 2000).

This flexible regulation will involve non-state bodies too. The 650 EWCs that were in place in 2001 have in some cases not just been influenced by the legislation of the EU but by the increasing impact of Global Union Federations as they develop social issues and codes of conduct with transnational companies (see Chapters 13 and 14 by Doug Miller and Jane Wills). By connecting with the social rights projects of the EU and interfacing with a range of regulatory bodies, EWCs will be part of a web of institutions and bodies which can provide them with alternative reference points, resources, trajectories and narratives. Hence, the closure that is assumed to be inevitable within TNCs will grate against these broader dynamics, especially as EWCs begin to co-ordinate a range of employment and social initiatives that emerge from the EU. This anticipated 'turn' in the role and behaviour of EWCs may be understood with reference to the gaps that Wills (2000) pointed out in her work regarding expertise and knowledge. As the ETUC and its national federation develop more focused education programmes and support networks these will inevitably impact on EWCs and their position as regulatory agents. The use of focused training programmes regarding communication processes, financial and business awareness, and comparative industrial relations issues, are being extensively developed within leading EWCs with the support, in many instances, of EU funding (see Chapter 12 by John Stirling). Hence, the decision to judge a new system of regulation and worker representation within a few years of its inception is difficult if not impossible.

There is also another dimension to this broader and more dynamic external environment that consists of the need to conceptualise their social and political context. There will come a time when the sociological and ethnic dimensions of the international labour networking and EWCs will need to become the subject of study as well. In what is considered to be quite eccentric, yet a telling, research on globalisation and capital, Kotkin (1992) has argued that underpinning the current phase of globalisation is a strong ethnic and cultural set of relations. In studying small business networks in sectors such as textiles he has pointed to the role of ethnic communities who through immigrant networks have created alternative forms of capital and product circuits. This is visible in the role of Korean communities in California or Asian communities in the UK. Much of the research on EWCs and international labour networking appears to be ethnically blind. It fails to locate such networks within the historic role of ethnic communities who provide linguistic and knowledge resources. It is these types of links and support processes that should move to the forefront of the study of how EWCs connect beyond the physical and ideological remits of management. In our study of General Motors the presence of Spanish immigrant trade unionists in Britain and Germany was central to providing connections with the Spanish worker representatives in Spain. Within food manufacturing and hospitality, the presence of immigrant communities facilitated not just linguistic support but an understanding of a variety of national systems and their industrial relations contours. This is not reducible to political campaigning but to actual exchanges of information within corporate contexts. Ethnic minorities constitute, therefore, a dynamic that provide social networks for worker representation that, whilst they may or may not develop in all circumstances, do nevertheless provide a further resource beyond the firm that can reinforce the broader educational dimension of international labour networks.

Politically, there is also a curious shift that has emerged in the past few years. The development of new types of international struggles based around the anti-capitalist movement is the subject of much debate in terms of its effect and potential (Hodkinson 2001). O'Brien (2000) has argued that we are seeing new types of international labour dynamic which are steadily rethinking the centrality of formal and industrial relations dynamics as the centrepiece of international collaboration. The new types of social protest, the interface between trade unions and Non-Governmental Organisations, and the relative opening of the International Confederation of Free Trade Unions as it moves away from a Cold War mentality, provide a different environmental context and diverse set of labour networks. Facilitating these changes is the role of the Internet and it's rethinking of trade union communication and transparency (Green *et al.* 2000). That the politics of the new international labour environment should not be encased in optimism is obvious. However, the debate on EWCs, with its limited prism of traditional industrial relations cannot continue to ignore these dynamics. These form part of a set of relations that can undermine the boundaries and logic of management action within TNCs.

Hence, EWCs are at the interface of *internal* transnational corporate dynamics and *external* social and political relations within labour. These interfaces point to the possibility of EWCs being used in a variety of ways in which they are not in themselves agents but conduits and vehicles for the actions of others. Through an appreciation of these complex environments we can visualise the tensions, possibilities and contradictions of EWCs in a way that is similar to our historical understanding of the tensions of unions more generally.

Conclusions and discussion

The above analysis of the dynamics that surround EWCs would suggest some explanation of the traditional meaning of 'solidarity' and worker action. EWCs have been contrasted with traditional forms of union activity and conflict strategies and have been measured in terms of the binarism of incorporation and militancy. Yet, as we stated earlier, the relations between these are always ambiguous due to the contextual factors and tensions that underpin trade unionism. The challenge of representation – economic and political – means that worker representation can be inconsistent and ambivalent in terms of their roles (Hyman 1989). The tensions between short-term delivery of outcomes (such as avoiding workplace closures) and the longer-term representation of interests (such as the ensuring of a broader framework of rights) can lead to uncertain and contradictory behaviour. What our work has shown is that these two elements of militancy and incorporation can exist side by side and emerge at different points of time, as in the ongoing rise and fall of collaborative and autonomous worker networks, for example. To a great extent EWCs are a part of this dynamic and are equally ambivalent as modes of worker representation. This ambiguity within international labour is not a weakness or failure but an inevitable feature of the reality of labour relations. We need to see EWCs less as given entities and more as *dynamic* developments which play varying roles and are influenced by (a) the linkages and tensions that envelop them and (b) the material tensions that underpin the reality of worker representation. The question becomes the way the balance of pressures and contextual factors, when coupled within a range of institutional dynamics such as deliberate strategies, influence the character and direction of such entities (Mouzelis 1995).

The need to go beyond a zero-sum analysis of EWCs is therefore vital and, moreover, we need a rethinking of the very concept of solidarity along the lines suggested by Durkheim (1933). To start with, Hyman (1999) suggests that the debate on organised labour has in great part rested on very traditional understandings of solidarity. If we apply this to the question of EWCs, the more negative views of them in terms of *mechanical* solidarity, that is, the imposition (or failure to do so as in the more pessimistic view) of an industrial relations bargaining logic or union co-ordinating function. In effect, this means the imposition of standardised rules on relevant constituencies through hierarchical relations (Hyman 1999: 97). This view assumes a clear series of exchangeable resources, which can be the outcome of bureaucratic manipulation, or negotiation between clearly established, hierarchically structured actors. Alternatively, it is possible to imagine new forms of action and relations in terms of *organic* solidarities. The basis of solidarity is the 'flexible co-ordination of individuals who were both more differentiated and (as a necessary consequence) more independent' (Hyman 1999: 107). The outcomes of this type of solidarity are more diverse and they do not necessarily rest on clearly identifiable outcomes but a broader, long-term set of exchanges and ongoing reciprocal relations. Whilst using these arguments to grapple with the challenge that the unions face in the context of a more differentiated and complex constituency of workers and economic environment, they are equally relevant to our discussion on EWCs. Mechanistic views of solidarity would argue for a disciplined and strategic/organisational view of EWCs, that in turn leads to quite tangible outcomes in economic and political terms whether oriented to wages or collective action. However, a more organic view would stress the need for constant negotiation and strategic alliances that transcend the EWC (Weston and Martinez Lucio 1998), along with a greater sensitivity to the relevance of intangible outcomes such as information exchange, knowledge resources and the development of broader social actors and processes in and around labour. Hyman (1999: 107) stated in relation to industrial relations generally:

> Any projects aiming to create such a model must recognise and respect differentiations of circumstances and interest: within the constituencies of individual trade unions, between unions within national labour movements, between worker in different countries. The alignment and integration of diverse interests is a complex and difficult task, which requires continuous processes of negotiation: real solidarity cannot be imposed by administrative fiat, or even by majority vote.

What is required therefore is an ongoing set of relations across a variety of actors and institutions both 'in and around' organised labour. These can create imaginative linkages and shared values. More importantly they can provide for relations and interactions that may limit the possibility of gaps and competitive relations being established between different workplaces as described earlier.

The answers to understanding the nature of EWCs rest 'outside' in economic, regulatory and social terms. International worker collaboration is the outcome of a variety of factors and environmental influences that connect with each other in a series of ways. The generation of trust within the labour movement is therefore premised on linking a variety of institutional sites and social relations. Hence, the landscape of 'solidarity' is changing and this requires an understanding of the new, flexible basis of solidarity and its less easily managed/regulated/output qualities. Isolating one dimension of these relations – what would be the varied elements of what Visser (1998) considers to be an increasingly layered network of cross-border activities – would be erroneous. These networks (including managerial ones) criss-cross EWCs, being perhaps contradictory but nevertheless rich developments, which best explain the variability and possibility of international union action. However, this contradictory quality is nothing new when one takes a historical view of labour representation and it should indeed be expected.

Finally, the discussions concerning EWCs are as much a 'methodological' one reviewing the challenges brought by studying developments at the transnational level. In the end we may need to go back to some earlier debates regarding the angst of understanding trade unions, and the significance of their political linkages, in order to reinvigorate a more realistic and subtle understanding of labour representation and the need to study it in relation to its new complex environmental contexts.

References

Abbott, K. (1998) 'The ETUC and its Role in Advancing the Cause of European Worker Participation Rights', *Economic and Industrial Democracy*, 19(4): 605–31.

Blyton, P., Martinez Lucio, M., McGurk, J. and Turnbull, P. (2001) 'Globalisation and Trade Union Strategy: Industrial Restructuring and Human Resource Management in the International Civil Aviation Industry', *International Journal of Human Resource Management*, 12(3): 445–63.

Coller, X. (1996) 'Managing Flexibility in the Food Industry: A Cross-National Comparative Case Study in European Multinational Companies', *European Journal of Industrial Relations*, 2(2): 153–72.

Cram, L. (1994) 'The European Commission as a Multi-Organization: Social Policy and IT Policy in the EU', *Journal of European Public Policy*, 1(2): 195–217.

Durkheim, E. (1933) *The Division of Labour in Society*, London: Macmillan.

Edwards, T., Rees, C. and Coller, X. (1999) 'Structure, Politics and the Diffusion of Employment Practices in Multinationals', *European Journal of Industrial Relations*, 5(3): 286–306.

EIRO (European Industrial Relations Observatory) (2000) 'Closure of Fujitsu Siemens Plant – a Repeat of Renault Vilvoorde?', online. Available HTTP: http://eiro.eurofound.ie/2000/02/feature/FI0002136F.html (accessed 30 December 2002).

Ferner, A. and Edwards, P. (1995) 'Power and the Diffusion of Organisational Change within Multinational Enterprises', *European Journal of Industrial Relations*, 1(2): 229–57.

Gill, C. and Krieger, H. (2000) 'Recent Survey Evidence on Participation in Europe: Towards a European Model', *European Journal of Industrial Relations*, 6(1): 109–32.

Green, A.M., Hogan, J. and Greco, M. (2000) 'E-collectivism: Emergent Opportunities for Renewal', online. Available HTTP: http://www.geocities.com/unionsonline/ebusiness2000e.html (*unionsonline* accessed 9 May 2001).

Hancké, B. (2000) 'European Works Councils and Industrial Restructuring in the European Motor Industry', *European Journal of Industrial Relations*, 6(1): 35–60.

Hodkinson, S. (2001) 'Reviving Trade Unionism: Democracy, Internationalism and the Internet', Working Paper presented to the 29th Joint Sessions of Workshops, Grenoble, France April.

Hyman, R. (1989) *The Political Economy of Industrial Relations*, London: Macmillan.

Hyman, R. (1999) 'Imagined Solidarities: Can Trade Unions Resist Globalisation?', in P. Leisink (ed.) *Globalisation and Labour Relations*, Cheltenham: Edward Elgar.

Jensen, C.S., Madsen, J.S. and Due, J. (1999) 'Phases and Dynamics in Development of EU Industrial Relations Regulation', *Industrial Relations Journal*, 30(2): 118–34.

Kotkin, J. (1992) *Tribes*, New York: Random House.

Knutsen, P. (1997) 'Corporatist Tendencies in the Euro-Polity: The EU Directive of 22 September 1994, on European Works Councils', *Economic and Industrial Democracy*, 18: 289–323.

Lecher, W., Platzer, H.W., Rüb, S. and Weiner, K.P. (2001) *European Works Councils: Developments, Types and Networking*, Aldershot: Gower.

Marginson, P. (2000) 'The Eurocompany and Euro Industrial Relations', *European Journal of Industrial Relations*, 6(1): 9–34.

Marginson, P. and Sisson, K. (1998) 'European Collective Bargaining: A Virtual Prospect?', *Journal of Common Market Studies*, 36(4): 505–28.

Martinez Lucio, M. and Weston, S. (1994) 'New management practices in a multinational corporation: restructuring worker representation and rights?', *Industrial Relations Journal*, 25(2): 110–21.

Martinez Lucio, M. and Weston, S. (1995) 'Trade Unions and Networking in the Context of Change: Evaluating the Outcomes of Decentralisation in Industrial Relations', *Economic and Industrial Democracy*, 16(2): 233–51.

Martinez Lucio, M. and Weston, S. (2000) 'European Works Councils and "Flexible Regulation": The Politics of Intervention', *European Journal of Industrial Relations*, 6(2): 203–16.

Mouzelis, N. (1995) *Sociological Theory: What Went Wrong?*, London: Sage.

Mueller, F. and Purcell, J. (1992) 'The Europeanisation of Manufacturing and the Decentralisation of Bargaining: Multinational Management Strategies in the European Automobile Industry', *International Journal of Human Resource Management*, 3(1): 15–43.

O'Brien, R. (2000) 'Workers and World Orders: The Tentative Transformation Of The International Union Movement', *Review of International Studies*, 26(4): 533–55.

Royle, T. (1999) 'Where's the Beef? McDonalds and its European Works Council', *European Journal of Industrial Relations*, 5(3): 327–47.

Schulten, T. (1996) 'European Works Councils: Prospects for a New System of European Industrial Relations', *European Journal of Industrial Relations*, 2(3): 303–24.

Sisson, K. and Marginson, P. (2002) 'Co-ordinated Bargaining: A Process for Our Times', *British Journal of Industrial Relations*, 40(2): 197–220.

Streeck, W. (1997) 'Neither European Nor Works Councils: A Reply to Paul Knutsen', *Economic and Industrial Democracy*, 18(2): 325–37.

Tuckman, A. and Whitall, M. (2002) 'Cultivating Consent within a new Workplace Regime', *Capital and Class*, 76: 65–94.

Turner, L. (1996) 'The Europeanisation of Labour: Structure before Action', *European Journal of Industrial Relations*, 2(3): 325–44.

UNCTAD (United Nations Conference on Trade and Development) (1994) *World Investment Report 1994: Trans-national Corporations and Integrated International Production*, New York: United Nations.

Visser, J. (1998) 'Learning to Play: The Europeanisation of Trade Unions', in P. Pasture and J. Verberkmoes (eds) *Working Class Internationalism and the Appeal of National Identity*, Oxford: Berg.

Weston, S. and Martinez Lucio, M. (1997) 'Trade Unions, Management and European Works Councils: Opening Pandora's Box', *International Journal of Human Resource Management*, 8(6): 764–79.

Weston, S. and Martinez Lucio, M. (1998) 'In and Beyond European Works Councils: The Limits and Possibilities of Trade Union Influence', *Employee Relations*, 20(6): 551–64.

Wills, J. (2000) 'Great Expectations: Three Years in the Life of a European Works Council', *European Journal of Industrial Relations*, 6(1): 85–108.

4 'Thriving on diversity' revisited

Sjef Stoop

Introduction

'Thriving on diversity' was the title of a document, published in 1993 by the Multinational Business Forum, an organisation especially created by employers to counter the proposed European Works Council (EWC) Directive (Stoop 1994). Employers argued that the EWC would be a bureaucratically imposed uniform model, which pays no attention to the diverse and often de-centralised nature of business and industry (see Chapter 2 by Paul Knutsen for a detailed discussion). However, this argument was already obsolete, as the European Commission had incorporated voluntarism into the Directive and open negotiations as the basis for establishing EWCs. Thus, EWCs could be established in any form and at any level that employers and employee representatives could agree.

One of the remarkable things to be noted in the years following is that the formal structures of EWCs do not differ greatly. The model based on the subsidiary requirements of the Directive has in fact become the standard (see Chapter 6 by Richard Hume-Rothery for a UK employer's perspective on this). Thus, the possibility of setting up alternative information and consultation procedures instead of EWCs has hardly been used; most EWCs are established at the parent company level (Carley and Marginson 2000: 18); only a few companies have used the opportunity to establish EWCs at lower level to fit their de-centralised character; EWCs regularly meet once or twice a year with meetings lasting two or three days and the majority, especially the 'Article 6' EWCs, have a select committee (ibid.: 44). It may also be assumed that the degree of uniformity between EWC structures will be even greater if the 'hollow EWCs' that have undoubtedly been set up to circumvent the Directive altogether are excluded.

Only two elements show any significant variation: the size of EWCs and their transnational composition, both of which are clearly related to the characteristics of the particular company. These are also shaped by the specific legal approach of the Directive, with 'transnational' and 'national' requirements affecting matters such as the role of trade unions, the way members are elected or appointed, and the facilities available to EWC members. However, the limited range of variations between formal EWC structures does not mean that there is no diversity between EWCs.

This chapter will argue that the actual diversity of EWCs is not to be found in their formal structures, but in their practices. It will focus on two sources of variation: the characteristics of the companies involved and the specific amalgamation of industrial relations systems that are represented in the EWC and leave to one side other possible explanations like the 'age' of the EWC. However, it will ask whether this diversity is a characteristic of the infant stage of EWC development, or whether diversity will remain a basic element in the overall picture of EWCs.

Differences in practice

Only a supreme optimist would have expected that EWCs, as a combination of a new form of transnational co-operation and a major innovation in the field of industrial relations, would be able to operate very effectively from the start. The existing body of research shows that the majority of EWCs encounter significant problems in realising their basic rights to information and consultation. In interpreting these results we should bear in mind Kerkchofs (2001: 8) comment that 'the problems in EWC practice are much more visible in these research findings than the progress made in improving their efficiency. The reason for this is that all case studies conducted up to now are snapshots taken at a certain moment'. To analyse the practice of EWCs the chapter will look briefly at the data from existing research showing the ways that they make use of their right of information, the consultation process itself, the items taken up by EWCs, and the use of extraordinary meetings. First, in terms of information giving there is mixed data with positive evaluations from Waddington's survey analysis (2001 and 2002) but less strong evidence from smaller scale, more qualitative studies (Syndex 1998). Overall it appears that information may still be superficial, not on time, or on subjects that do not have a high priority for employees. Second, the general experience of consultation has also been imperfect as was highlighted by the Renault-Vilvoorde case.[1] Again Waddington's survey evidence (op. cit.) is the most positive whereas Stoop and Donders (1997), Lecher *et al.* (1998) are more pessimistic. However, there appear to be slow procedural changes as EWCs move from written questions often to be submitted in advance, to a more open discussion.

Third, there is some indication of EWCs beginning to develop their own agendas. Key issues may include health and safety, training, equal opportunities and the environment. Recently, the scope of EWC involvement in various kinds of negotiations has been extended. According to some recent surveys, EWCs are seeking to negotiate a range of issues (Krieger 2000) including codes of conduct (Baur 2002) and in relation to issues arising from corporate restructuring (Cremers 2001: 26–8). For example, the GM agreement 'Fair-teilen', resulted in spreading the effects of the lowering of car production over a number of European plants and has prevented plant closures.

A final indicator of practice is the use of the facility to have extraordinary meetings. This is particularly important as issues such as collective redundancies are unlikely to coincide with the annual meetings. Different research reports give varying outcomes to the question of how many extra meetings have been held. Of the eight cases that Lecher *et al.* (1998) studied, only one has had an extraordinary meeting. Stoop and Donders (1997) found five out of 10 cases, and Lamers (1999) five out of 17 cases to have held extraordinary meetings. The recent DTI survey reports about half of the EWCs to have had extraordinary meetings (DTI 2000: 28).

Lecher and his colleagues have tried to draw on characteristics such as these to provide an overall assessment of EWCs practice. In research involving twenty EWCs they conclude that about 50 per cent belong to the 'symbolic' type, 'their activities are mainly confined to the annual plenary meetings and EWC members are, for the most part, passive between meetings and do not prepare for the plenaries' (Lecher *et al.* 2001: 85).

The other 50 per cent are more or less evenly spread amongst a further three categories. The 'service EWC', where members forward information to their colleagues between meetings and where the EWC can put national or local problems to central management. The 'project-oriented' EWC. That can organise 'everyday business' via its own structures and use resources specifically attributed to the EWC. An active select committee, the establishment of its own information system and the ability to define and tackle areas of work, are the main characteristics of this type of EWC. The 'participative' EWC, where the EWC seeks to participate in the corporate decision-making process.

These categories show that EWCs can and do operate in different ways but what are the explanations for this diversity?

Company characteristics as an explanation for differences in European Works Council practices

A key to differences in EWC practice is to be found in company structure and organisation and specifically size, international spread and corporate strategies. Smaller companies clearly give EWC representatives more opportunity to develop detailed knowledge and integrated activity. Companies with a focus of the home country rather than a wider international spread will inhibit EWC development and confine them to the symbolic role identified by Lecher *et al.* (2001: 85). Finally, there is the question of whether companies develop genuinely international human resource strategies beyond senior management levels. The reality appears to be that policy development in this area is most commonly informal and arranged more through internal communication and the international exchange of management.

These characteristics of size, international spread and global management strategies are relatively straightforward. However, to determine the precise relations between sites in different countries, a more detailed analysis of the company is needed. An analysis in terms of the diversity of the company and the level of integration within the company may be a useful tool (Bartlett and Goshal 1989). These two dimensions determine to what extent common interest can be found amongst workers' representatives.

The level of differentiation indicates the extent to which subsidiaries do not produce identical goods or services or perform the same tasks. When the level of differentiation is low, it is easier for representatives from different subsidiaries to understand each other's background, as everyone is involved in the same kind of production. But with a low level of differentiation, workers in different subsidiaries may also find themselves in competition with each other, especially when the subsidiaries produce goods or services that can be exported. If the level of differentiation is very high it may be difficult to find concrete issues that are of interest to everyone in the EWC.

The level of integration indicates the extent to which subsidiaries are tied to the group as a whole or can run their own business more or less autonomously. Integration is high where subsidiaries are tied to the group and low where they are more or less independent, as long as they fulfil certain financial standards. For example, where production locations have their own R&D and sales and marketing they may hardly be integrated into other networks of the company at all.

International, multinational and transnational companies

The two elements of integration and differentiation can be very useful in classifying different types of companies and linking this to types of EWC. This classification can help clarify the multitude of experiences of worker representatives. This is summarised in Table 4.1, which combines three dimensions: the degree of internationalisation as against dominance of the home country, and the levels of differentiation and integration.

Whereas the above-mentioned classification is based on the internal structure of the company, the Construction unions' federation (EFBWW 1995) has developed a further categorisation on the basis of Dunning's classification of MNC strategies. Although the EFBWW categorisation specifically refers to the construction industry it can easily be generalised (Table 4.2).

Both the analysis of company strategies and of company structures may help in understanding the differences existing in EWC practices as these company characteristics may impede the development of the EWC into one type and may foster another. However, there is no necessary one-to-one relation between company strategies and structures and the EWC practice. Other factors come into play too.

Industrial relations systems as an explanation for differences in European Works Council practice

Apart from the differences between companies, a second explanation for differences is that every EWC has a different blend of industrial relations cultures. The experience with a particular system of consultation at national level causes differences between both managers and participants in EWCs from different countries. The following discussion looks at the impact of the national system of

Table 4.1 Classifications of EWC prospects by company type

Company type	EWC prospects
International: Dominance of parent company, no links between foreign subsidiaries except through company headquarters. Transfer of knowledge and strategy from centre to subsidiaries. Little integration between foreign subsidiaries, strong ties between centre and individual foreign subsidiaries. (differentiation = low; integration = medium)	Dominating role of representatives from the centre. The EWC as 'extended' national structure where the greatest interest of representatives from subsidiaries is to get information from the mother company.
Multinational: International federation of national companies, working for their own national markets. Local-for-local structure with little integration between subsidiaries. No danger of transfer of production. (differentiation = medium; integration = low)	The EWC is no more than the sum of its national delegations, which use the EWC to improve their position in local/national consultation or negotiation structures. The company might proceed to more international integration.
Transnational: network of interlinked foreign subsidiaries, many of them having roles beyond their own region. A transnational does not mean necessarily a centre-less company. A two-way communication between centre and subsidiaries exists. (differentiation = high; integration = high)	EWC becomes a necessity because national consultation rights are becoming less relevant in respect to an international company strategy. EWC develops dimension of its own. Some items may be co-ordinated or even regulated on European level. For management the EWC can become a check on whether the international company strategy is being implemented at local level.

Sources: Stoop and Donders (1997) based on Bartlett and Goshal's 'Managing across borders' (1989); Lecher *et al.* (1998: 37–9).

industrial relations on the EWC, including the so-called 'country-of-origin effect'. It then turns to the question of the possible impact of the EWC on national systems of industrial relations.

The impact of the national systems of industrial relations

In general, a German-based multinational may have a different type of EWC when compared to a UK-based or a French multinational. However, care should be taken when tracing country-of-origin effects back to basic characteristics of the industrial relations systems. Knudsen and Bruun (1998) analysing 66

Table 4.2 Classifications of EWC prospects using the EFBWW typology

Company strategy	EWC prospects
Low wage. Leading principle is cost cutting. Structure: Overhead functions concentrated at company headquarters. No autonomy for foreign establishments. The level of differentiation is often low; companies concentrate on basic activities. The level of integration is medium: subsidiaries do not form an intricate network, but they compete with each other on costs.	Difficulties because of internal competition and large gap between (central) staff and (peripheral) production workers. Need for information dissemination from central office to peripheral subsidiaries. Need for introducing company labour standards across subsidiaries to limit internal competition based on bad employment conditions.
Market expansion. Leading principle is conquering new markets. Structure: Level of integration is low. Subsidiaries will to a great extent operate independently from company headquarters to serve local markets and obtain government contracts.	Position of workers outside home market might be vulnerable because strongly dependent of market development. Need for information dissemination from central office to other countries. Need for codes of conduct, for example, on closing subsidiaries.
Efficiency seekers. Leading principle is smart production and using economics of scale. Structure: Business units with internal competition. Level of integration is high. Transfer of management and technological expertise to the different units.	Relatively equal position of workers from different countries. Need for comparison of labour conditions/terms of employment and of best practices. Need for setting general labour standards across subsidiaries.
Asset seekers. Often (former) National monopolies. Leading principle is a portfolio strategy, often by strategic acquisitions and disposals. This category often overlaps with other categories. Level of integration may vary, but level of differentiation is often high: all kinds of companies may be subsidiaries of these kinds of conglomerates. Central role for overall strategy.	In home markets the company dominates and can offer good terms of employment. Position of 'foreign' workers might vary greatly across subsidiaries. Great need for understanding company strategy. Need for codes of conduct, for example, on buying and selling of companies.

Source: EFBWW 1995, levels of integration and differentiation added by the author.

Note
This last type of company seems to be specific for the construction industry, compare Suez, Vivendi or Bouygues.

agreements in the Nordic countries found no clear differences between them and conclude that, 'we are sure that country is not the important factor' (ibid.: 148). Another indication that the 'country-of-origin' effect should not be overstated can be found in the fact that the 'French' EWC model of a joint employer/employee body is used in far more companies than those with their headquarters in countries which have this model for national representation systems (69 per cent of all Article 13 EWCs according to Carley and Marginson 2000: 19).[2] Japanese and US companies overwhelmingly opt for this model (96 and 93 per cent, respectively). However, in moving our analysis from the formal structures to differences in practice, the importance of differences between national backgrounds becomes quite crucial.

One important difference between industrial relations systems is the role played by unions and this is also critical in EWCs. In some countries unions might be able to play a very constructive role in EWCs, in others seats legally designated to them may be left vacant because they have set other priorities. For example, in their analysis of the Merloni case, Lecher *et al.* (1998) come to the conclusion that an important reason for the poor functioning of this EWC is the central role designated to unions, as the unions have 'forsaken' the EWC (ibid.: 206). The picture becomes even more complicated when the differences within unions are acknowledged. For example, in the Nordic countries, with their generally strong trade unions, the quality of voluntary agreements is often below the minimum requirements of the subsidiary requirements in the Directive. Knudsen and Bruun (1998) explain this by pointing to the de-centralised trade union structure, this means that the union representatives in the company have often negotiated the agreements: 'the trade unions at national level did not fully control events: some agreements were signed by employee representatives against the advice of their trade union' (ibid.: 138). The Nordic union delegates at shop floor level, 'are not automatically prepared to present broader trade union interests and aims. They may interpret employee interest as more closely linked to the success of the company' (ibid.: 152).

Apart from the different styles or models of industrial relations the position of a particular country delegation in the overall setting of the EWC is of importance. In practice, a major 'home-country advantage' exists with employee representatives from the parent company feeling much more confident with 'their' procedures and 'their' managers and having more chance to successfully intervene in proceedings than 'foreign' representatives. There is a marked tendency for employees at the parent company to show more loyalty to their employer than to foreign colleagues, or at least feel responsible for maintaining good relations with central management. Thus, at ICI, the British delegates are trying to prevent confrontations, whereas at the Italian company Merloni the British delegates tried to mobilise the EWC to take action against job cuts, but this was blocked by the Italian representatives (Lecher *et al.* 1998: 186–202).

These attitudes sometimes even stop representatives from starting the negotiation process. Home-country workers representatives 'with experience of co-determination feared to lose some of their privileges with the advent of EWCs' (Kerckhofs 2001: 3). Experience has also shown that there is often a marked difference between the attitudes of Dutch participants in EWCs from a 'Dutch' parent company compared to those working for a foreign-owned company. Many central works councils in the Netherlands have extra rights by agreement with central management and this may include rights on information or consultation over international matters, which they are afraid to loose. However, for Dutch representatives working at a company owned by a foreign parent, the EWC is often seen as an opportunity to improve the feeble position that the Dutch works councils have *vis-à-vis* that parent.

The impact of European Works Councils on national systems of industrial relations

National industrial relations cultures are not homogenous and are in a period of transition in many countries that leaves them open to changes. In an overview of the impact of EWCs on national industrial relations systems the EIRO Observer (1998) concluded that the direct influence might be rather limited as the implementation of the Directive generally fitted EWCs into existing systems. However, this conclusion is drawn from a rather legalistic or structural viewpoint with little attention to cultures and issues of industrial relations systems. Other researchers expect that EWCs will contribute to convergence in the EU (Bobke and Müller 1995: 991; Jacobi and Marginson 1998: 3).

To clarify this complex question the structure/conduct/performance distinction that originates from industrial organisation studies (Jacquemin and de Jong 1977: 5–8) can be applied. Convergence may or may not occur on different levels: structures (e.g. dual systems), conduct (i.e. cultures and practices such as more co-operative labour relations or company trade unionism[3]), or performance (such outcomes as employment conditions).

Structure convergence

According to Lecher *et al.* (1998: 272) the introduction of the EWC Directive signifies the basic decision to introduce a dual model in Europe. The Directive on national information and consultation (2002/14/EC), in effect, makes works councils mandatory and will strengthen these developments. Indirect effects include the incentive for building up group-level structures in Spain and Belgium (EIRO Observer 1998). Also in the UK and Italy the EWC stimulates the development of national structures to co-ordinate representation above plant level, similar to those already existing in, for example, Germany, France, Finland and the Netherlands.

The implementation of EWC legislation also marks a break in the UK and Denmark, from the national traditions of modelling the relations between employers and employee representatives solely on the basis of agreements concluded with trade unions (Knudsen and Bruun 1998: 135). In Germany on the other hand, the establishment of EWCs on the basis of negotiations marks a break from the strongly legalistic basis of the German co-determination system. In the Netherlands this strengthens a tendency that is already present, for example, in the change of working-time legislation, from detailed legislation to framework legislation where the social partners or works councils arrange the details in specific agreements.

Conduct convergence

Besides the convergence in regulatory frameworks the EWC Directive has caused, one can also observe a certain convergence in industrial relations cultures towards more co-operative relations, based on specific workplace related problems and solutions. General indicators of this are falling strikes in most countries, the growing importance of alliances for jobs, and collective bargaining policy geared to competitiveness and leading to wage restraint (Hoffmann 2000: 629). National examples also illustrate this point. In recent years, the British unions have been advocating the introduction of works councils on a European level, and at national level the idea of 'social partnership' is also supported. The development of the EWC also provides a stimulus for British managers to rethink and reshape the employee–management practice in the UK (Wills 1998: 27).

According to the EIRO Observer (1998), the EWC might strengthen the development of the existing system of works councils in Greece by helping create a 'participatory climate'. In France EWC practice highlights differences in industrial relations culture, both between French representatives and also with other countries, for example, over the issue of confidential information and over the degree to which employees representatives should use a confrontation policy (e.g. see Lecher *et al.* 1998: 140–2, 144). Indications are that the more co-operative attitude is winning ground, but this tendency is anything but clear-cut.

Performance convergence

Some convergence in the 'output' of industrial relations systems (employment conditions), might also occur. European collective bargaining on wages still seems a far-fetched project. Most employers are firmly opposed to this and refuse to authorise international employers' organisations to negotiate on their behalf. However, on other items such as health and safety, training, and some aspects of working time, a negotiating role for the EWC, and thus some international convergence might be conceivable (Hoffman 1998: 163) and indeed is taking place. This may be an objective both for management (e.g. at ENI concerning health and safety, or at Bull concerning mobility), and for employees (e.g. at Unilever and Sara Lee where workers started to compare redundancy packages). This may lead to some convergence in the way companies handle restructuring as in, for example, the Unilever 'Responsible restructuring' code or the 'Closures and social responsibility' programme by which Hydro Agri monitored the consequences of its plant closures. Both examples concern company initiatives that have been discussed in, but not negotiated by, the EWC.

Industrial relations and the European Works Council

National industrial relations systems are not homogenous and multinational companies 'export' part of their culture to their foreign branches. Indeed the greatest danger perceived by unions is that of EWCs becoming a system of their own with

Table 4.3 The influence of national industrial relations systems on an EWC

Perceived quality of industrial relations in home country	Progressive strategy	Defensive strategy
Good	Use the EWC to export 'good relations' from the home country to other countries.	Delay the establishment of EWCs to prevent the 'dilution' of quality by the EWC.
Poor	Use the EWC to import 'good relations' from other countries.	Delay or obstruct the establishment of EWCs instead of using the EWC to improve relations.

transnational industrial relations for workers directly employed by the 1,500 or so core companies in Europe (Hoffman 1998: 163). In periods of heavy restructuring the EWC system seems to be perfectly fitted to an accommodation of workers demands and aspirations to the policy of the company (Streeck 1984: 292). Thus, the emergence of EWCs might lead to increased segmentation or even fragmentation of industrial relations.

To understand how the mutual influences between the EWC and national industrial relations systems might work, it is useful to use an analysis derived from strategic perspectives. For simplicity's sake a model is used with two variables: the perceived quality of industrial relations in the home country and the (explicit or implicit) strategy of the actors. This is outlined in Table 4.3.

For some countries this may have some explanatory power, for example, in countries like Sweden and the Netherlands where it seems that both social partners have not been in a hurry to establish voluntary EWCs. This then could be explained as a defensive strategy in a situation where the perceived quality of industrial relations are good. A common pattern in existing EWCs seems to be that, at the parent company good relations exist, but the group is growing by international acquisitions, which introduce a range of atypical relations in the group. Therefore management wants to use the EWC to export the good relations 'at home' to the newly acquired companies. ICI, Bull, Rhône Poulenc, Merloni and ENI, all seem examples of this trend, which is not confined to certain countries.

Conclusions and policy implications

In this chapter, it has been argued that significant differences exist between the practices of EWCs. The central question to be answered is whether these differences belong to the development stage of the EWCs or whether they will persist. Two possible sources of diversity, company characteristics and industrial relations systems have been discussed. How will they evolve?

Some differences will remain or may even become more deeply entrenched. In particular, differences caused by company characteristics are unlikely to be reduced. On the one hand, there are some general trends in companies that might suggest convergence. For example, in the 1950s and 1960s one could see the rise of divisional structures, in the 1960s of diversification, and in the 1990s 'back to core businesses' but this has not led to identical company structures. Differences in size and in international spread will continue to exist, as will differences in products and markets that call for specific structures.

For the other source of diversity discussed, national industrial relations systems, the answer to the question whether these will continue to exist is more controversial. It has been argued that the role the EWC plays in the possible convergence depends on the strategies of the industrial relations partners in combination with the perceived quality of the industrial relations systems. The outcomes may differ for different aspects of the industrial relations system and an analysis in terms of the structure–conduct–performance paradigm may prove useful to clarify the debate on this question. Convergence may be most pronounced in the structural elements of the industrial relations system, as in many countries these are going through a period of transition. This convergence may be helped by other European legislation, which creates a European space for the EWC to work in, for example, the recent EU proposals to make works councils mandatory at national level and in the European Company Statute. Reflecting on these Directives, and the rejection of the 13th take-over Directive by the European Parliament, Reberioux (2002: 126) observes 'substantial progress towards establishing a European model of corporate governance, rooted in a European social model'. On the other hand, without the creation of a European space for the EWC to work in and a convergence of national industrial relations structures, the EWC project may well collapse. In this respect the EWC is part of a virtual or a vicious circle of convergence or blocked internationalisation of industrial relations.

The conduct of industrial relations systems may also converge but as this is also dependent on cultures the movement is much slower. On the other hand, this is less prone to political stalemates as it is more dependent on learning processes. The international exchange of experiences that the EWC stimulates will certainly contribute to such learning processes. Discussions in the EWC and with management can lead to developing European models, for instance when dealing with restructuring or privacy. Indeed Hoffmann (1998) sees these learning processes as the main reason why EWCs 'can play a leading role in Europeanising industrial relations ... [although he warns] ... against having any euphoric expectations' (ibid.: 162). As for the outcomes of industrial relations, nothing much may be expected on the level of wages. Any convergence in this field will be more probably caused by larger economic forces than by the EWC.

These mutual feedbacks in the development processes of EWCs and convergence of national industrial relations systems, provide for a very dynamic and unstable development path, as the feedbacks do not correct but enforce existing tendencies. So we may expect either a virtual circle of EWCs improving their effectiveness in a context of converging industrial relations systems and the development of the social dimension of the EU or a failure of the EWCs to become more effective, in the context of a 're-nationalisation' of industrial relations systems.[4]

Much will depend on the prospect of embedding the EWC in national systems. Even if a full-grown system of EWCs might involve 30,000 employee representatives or more all over Europe (Lecher *et al.* 1998: 270), this still is a very small number compared to those active in national and/or local structures. So, perhaps the most fundamental observations to be made from studying EWCs can be summarised under 'diversity' and 'learning processes'. The interplay of these fundamental characteristics of the general EWC phenomenon results in EWCs being in different stages of development to diverging models.

Without a stronger position for workers representatives' *vis-à-vis* central management and more internal cohesion of the EWC (including a common strategy) any consultation rights are bound to run into practical problems. The solutions to these are to be found in holding more than one meeting each year, having training, improving the co-operation between EWCs delegates and ensuring that EWC members really are the representatives of their national colleagues. This is partly defined by their EWC agreement, but to a large extent it is defined by what the representatives can make out of it, depending also on their local power resources. There is already some difference in many EWCs between what the agreement officially allows for and what is possible in practice. Especially in countries like France, Germany and the Netherlands where there is already a well-developed and well-equipped central works council structure that the EWC may be able to utilise. Therefore, we may conclude that to improve the position of EWCs, we should not concentrate only on improving the legislation, but also put much more effort into improving the practical work of the EWC.

Acknowledgement

Thanks to Boudewijn Berentsen for comments on an earlier draft.

Notes

1 This is one of the conclusions in the survey by the EIRO Observer (1998). This is supported by case-study research. The Syndex study (1998: 1) states that EWCs are not consulted by management. Stoop and Donders found that no consultation had taken place in the nine cases they studied (1997: 24).

2 This can be explained partly by the fact that in practice the difference between the French or German model turns out to be not very important. The reason is that almost all EWCs, which do function at all, have a pre-meeting of employee representatives only and a meeting with management.

3 Company unionism holds a negative connotation in this respect as it is associated with 'Betriebsegoismus' (company egoism) or productivity coalitions, whereby broader interests are ignored in favour of improvement of the employees of just one's own company (Stoop 1994: 49; Hoffmann 1998: 163).

4 This re-nationalisation is not just an abstract possibility, it did occur in the 1970s as Streeck has argued (1992: 208). Visser has argued that the loss of other policy instruments due to the introduction of the Euro, makes a national co-ordination of wages more crucial for European governments (2001: 7–8).

References

Bartlett, C.A. and Goshal, S. (1989) *Managing Across Border: The Transnational Solution*, London: Hutchinson.

Baur, B. (IG Metall) (2002) *EWCs and Negotiations*, presentation for the EMF Task Force, 25 June 2002, Bad Hofgastein.

Bobke, M. and Müller, T. (1995) 'Chancen für eine Neugestaltung des Systems der Arbeitsbeziehungen auf der Europäische Ebene', in *WSI Mitteil-lungen*, 1995/10.

Carley, M. and Marginson, P. (2000) *Negotiating EWCs under the Directive: A Comparative Analysis of Article 6 and Article 13 Agreements*, Dublin: European Foundation for the Improvement of Living and Working Conditions.

Cremers, J. (2001) 'Worker Representation on Large-Scale Construction Sites', *CLR News*, no3/2001: 3–11.

DTI (Department of Trade and Industry) (2000) *Cost and Benefits of the European Works Council Directive*, Employment Relations Research Survey No. 9, London: DTI.

EFBWW (1995) *The Strategic Conduct of Multinational Companies: A Discussion Paper for European Works Councils in the Building and Woodworking Sector*, EAFBWW Multi-project Booklet No. 2, Brussels: EFBWW.

EIRO Observer (1998) 'The impact of European Works Councils', *EIRO Observer*, supplement to issue 4/1998.

Hoffmann, R. (1998) 'The Europeanisation of Industrial Relations – Prospects and Limits', in R. Hoffmann, O. Jacobi, B. Keller and M. Weiss (eds) *The German Model of Industrial Relations Between Adaptation and Erosion*, Düsseldorf: Hans Böckler Stiftung.

Hoffmann, R. (2000) 'European Trade Union Structures and the Prospects for Labour Relations in Europe', in J. Waddington and R. Hoffmann (eds) *Trade Unions in Europe, Facing Challenges and Searching for Solutions*, Brussels: European Trade Union Institute.

Jacobi, O. and Marginson, P. (1998) *European Works Councils: Trends and Prospects*, Brussels: European Trade Union Institute.

Jacquemin, A.P. and de Jong, H.W. (1977) *European Industrial Organisation*, Macmillan: London.

Kerckhofs, P. (2001) *There are no Good or Bad Companie: 20 Years of European Works Council Dynamics*, Brussels: European Trade Union Institute, online. Available HTTP: http://www.iira2001.org/Documents/Papers (accessed 30 December 2002).

Knudsen, H. and Bruun, N. (1998) 'European Works Councils in the Nordic Countries: An Opportunity and a Challenge for Trade Unionism', *European Journal of Industrial Relations*, 4(2): 131–55.

Krieger, H. (2000) 'EWCs Acting as Platforms for Agreements', presentation at the ETUC conference, Paris 20 November 2000.

Multinational Business Forum (1993) 'Thriving on diversity'. Brussels.

Lamers, J. (1999) *The Added Value of European Works Councils*, AWVN, the Netherlands: Haarlem.

Lecher, W., Nagel, B. and Platzer, H.W. (1998) *Die Konstituiering Europäischer Betriebsräte – Vom Informationsforum zum Akteur? Eine vergleichende Studie von acht Konzernen in Deutschland, Frankreich, Großbritannien und Italien*, Baden-Baden: Hans Böckler Stiftung.

Lecher, W., Platzer, H.W., Rüb, S. and Weiner, K. (2001) *European Works Councils: Developments, Types and Networking*, Aldershot: Gower.

Stoop, S. (1994) *The EWC, One Step Forward: A Study into the Success of EWCs*, Amsterdam: FNV.

Stoop, S. and Donders, P. (1997) *EOR-en in functie. Een onder-zoek naar het functioneren van Europese ondernemingsrade*, Amsterdam: FNV EOR-service.

Streeck, W. (1984) 'Neo-corporatist industrial relations and the economic crisis in West Germany', in J. Goldthorpe (ed.) *Order and Conflict in Contemporary Capitalism*, Oxford: Clarendon Press.

Streeck, W. (1992) *Social Institutions and Economic Performance: Studies of Industrial Relations in Advanced Capitalist Economies*, London and Beverly Hills: Sage.

Syndex (1998) *Methodological Guide on the Informing and Consulting of European Works Councils in the Case of Restructuring*, Volume 1, Paris: Syndex.

Rebéroux, A. (2002) 'European Corporate Governance and Worker Involvement', *Journal for Common Market Studies*, 40: 111–34.

Visser, J. (2001) 'Europa en de CAO, drie scenario's en een toekomstverkenning'. *AIAS online research paper, Amsterdam*.

Waddington, J. (2001) *What do European Works Council Representatives Think? Views from Five Countries*, Warwick/Brussels: ETUI.

Waddington, J. (2002) *The Views of European Works Council Representatives in the Engineering Industry*, preliminary results of a survey for the EMF, Warwick/Brussels: EMF.

Wills, J. (1998) *The Experience of European Works Councils in the UK*, Working Paper No. 4, University of Southampton.

Part II

Assessing the Directive in action

The single market is the European backdrop of a global economy that has change as its maxim. As there is global expansion through company mergers and acquisitions that often, if not always, lead to closures and redundancies, so there is change. As companies restructure the shop floor with new production techniques and acquire new businesses to enter expanding/changing markets. The Social Charter was the European response to the major change that was taking place then and is continuing now. The chapters in this part continue two of the themes introduced in Part I. First that of employer recalcitrance to an undermining of their managerial prerogative to follow global markets, which was an important factor in the slow progress of any significant form of European employee participation, finally broken by the European Works Council (EWC) Directive. Second, the problems with the current legislation whose Articles currently influence the agreements of over 700 EWCs.

The first two chapters have the theme of change at their heart. With Buschak discussing what should go in a review of the Directive and the type of information and consultation the ETUC expects when employees' lives are affected by company restructuring. In a contrasting vein Hume-Rothery concerns himself with a management view of change noting that EWCs can be useful for communication when restructuring occurs but are more likely an opportunity lost for company communication of indisputable business decisions. Whilst Gilman and Marginson provide an analysis of the agreements that form the basis of these EWCs, providing an objective account of the influences that frame agreements.

The European Works Council Directive review

Chapters 5 and 6 by Willy Buschak and Richard Hume-Rothery, respectively, concern themselves with the Directive's review, one explicitly the other implicitly. Buschak gives an insight into the European Trade Union Confederation's (ETUC) views on what a review of the Directive should contain. Central to his chapter is the theme of information and consultation with a proposed definition for each that mirrors the recently adopted European Company Statute. He argues for stronger controls on company restructuring through the EWC, turning it into a channel to slow this down, a view that Hume-Rothery would certainly not share.

Buschak discusses EWC agreements arguing that employers have an important advantage in negotiations, not only because of their greater resources but also because trade unions are not always involved. He believes that to help counter this a review of the Directive should contain a right for European Industry Federations to participate in all negotiations. Chapter 5 finishes by identifying the main functions that need to be strengthened if an EWC is to operate effectively. These include a right of access for EWC representatives when they need to discuss issues with national employee representatives. An appropriate level of EWC financial and material resources and the right to have an adequate number of meetings. This sharply contrasts to the views of Hume-Rothery who argues that meetings are an expensive business.

Chapter 6 by Richard Hume-Rothery does not openly concern itself with the review of the Directive but instead focuses more on the spectre of co-determination. He directly challenges the ETUC's views on consultation arguing that their proposals, which would mean employees being involved in management decision making, are contrary to what most employees want. The chapter offers a personal account of somebody with intimate knowledge of British multinational reservations to the Directive. Implicit is the potential challenge to managerial prerogatives and Hume-Rothery argues that the British business community saw the Directive as a potential trigger for a pan-European collective bargaining platform based on the constraints of co-determination. From this he believes that companies chose Article 13 French rather than potential Article 6 German models for their EWCs, the French having a constitutional role for management on the EWC (see Chapter 7 by Mark Gilman and Paul Marginson, which offers evidence to support this proposition). He believes, though, that these agreements were a management opportunity lost to provide a channel for effective management communication. He supports his argument for management communication, rather than employee participation, by arguing that for EWC representatives to take a participative role they would need to be educated to the level of an MBA. He finally notes that the slow rate of progress of agreements (identified in Kerckhofs 2002) is evidence of the lack of enthusiasm for the Directive from both employees and management.

The influence of the Directive on EWC agreements

Gilman and Marginson focus on the main factors that influence EWC agreements, and whilst not denying that inequalities between employer and employee are a factor in the final content of agreements, they offer a number of other propositions. They view the negotiation of agreements from a position of 'constrained choices' for management and employee negotiators arguing that a series of factors influence their decisions. Four propositions are explored, a 'statutory model effect' where agreements conform to the Directive's EWC model; a 'learning effect' where provisions of prior or current agreements are 'diffused' to future agreements; a 'country effect' in which the headquarters of a multinational influences its EWC agreement such that it resembles the national information and consultation provision; and a 'sector effect' where EWCs in the same sector resemble each other. Introducing a multi-variate analysis that includes three groups of key features that shape EWCs, including one set that is contained within the Directive, one that is not, and one which relates to country-of-origin/or sector influences, they test each of the propositions. The results provide strong evidence that a statutory model effect is in operation; there is also support for the 'country' and 'sector' effects; and the presence of a 'learning effect'.

Reference

Kerckhofs, P. (2002) *European Works Councils in Facts and Figures*, Brussels: European Trade Union Institute.

5 The practical and legal problems of European Works Councils

Reviewing the Directive

Willy Buschak

Introduction

Every day, newspapers are full of news about mergers and mega-mergers, about acquisitions, restructuring, closures, relocations and reorganisation of business on a transnational scale. Decisions of transnational central management affect workers in all European subsidiaries. In contrast, the rights of workers and their representatives have their limits at national borders. The Directive on European Works Councils (EWCs) was a first step to remedy this situation. Since 1994 practice has shown that, thanks to EWCs, 'undertakings' have gained the advice of the best possible consultants: workers and their representatives. Information and consultation with workers and their representatives is a basic social right, but at the same time one of the most important elements of modern corporate governance.

Thanks to the EWC Directive, workers of the same undertaking have the right to come together across borders and form joint opinions. The EWCs of Unilever, of Opel/General Motors, of Ford and many others have used the opportunity to influence restructuring all over Europe, often successfully. Practice has shown, however, that there are many shortcomings.

This chapter examines the most common practical problems EWCs have to face by reviewing what the Directive states. It does this in order to see where a strict interpretation of the current text can help to remedy problems or where the Directive needs to be changed. The first section, 'Primary considerations', identifies the basic elements that give birth to the form of the EWC. The second, 'Agreements', briefly discusses the agreements that provide the governing rules of an EWC. The third, 'The basic requirements of an EWC', considers the main requirements needed to provide an effectively functioning body. It closes with a short conclusion which details the ETUC's view of the main elements that should be considered in the review of the EWC Directive.

Primary considerations

This first section discusses the basic principle contained in the EWC Directive, information and consultation, an area that every author in this book touches on in one way or another. It follows this by reviewing the nature of the term controlling interest, a prerequisite for the formation of an EWC. It also discusses the problems with identifying controlling interests when they are part of a franchise or joint venture and asks how to resolve the situation when two or more organisations merge. It recommends changes throughout that will begin to resolve some of the problems identified.

Information and consultation

Information and consultation is the primary consideration of an EWC and the 'timeliness' of these continues to present the biggest problem they face. There is still evidence that company managers are not only failing to provide information and consultation in good time, but are often failing to provide it at all. Unfortunately, despite the notorious Renault case, there have also been problems with Marks & Spencer, Kone and Danone. These are undoubtedly just the tip of the iceberg, since not all cases become public knowledge.

Constantly over the past five years, EWC members have had similar experiences, information given late, incomplete and thus not permitting EWC members to evaluate a situation. Management have not taken seriously their obligations to inform and consult worker representatives. When companies restructure the EWC members have been informed at the same time as the general public or at the very best shortly before the *Financial Times* goes to the printers. Big reorganisations are carried out without any consultation with the respective EWCs; there is no consultation on the general plan, only its implementation in the respective countries when it is announced publicly. When the EWC demands consultation, the same answer is always given, that this is a purely national affair, hence no concern of the EWC, until the next restructuring takes place in the next country.

According to the EWC Directive, consultation is an exchange of opinions and dialogue. Dialogue is only possible, if a decision has not yet been taken and there are still different options available, in an early phase of the decision-making process. Otherwise, there is no dialogue only a monologue! Unfortunately, there are too many representatives of central management who cannot understand this self-evident truth. The ETUC therefore suggests improving the EWC Directive in the following ways:

- *Adding a definition of information*: information must be written and comprehensive, it must be presented to employee representatives in good time and on a con-tinuous basis. As such it should be given at a time, in a manner, and with a content that allows employee representatives to undertake an in-depth assess-ment of the possible impact of change. This will allow, where appropriate, employee representatives to prepare for consultation with central manage-ment or any other more appropriate level of management. Information and documents should also be given in the appropriate languages of the employee representatives concerned.

- *Modifying the definition of consultation*: so that consultation should mean an exchange of views and the establishment of a dialogue between employee representatives and central management, or any more appropriate level of management. To achieve this it should take place in good time before a decision is made by central management, or any other more appropriate level of management, allowing the opinion of employee representatives to be considered during planning. The employee representatives shall be given adequate time to deliver an opinion. If they deliver their opinion in writing, they should have the right to be consulted orally. The EWC shall be considered competent for all questions that are beyond the decision-making capacity of local management.

The notion of a controlling undertaking

An EWC is founded when a controlling interest meets certain criteria laid down in the Directive. This notion of a controlling undertaking is an idea that is far-reaching and comprehensive and is developed in Articles 3.1 and 3.2 of the EWC Directive. For the purposes of the Directive, a controlling undertaking means an undertaking, which can exercise a dominant influence over another undertaking by virtue, for example, of 'ownership, financial participation or the rules that govern it' (Article 3.1). Other possibilities to exercise a dominant influence are not ruled out and the Directive mentions ownership, financial participation and rules, only as an example to illustrate the notion of domination. As the Directive does not mention any percentage of financial participation, the notion of financial participation covers any form of minority participation, if the owner of the minority participation has the ability to exercise a dominant influence.

Often it is difficult to say what percentage of shares somebody holds and difficult to determine whether the minority participation is really the basis for controlling another undertaking. In this context, part of a judgement by the European Court of Justice is important. On 29 March 2001, in Case C-62/99, the Court ruled as follows:

> where information relating to the structure or organisation of a group of undertakings forms part of the information which is essential to the opening of negotiations for the setting-up of a European Works Council, an undertaking within the group is required to supply the information which it possesses, or is able to obtain, to the workers' representatives requesting it.

Communication of documents clarifying and explaining the information, which is indispensable for that purpose, may also be required. The Court's decision means that undertakings must supply employee representatives with all the necessary information and documentation which enables them to decide whether they can set up a Special Negotiating Body with a view to opening negotiations for the estab-lishment of an EWC. In order to avoid confusion in future, the ETUC suggests:

- *Amending Article 11.2 of the Directive*: to ensure that employees and their repre-sentatives receive, upon request, information and documentation concerning the structure of the undertaking and the group of undertakings, the quota of shares and the ability to exercise control.

Problems with identifying a controlling undertaking: franchising and joint ventures

An EWC will normally be installed at a central management level, although, sometimes it is not evident where this is. In particular, this happens when an undertaking or group of undertakings are constructed upon certain governing rules or franchising contracts. Franchising can frequently be found in the catering or food industries, but is also present in other sectors such as the retail trade.

Can the undertaking that is the franchiser be considered as a controlling undertaking as defined in the Directive and required to create a Special Negotiating Body with a view to setting up an EWC?

Article 3.1 of the Directive stipulates that; 'For the purposes of this directive, a "controlling undertaking" is understood to be an undertaking which can exercise a dominant influence over another undertaking, (the "controlled undertaking") by virtue, for example, of . . . the rules which govern it'. The reference made to the rules that govern an undertaking emphasise the European legislator's intention to encompass in the scope of application of the Directive the different possibilities of a 'co-operation of undertakings'. According to the spirit of the Directive, franchise agreements are included amongst the 'rules which govern (an undertaking)'.

An analysis of the 'whereases' (terms) of the Directive leads to the same conclusion. In the 'whereases', reference is made to the constantly evolving structures of undertakings, to the different cross-border forms of concentration of undertakings and to the transnationalisation of undertakings. With a view to improving the rights of workers to information and consultation, the Directive has elaborated a definition of a 'controlling undertaking' which applies only in the framework of the Directive, designed to ensure that workers can be informed and consulted despite differing structures and concentrations of undertakings.

Where it happens that an undertaking is run by two or more other undertakings (a joint venture), none of which can exercise a dominant influence, the ETUC suggest:

* *Amending Article 3 of the Directive*: this can be done by inserting a new paragraph saying that the joint venture shall be regarded as an undertaking controlled by each of them. This will mean that its employees can be represented on the EWCs of both undertakings. Unless an agreement exists that the joint venture is controlled by one of the undertakings only, in which case this undertaking is considered to be the controlling undertaking.

European Works Councils and a merger of undertakings

Due to changing market conditions undertakings are increasingly viewing the strategy of merger as an important competitive tool. Should two or more undertakings decide to merge and this merger will have an impact throughout the European Community it must be formally registered for approval with the Commission. The undertakings must provide the Commission with detailed information and documentation. The Commission then checks, on the basis of various criteria, whether the merger of undertakings is compatible with Common Market regulations and whether approval can be granted. The Commission is entitled to demand further information from the undertakings, this means that they have to plan and arrange the merger in fine detail before drafting their application for approval.

However, undertakings often fail to meet merger information and consultation duties with respect to their EWCs. The reason they give is that they are only in a position to provide accurate information once the Commission has reached a decision on their application.

An example of this lack of consultation was with the Renault affair and here the Nanterre court found in favour of the EWC and ruled that it should have been consulted over the company's decision, justifying this ruling with reference to the Community Charter (9 December 1989) on workers' basic social rights.

Experience has also shown that mergers constantly affect employment, which is why EWCs must be informed and consulted at an appropriate time. In principle, information and consultation can be provided as early as the planning phase and can actually only be considered as appropriate if it takes place during the planning phase.

Another reason for informing EWCs at an early stage is that if worker representatives believe it is necessary they can apply to the Commission to be consulted on a merger application (according to Article 18.4 of Regulation number 4064/89). However, they cannot voice an opinion if the company has not informed them in advance.

The Commission currently examines applications for mergers of undertakings without any due consideration to the effect of mergers on employment. This should not prevent the EWC from informing the Commission in detail and as clearly as possible, pointing out the foreseeable early and subsequent effects on company employees. The ETUC is of the opinion that:

- *When the European Commission is approving a merger*: it should take into account the effect mergers have on workers. Article 127 Paragraph 2 of the Treaty on the Founding of the European Community (the consolidated version as amended by the Treaty of Amsterdam dated 2 October 1997, known as the Amsterdam Treaty) states, 'the objective of a high level of employment shall be taken into consideration in the formulation and implementation of Community policies and activities'. This obligation applies to all community policies, merger control policy included.
- *The European Commission*: should also consider whether or not the company has met its obligations with regard to EWC information and consultation.
- *The opinion of worker representatives on a merger*: is of major importance for the Commission. There should be a review of the merger control regulation to ensure that worker representatives play a proper role in the merger control

procedure. We believe that the Commission should inform the respective worker representatives (an EWC exists in most cases) if a company asks for approval of a merger or acquisition. The European Commission should invite the views of worker representatives.

- *The deadlines given to worker representatives are inadequate*: the current merger control procedure is too short. Company management has sufficient time to plan and prepare for a merger before the approval of the Commission is requested. Worker representatives only have a short period to prepare for a meeting with the merger control unit, if they request one. It is in the interests of all parties concerned that worker representatives have sufficient time and can prepare as thoroughly as possible before they meet with the Commission. This is only possible without further delaying the entire procedure, if the Commission informs worker representatives at an early stage that the undertaking has asked for approval of a merger.
- *Often a merger once approved by the European Commission*: has important consequences for the structure of worker representatives in a company or in the companies, which are going to be merged. The consequence may well be that for a certain period there is no worker representation at all. The Commission should not approve a merger without it being guaranteed that undertakings maintain worker representatives in office for a transitory period. They can then accompany the first phases of the merger and lay the foundations for the establishment of joint worker representation.

Agreements

An EWC is a growing, changing body but at its heart is the constitution or governing rules that are based on the agreements that were originally achieved. This section discusses a number of issues surrounding these agreements and recommends certain changes so that EWCs can continue, and in some cases begin, to function.

Article 13 agreements concluded for an indefinite period

The Directive does not apply to agreements that were already in force on the date laid down for its transposition (22 September 1996). Between September 1994 and September 1996, there was an urgency to conclude such agreements. However, a number of these agreements do not have a stated term; they have been concluded for an indefinite period. Article 13.2 of the Directive assumes that the agreements referred to in Article 13 do have a term. It states: 'When the agreements referred to in paragraph 1 expire, the parties to those agreements may decide jointly to renew them'. Article 13 agreements must therefore include a term, either they are limited in time or they provide for the possibility of termination. In light of this, the Directive should be revised.

Also according to the legal systems of the Member States of the European Union (EU), no one can be compelled to continuously comply with an agreement.

However, this is precisely what happens if a company management refuse to revise an Article 13 agreement.

Further important grounds for terminating an agreement of the type referred to in Article 13 include company restructuring measures, mergers and the resulting changes on the employees' side of an EWC. Other important considerations include any changes to the underlying basis of the contract, for instance if substantial parts of the agreement no longer correspond to the ideas of the parties at the time, or for example if it differs sharply to the Directive's intentions. The ETUC therefore suggest that agreements:

- *Which do not contain a clause concerning the term of the agreement or the possibility of termination*: shall be amended to include one of those possibilities, should this not be the case, then agreements should be terminated on a certain date and the Directive can be applied.

Renegotiation of Article 13 agreements

An increasing number of Article 13 agreements are expiring and EWCs are deciding whether or not they should continue to apply or be amended. Employee representatives in Europe-wide undertakings often ask the question, who on their side is responsible for any renegotiations? Is it those who negotiated and signed the first agreement, or is it those who, under this agreement, are now the European employee representatives?

Article 13 of the Directive is unclear on this point. Article 13.2 states: 'When the agreements referred to in paragraph 1 expire, the parties to those agreements may decide jointly to renew them'. The question then becomes how the notion 'parties' (which is also used in most national transposition law) is to be understood.

The ETUC believes that the notion 'party' does not refer to a physical person, but to the employer (central management) or the worker representation as an institution. Those having signed an agreement for one or the other side are their representatives. Representatives can change in the course of time but the 'parties' remain. Those employee representatives who negotiated and concluded an agreement with the company management are possibly no longer in post or working for the company. Agreements that were negotiated and signed by employee representatives, who have now left their posts, nevertheless continue to apply. The employee representative body currently in office is entitled to decide whether to cancel the agreement or begin renegotiations, taking into account any stipulations that an agreement might have regarding additions/amendments. If, though, the central management refuses to discuss the situation then the provisions of the Directive/implementing laws apply.

A request then has to be made according to Article 5.1 of the Directive and a Special Negotiating Body set up. Negotiations start with the central management on an agreement in accordance with Article 6 of the Directive. It may even be possible that an EWC according to the provisions of the Annex is constituted, if the respective provisions apply.

Negotiations

If an agreement cannot be reached to form a newly constituted EWC then the subsidiary prescriptions in the Directive come into play. At an initial stage of the overall EWC process this situation spurred on the negotiating partners in their search for tailor-made solutions. However, the negotiating parties did not, and still do not, approach the negotiations on an equal footing, so that even Article 6 agreements are still far from satisfying the key requirements for proper cross-border information and consultation. The reason for the lack of 'equal firepower' in negotiations is mainly that the Directive has not made the role of experts on the Special Negotiating Body sufficiently clear. Given this, these experts are often excluded from negotiations. Another reason for the lack of 'equal firepower' is that the list of issues in Article 6, for which the negotiating partners must find appropriate solutions, is incomplete. The ETUC therefore proposes these amendments to remedy this:

- *Trade unions must be given greater rights*: the competent European Industry Federation has to be informed of the beginning of negotiations and a representative of the European Industry Federation shall have the right to participate in negotiations. The Special Negotiating Body is dependent on the support of expert trade union representatives. Unfortunately, in view of the present legal situation, company managers are constantly able to prevent such support and in this way to avoid equal negotiations and to succeed in excluding important regulations from agreements.

Sanctions

If a central management breaches an EWC agreement then appropriate sanctions should be brought to bear. The ETUC believes that a review of the Directive should include sanctions and that:

- *The Member States should provide (legal) sanctions in the event that valid agreements are breached*: when employees are affected by exceptional circumstances, such as transfers, closures or redundancies, there should be provision for immediate legal proceedings. Any measures which have already been implemented – or which are in the process of being implemented – should be declared null and void.

The basic requirements of a European Works Council

This section identifies the basic requirements needed for an effectively functioning EWC. It discusses how the basic principle of the Directive, to provide information and consultation, can be effectively established. It does this through identifying the scope of information and consultation, how it should be correctly delivered and through clarifying the rights of those EWC representatives who are the focus of it.

Access to establishments

As indicated, the aim of the Directive is to improve employee rights to information and consultation in community-scale undertakings. This calls for appropriate communication between the EWC and national employee representatives, unfortunately, EWCs are repeatedly denied access to national employee representatives. This means that instead of removing obstacles they are being perpetuated. Even when an agreement does not expressly regulate for a right of access for the EWC to the establishments and undertakings concerned, this does not automatically mean that this refusal to grant access is lawful.

The EWC is not a body that can act without contact with national employees and their representatives. On the contrary, in order to be able to fulfil its tasks, it must have close contact with national employees/employee representatives in the establishments and undertakings concerned. They have a wealth of information and knowledge concerning the establishment, which the EWC (independently of whether the agreement is an Article 13 or Article 6 agreement) does not. The EWC is therefore dependent on co-operation with employees/employee representatives in order to be able to hold a dialogue with the management of an undertaking.

Both the national transposition laws and the EWC Directive work on the assumption of this fact. The transposition laws in Belgium (Article 44), Greece (Article 20.3), Ireland (Article 12), Luxembourg (Article 54), Finland (Article 11d), Sweden (Article 32) and Norway (§§2.5) contain express regulations that an Article 6 EWC should inform the national employees/employee representatives in the establishments and undertakings concerned. Denmark, Spain, France and Italy have not included such express regulations on information in their national transposition laws but stress, in the same way as the EWC Directive, that the employees' right to information and consultation is to be improved.

The explanatory statement of the EWC Directive points out that the establishment of an EWC is necessary in order to guarantee appropriate information and consultation for employees affected by decisions taken by transnational undertakings. The explanatory statement stresses that the unequal treatment of employees with regard to decisions by transnational undertakings is to be overcome by the Directive. It therefore involves employees and their representatives in the establishments and undertakings concerned who should be informed and consulted. The EWC is the means of guaranteeing that an equal level of knowledge is ensured in the establishments and undertakings concerned, and hence equal treatment.

According to Article 6.1 of the EWC Directive, Article 6 agreements are to lay down the terms and conditions of the implementation of employees' information and consultation provided for in Article 1.1. According to Article 1.1 the purpose of the EWC Directive is to, 'improve the right to information and to consultation of employees in Community-scale undertakings and Community-scale groups of undertakings'. Article 1.4 makes it clear that this refers to employees in all establishments of the undertaking operating throughout the Community and in all undertakings in the group of undertakings. The areas of competence of the EWC extend to all these.

It follows from the above that the point of the EWC Directive is that the EWC passes on any information given to it and discusses this with the employees and employee representatives. If it does not then the EWC cannot enter into a dialogue with the management of the undertaking on any planned measures. The EWC should not be a 'withdrawn' body, as this will weaken the employees' rights.

Information and discussion (consultation) with the employees/employee representatives concerned implies in turn the right of access to the establishments and undertakings affected by decisions taken in transnational undertakings. Refusing the right of access would reduce the whole point not only of the EWC Directive but also of the national transposition laws to absurdity, since this would mean that any information could be refused to the employees concerned and their representatives. This is clearly not the point of the directive.

The logic is that an EWC should not be refused access to the establishments and undertakings concerned. It is possible that the EWC will have to accept that they will not be able to arrive with the entire body, but possibly only, to the extent that this exists, with the more limited Select Committee.

Agreements, which are covered by Article 13 of the Directive, are only effective if they exist for all employees of undertakings or groups of undertakings operating throughout the Community and when transnational information and consultation of employees is planned. This means that access to the establishments and undertakings concerned may not be refused to an Article 13 body. If it is, it undermines the aim of Article 13 of the EWC Directive which guarantees information and discussion with all employees/employee representatives concerned. Given this overall situation, the ETUC calls for:

- *An EWC right of access*: to national employee representatives to be explicitly enshrined in the Directive.

Financial and material resources

EWCs operating on the basis of Article 6 agreements often face the problem that they receive insufficient, or no, financial and/or material resources. They may also not meet frequently enough to be able to fulfil their tasks as required by the Directive. In many cases when these agreements were concluded it was not possible to foresee what would be required in terms of resources and meetings. As a result, there are agreements that do not cover this issue adequately, if at all. Hence, for many EWCs the question is whether these problems can be resolved by applying the appropriate national transposition law and the Directive.

The exact wording of the EWC Directive, or a virtually identical formulation, was used in the transposing laws of Denmark (§ 17 point 5); Germany (§ 18 point 5); France (Article L 439–9e); Ireland (Article 12 point 4d); the Netherlands (Article 11 point 3f); Austria (Article 189 point 5); and Sweden (Article 21 point 5). In addition to using a virtually identical formulation, Italy has also stressed that the resources to be provided include funding for interpreting costs (Article 9 point 2e). Finland provides for 'a settlement for all other expenditure relating to group cooperation. This also includes reasonable expenditure incurred by calling in experts' (Article 13). Belgium (Article 24 point 5); Greece (Article 10 point 1g); Luxembourg (Article 25 point 5); Norway (Article 5b); and Spain (Article 12 point. 1f); stipulate that appropriate resources should be made available so that the EWC can fulfil its tasks. Whilst Greece, Spain and Luxembourg also point out that this means the effective, proper fulfilment of tasks (s. FN 5). Article 44 of the Belgian transposing law also stipulates that the EWC must be accorded adequate time and resources. Given this it is clear that the Directive, and all those countries referred to, stipulate in their legal provisions that Article 6 agreements must contain regulations on both financial and material resources.

However, the national laws and Directive do not make any stipulation regarding the amount and extent of these financial and material resources. The provisions in Belgium, Finland, Greece, Luxembourg and Spain go furthest (s. FN 4, 5). According to these, the extent of resources should be determined on the basis of what the EWC requires to fulfil its tasks properly and effectively. These regulations are based on an explanatory statement in the Directive, which notes that financial resources should be established by mutual agreement in such a way 'that these correspond to the particular circumstances in each case'. The particular circumstances refer to the tasks of the EWC, which arise from the company-specific situation. The EWC must visualise its tasks and then request the resources required to fulfil them. These may range from pencils and computers to travelling expenses or interpreters'/experts' costs, which are to be provided for the EWC when it could only work to a limited degree without them.

If the EWC does not receive the resources it needs, then it weakens employee rights to information and consultation. Therefore, if the EWC needs interpreters because it cannot communicate with national employees and their representatives then it should get these. If it requires an expert to understand facts submitted by company management, then these costs should also be borne by the company.

Article 6 agreements, which do not contain adequate regulations on financial and material resources must be supplemented in line with the Directive. For the sake of clarity, in order to avoid any unnecessary discussions in the future, the ETUC suggests:

- *Amending Article 6 of the Directive*: any agreement must include provisions on the financial and material resources to be allocated to the EWC. These should include financial resources to establish communication structures between employee representatives on the EWC and national worker representatives.

This is in addition to the annual meetings with central management and adequate resources for training.

Rights of European Works Council members

Very often an EWC and its worker representatives are handicapped because the meetings scheduled are not adequate for the existing workload. There is often only one meeting, and a very short preparatory meeting, each year. Again, reference needs to be made to the explanatory statement of the Directive, which states that the areas of competence and working methods of the EWC must in each case correspond to the particular circumstances involved. The clear interpretation here is that the EWC must have an opportunity to hold additional meetings to those scheduled if it cannot deal with problems adequately; or if circumstances have arisen which make it necessary for the EWC to meet outside the regular meetings. Again the ETUC believes in clarifying matters through a review of the Directive. It suggests:

- *Meetings with central management*: shall take place at least once a year, although, our experience is that 3–4 meetings per year are a necessary minimum.
- *Members of the EWC*: shall be entitled to take time off in fulfilment of their duties and for training with no reduction in remuneration.
- *That time off*: is to a level necessary in order to inform national worker representatives immediately of the content and results of information and consultation from the EWC.
- *That central management*: covers the expenses for the required training and travelling.

Conclusion: central elements for the review of the European Works Council Directive

EWCs are an option for a different model of innovation and change that is based on social dialogue and produces long-lasting results. In order to make the most of this option, the EWC Directive needs to be reviewed.

The review has to be accompanied by changes in trade union practice to allow EWCs to function effectively. EWCs are male-dominated bodies and the ETUC requests an equal opportunities paragraph in the EWC Directive. It also urgently requests trade union negotiators to deviate from the 'easy way' and to include more women in Special Negotiating Bodies and EWCs. The ETUC believes that its member organisations should dedicate even more assistance to EWCs and training is urgently needed, but practical help is also required, above all practical legal assistance. With regard to a review of the Directive, the ETUC suggests that the following should be included as central elements:

- Worker representatives in EWCs must have comprehensive and on-going information.

- Consultation has to take place before decision making in the planning-phase, when decisions can still be influenced. Only then can the consultation of workers be helpful for both sides.
- EWC members need resources to undertake their work properly. They need training, communication facilities, access to e-mail, and the right to meet each other and their colleagues at a national and local level.
- Trade unions have a key role in keeping EWCs running. They act as moderators between different cultures. This role should be recognised in the Directive.

6 Implementing the Directive
A view from UK business

Richard Hume-Rothery

Introduction and background

The business community, if asked what it really thinks of the concept of European Works Councils (EWCs) is quite likely to be reminded of the traveller who, on asking a local person for directions to a particular place, got the response 'Well I wouldn't start from here'.

To understand the business perspective of EWCs, especially UK-based ones, it is probably helpful to track the evolution of the Directive and with that the perceptions of people from the management community. First of all, 'Europe'. Most of the major UK-based multinationals that are in scope of the EWC Directive have been in business for a long time, often going back into the nineteenth century. In this day and age, it comes as something of a surprise to realise that the UK 'discovered' the European mainland as a place to do business only some 25 or 30 years ago. The main UK export and investment markets had been the US and those countries that used to be red on the map. As British investors moved into Europe, by buying local businesses, mostly since the 1960s, they generally regarded the way in which the local management ran their businesses as distinctly 'foreign'. UK management deliberately did not involve itself in understanding local practices and would normally hire a local management team, usually the one that it had bought, and from an employment or HR perspective, the only interest which it would then take would be to control the top local person's salary package. The view was that the rest of the detail of employment matters was best left to the local management.

The publication of the Social Charter and Action Programme in 1989 went almost unnoticed in the UK. A few of us who worked for multinational corporations realised that even if the labour market reforms, which Margaret Thatcher had by then introduced in the UK, were presumably going to protect the country from some of the weirder ideas which seemed to be emanating from the Continent to our main UK base, at least we had to start to think about their impact on our mainland European operations. As we looked at the Jacques Delors wish list, the one proposal which caused us more concern than the others was that for a construct called a 'European Works Council'.

The more that we thought about this EWC idea, the more it looked to be a template for a pan-European employee relations system, and one that might even create a platform for pan-European collective bargaining. Indeed, in its original drafts the EWC Directive even had something included in it called participation, which is Euro code for co-determination. The British business community did not like that one bit. To understand this reaction, one needs to understand the mindset of the global business player. If one is trading around the world, one is constantly faced with threats and problems, be they competitors, economic instability, political risk, etc. The name of the game therefore is 'damage limitation'. As a competent manager, your job is to contain and control any perceived threat to your company. That is how EWCs were perceived, except by a very tiny minority of the MNC business community in the UK. It explains why, despite the opt-out from the Maastricht Social Chapter, the UK produced proportionally such a high number of Article 13 EWCs, or Forum agreements – Forum being a softer and more inclusive name.

It should also be appreciated that the UK manager is, by world standards, a highly legally compliant individual. Competitive, yes, seeking flexibility, yes, but in the world of the highly disciplined major corporations, legal compliance is very high up the list of key attributes of the successful executive. And there is a herd instinct that plays a major part in behaviour too. CEOs talked amongst themselves to a considerable degree in their top-level networks about whether or not to have an Article 13 arrangement. The peer pressure on the HR community from their bosses was considerable.

But there is another piece of EWC history that the reader needs to understand and this is the role played by corporate lawyers. Top UK management cover their backs with lawyers. If in doubt, they ask for their law firm's opinion, and with something as strange as EWCs, this was definitely the case. But the lawyers also need to cover their backs since they have concern for their professional indemnity policies. The safe route for the lawyers is to give advice based on precedent, but the problem here was that there was no obvious precedent in English Common Law. So, in looking at the EWC Directive, the only safe haven which they could find was – in their opinion – the Annex to the Directive, and almost universally, they advised their clients to produce an Article 13 Agreement, the content of which looked like that of the Annex (see Chapter 7 by Mark Gilman and Paul Marginson).

It was a serious lost opportunity, as Article 13 was actually an opportunity for creativity. Instead, most companies just implemented the process that the Annex offers with no added value. I have many rueful memories of meetings with CEOs ahead of their annual EWC gathering, when they would say that they had nothing of real transnational interest to talk to the EWC representatives about. They had talked about the Millennium bug and the single currency *ad nauseam*. Did I have any good ideas of new safe topics? What a wasted opportunity... Happily, that has mostly changed now, or at least improved, as EWCs have matured.

But I digress, the British are not a very process-driven people. It is reflected in our Common Law, where issues tend to be much more absolutist than in continental Europe. The fundamental premise that the UK management spotted about the EWC Directive was that it is a purely process-driven concept. So the safe response that they adopted was to allow the appetite of the process to be fed, in reasonable measure, in the knowledge that although it might be rather a waste of time and money, it did not deflect them from any ultimate end objective. I am glad to be able to say that that attitude has now receded in most UK-based EWCs, though if the management feel threatened they revert to process and the end result of such behaviour is that, in reality, nobody gets any long-term value.

Mindful, in part, of the fact that in the context of this book, a business viewpoint is distinctly in the minority, it is worthwhile to concentrate on a limited number of sensitive and key areas of the EWC debate. So this chapter will continue by addressing:

- EWC constituencies and their make up.
- What EWCs can and do discuss.
- The three C's – consultation, co-determination and confidentiality.
- Conclusion: the future of EWCs.

European Works Council constituencies and their make up

In the earliest days of Article 13 agreements and since then with Article 6 negotiations, the issue of how the European workforce is to be represented and who will actually do that representation has usually been amongst the most sensitive negotiating issues. It has been plain to see that certain representative factions have felt their reputations and their future hung on the outcome. In addition, the question of the extent of management's involvement and the question of including representation from European Union (EU) Candidate Member States (CMS) have had to be considered.

Taking the last two questions first, the issue of contractually involving management in the Agreement was a simple choice for most UK-parented companies. Faced with the choice of the German model of an employee side only EWC, or a French model of the management having a constitutional role in the EWC, usually chairing the body, etc., the choice was simple. Given the UK's past history of confrontational industrial relations, the inclusive French one was almost invariably deemed the only choice. The hope that the EWC could become an inclusive communications body also clearly favours the French approach. The last thing that UK management wished to see was a structure where the EWC became the 'official opposition to management'.

Until recently, the inclusion of representation from such places as the Czech and Polish Republics was not an important issue. Maybe that was due, in part, to the uncertainty and distant prospect that these countries would join the EU. Generally, there has been reluctance by UK management to include their CMS operations. This has been prompted by two primary considerations. First, the CMS workforces have been less directly involved and included in the EU-level operations and second, there has been real concern by management over the protection of confidential information involving people where the EWC Directive and its confidentiality protection legislation has not been made enforceable law, under EU Treaty.

In addition, serious problems have been encountered in getting interest in involvement from CMS employees, or indeed from CMS management people. Their Iron Curtain history, culture and lack of experience of an employee voice, together with surprisingly low levels of trade union or works council membership, have held many possible candidates back from trying to join their colleagues in the West.

It also has to be said that there has been surprise in management circles that EU-level trade union bodies have pushed for the inclusion of CMS representation. Especially in light of the transfers, in particular, of production from Germany to CMS countries, they found such calls very difficult to understand. When they heard that the union motivation was in fact to use this move to add pressure towards the raising of CMS levels of earnings – and therefore cost bases – to those of the existing EU countries, they received this news with complete incredulity, in particular, given the comparative circumstances of the various CMS economies.

Turning now to the general question of employee representation, the allocation of seats at the council table and who fills them, the practice has varied fairly widely according to the size, geographic distribution, divisional make up and union history of the businesses. There are EWCs where the representations range from six to 57 employee representatives. The number of Forums per company can range from one (the great majority) to three, and in one case five separate bodies. Structural differences between businesses are enormous. Some, such as the finance industry, tend to do pretty much the same thing everywhere; some are very geographically limited in their field of activity, such as food, which has unique storage and transport challenges. Some, such as the hotel industry, have very large numbers of separate and small groups of employees who are spread very wide apart geographically (see Chapter 4 by Sjef Stoop for a fuller discussion of the range of EWCs).

The biggest challenge that I have observed has been where there are both clear divisional and geographic differences in a business. The pressures to reconcile the demands for the employee voice which includes very different types of operation and geographic origin are often difficult.

Usually it has been the geographic base that has prevailed. There are quite a number of refinements whereby there is a cut-off point. For example, if the number of employees in a given country is below a given number or percentage, they do not qualify for a seat and will be represented by a colleague from another country, usually in a Division which has regular links with that small population.

My experience to date is that there is a healthy competition between unions for seats. Here it is only right to pay tribute to some of the EU-level trade union 'industry' bodies, that have done sterling work when faced with a collection of representatives from a wide variety of European countries. Many of these people are local 'gods' in their own home countries, sometimes with egos of a size to match, and have needed to be organised and moulded into a single European-level body. No easy task.

One of the best indicators of the value of an EWC, in the eyes of the workforce, is the type of representatives who come 'up through the system' and the degree of local support which they enjoy. In continental Europe, the legal norm is for the representative to come from a local works council, or equivalent. Here it has to be reported that in quite surprising numbers, we have found that there have been problems getting representatives from such bodies. That local works councils do not always exist, even in places like Germany, is not what people in the UK are led to expect. And where a secret ballot is held, as is the norm in the UK and Ireland, the level of turnout is often disappointingly low, even at lower levels than for European Parliament elections. This makes us question the value that the workforce sees in an EWC.

Having been involved in a wide variety of EWCs, some of non-UK parentage, I will offer three observations, all of which are important. The first is that the representatives are overwhelmingly white, middle-aged and male. This may be a particularly British viewpoint, but since my career has taken me to work in continental Europe, Africa and Asia, it will be made all the same. I have yet to see an Afro-Caribbean or Asian employee representative on an EWC. Why not? The second point is the extent to which I have heard employee representatives articulating in any detail the wide range of views, interests and concerns of *their* constituents – as opposed to single-issue type matters – is sadly very, very low and infrequent.

The third and probably most important issue I have observed is the lack of ability of the individual representatives to cope with the type of challenging issues an EWC may be asked to consider. By definition, if an EWC is to be positioned at the controlling undertaking level of the organisation, it is going to be addressing key strategic issues of a level of complexity and detail which is going to tax the intellect and skills of the best of people (in this context see the discussion on training in Chapter 12 by John Stirling). The reason why the original designers of the EWC Directive positioned it where they did, at the very top of the corporate hierarchy, was so that it could be a body that could have a consultative role in what, at the end of the day, are going to be major strategic investment-based decisions.

What European Works Councils can and do discuss

The agreements that form the constitution for EWCs, be they Article 13 or Article 6, almost invariably specify a similar broad list of items which will form the topics for discussion. These, not surprisingly, tend to follow fairly closely the list in the Directive, for the reasons mentioned earlier. There are, however, two key areas of tension, the non-transnational and the collective bargaining-type issues.

As far as non-transnational subject matter is concerned, it is easy to see why a particular employee representative wants to air a particular point, often a grievance, which is a purely local issue. He or she has probably been given a mandate by his or her colleagues back home to bring up an issue when they meet the top bosses, which they have not had satisfaction on from their local management. Quite possibly, they view the EWC as being a court of appeal. Top management has the duty to rule this out of order so as not to be seen to undermine their local management over an issue, the detail of which is probably pretty sketchy at controlling undertaking level anyway.

Similarly, collective bargaining-type items are deemed to be a clear local area of responsibility. There are clearly pressures – especially now that the euro-zone is with us and due to some of the more energetic European-level trade union 'industry' bodies – to turn EWCs into pan-European negotiating Forums. Corporate management will resist this most vigorously. In both the non-transnational and the negotiating issues, the firm view of business is that to undermine the competence of local structures is rank irresponsibility.

A particular problem also observed, is the type of presentation given by management to the EWC. Usually, the annual Forum meeting takes place as soon as is reasonably practicable after the Annual Results are released. The Board of Directors has a well-prepared presentation which they have given to the financial analysts in the city and which they then produce at the Forum meeting. In as much as it is geared to the demands of the financial community, it is almost guaranteed to be unsuitable for an EWC type of audience. That said, there has been considerable improvement in this area in the last couple of years.

EWC meetings have tended, in the main, to settle down as healthy sessions of information provision and dialogue on 'the state of the nation' for the business. If the venue is rotated around company sites and factories across Europe, it is usually an added bonus as it lets the Forum members see the different locations and what they do and it has the benefit of letting local workforces actually see that this body exists – a valuable piece of PR all round. But beware the charge of 'Euro-Tourism'. The Forum must also be seen to be doing its job in a professional manner.

Most EWCs started out with just one meeting a year, apart from the 'exceptional circumstances' occasions. There is a growing trend now to increase the frequency of meetings to every six months, as it is often felt that a gap of twelve months is too long.

But the decision to spend, on average, another £60,000 for a second meeting is not one which most management take lightly. There has to be reasonable justification for such additional expenditure, so it is increasingly a joint effort by both 'sides' to try to get more out of their dialogue of common benefit that leads to more meetings.

From an employer's viewpoint, and to be fair, from the viewpoint of employees too, the most 'successful' EWCs are the ones that are deliberately used as an active agent for change. Like it or not, we live in a world which is changing at a frightening speed; business is the front line of this process of change and any competent company management needs to take the workforce with them in the change process. The employees can sometimes be forgiven for feeling threatened by the speed and nature of the change process, especially as its impact is so often of a transnational nature. So there is a clear role here for the EWC to be, and be seen to be, consulted and involved in this change process.

For example, the Chief Executive of a major manufacturing company which has been going through a massive and very successful change programme across Europe, recently said very frankly that if the EWC Directive were to disappear tomorrow, he would continue to run his Forum for the benefit of all in the Company. Without the Forum they would not have been able to deliver the change in the efficient, acceptable and generally accepted way that they had, despite the fact that it involved some plant closures and consequential job losses.

The three C's – consultation, co-determination and confidentiality

These three C's are regarded by many as being the main issues that prevent EWCs or Forums from realising any potential they might have for being an added-value constituent of the people-management process of a business.

Consultation

Most employers readily acknowledge that benefit can accrue to a business by keeping employees informed about the progress of the business, the decisions that are being taken by executive management to maintain the business and keep it profitable and most bosses are willing to spell out the potential threats to the business that could blow it off course.

Very many managements are also willing to recognise the benefits that can accrue from listening to the views that their employees express about the information they have been given. These managements are equally willing to actively engage with their employees to discuss the impact their decisions might have on employees and how such impact might be dealt with. A willingness to listen to employees' views as to how any potential threats to the business might be countered is also a part of the way these managers manage their people.

In other words, many managements are very ready to consult employees on relevant issues and very often, depending on the subject matter and the structure and geographical location of employees, such consultation takes place in a variety of ways. Sometimes it is direct with all employees in small and/or large groups, sometimes with fellow employees acting in a representative capacity on behalf of their colleagues, sometimes with employees acting as representatives of a recognised trade union (shop stewards), and sometimes consultation will be with full-time officials of recognised trade unions. The route chosen is very often dependent upon the nature of the discussion in hand and the history of the relationships that have been built-up.

Where many of the managements have an issue with consultation in the context of the EWC is that they fundamentally disagree with the agenda for consultation that is being promoted at European level by both the Commission and the European Trades Union Confederation. The premise is that employee representatives (and the Commission have only legislated for employees' representatives to be consulted) should be involved (consulted) in the management decision-making process as well as in the implementation of management decisions. Whilst nobody has been able thus far to be specific about precisely which management decisions employee representatives should be party to, everyone assumes that the promoters of this agenda regard *all* decisions as coming within the ambit of consultation.

The reality of course is that the vast majority of employed people actually want to go to work and be well managed, to be given interesting work to do, to be properly paid for the skills they have and to be able to share their time sensibly between their occupation, their families and their outside-of-work interests. In this context, therefore, employees expect their managers and executives to make the decisions that are necessary for the profitability and continuity of the business, such that the lifestyles they create for themselves can be sustained.

In my experience, another issue that managements have with the EWC concept is that they have to reluctantly accept that the only practical way of delivering transnational consultation is through some form of representative structure. Many of them believe that such structures can be notoriously ineffective vehicles of consultation such that the real views of the majority of employees are never heard. In such constructs it is often only the views of the 'activists' that are heard, which of course can have the effect of minimising the value of the contribution of employees' representatives since activists can very readily turn their role into one of 'the official opposition', often acting as single-issue lobbyists.

A further source of difficulty arising from the legal obligation to consult at a transnational level is that for some subject areas, like collective redundancy and business transfers, it can conflict with the legal obligation existing in all Member States to consult on these same matters at country level. Neither the transnational law nor the country law recognises the existence of the other and consequently neither of them makes any reference as to which takes precedence. The resolution of any conflict, which inevitably does arise, is left to the management to resolve. Experience has shown that almost without exception, domestic consultation takes precedence and transnational consultation follows. The explanation for this is that it is at the domestic level where the contracts of employment are struck and the concept of a transnational employee has not yet reached us and probably never will.

The EWC Directive could be subject to revision and a very likely demand is that the definition of consultation may be significantly expanded. Currently it simply refers to 'an exchange of views and establishment of dialogue' and is not expanded upon any further in the Articles of the Directive. In any revision, however, it is reasonable to expect that the demand will include a reference to the timing, method and content, the fact that employer and employee opinion must be considered, with employees being entitled to a response to their expressed opinion, and that consultation should be conducted *with a view to reaching agreement* (see Chapter 5 by Willy Buschak).

In industrial relations systems, it has long been recognised that the boundary line between consultation and negotiation has always been very fine. With a change such as that just described, management would expect the boundary line to become even thinner.

Co-determination

In the UK, the informed view is that German style co-determination, or co-decision making, is inextricably bound up with the very creation of Germany as a nation. Indeed, one can actually trace the origins of co-determination back to the days of the Bismarck Government. The creation of a single German nation was not without its serious tensions and problems, being a Federation of often competing and different small states or Principalities. Nor should it be forgotten that German unification was forged in the aftermath of what is called the Franco–Prussian war.

Particularly given Germany's subsequent history, it is not difficult to see that one of the inherent aspects of co-determination, which singles it out from other countries' social models, is the basic message of a fundamental lack of trust in social institutions, including corporate institutions. This prompts the need to have a system which inherently has the potential to dis-empower such institutions through a complicated structure of checks, balances and 'second guessing'. The message this gives to the outside observer is of a fundamental lack of trust and a clear attempt to contain the power of management to manage. As far as the UK is concerned, notwithstanding the fact that we have a history of confrontational relationships, at the end of the day we do still place our trust in our institutions, even if we give them a hard time, as successive UK Governments consistently find out.

Given this background, it is not too surprising that some of the northern European jurisdictions within the EU, including Germany and Austria, provide for employees' representatives to participate in the management decision-making process through their system of two-tier management boards.

As an extension of the information and consultation works council structure, employees can be appointed to the supervisory boards of their companies and thus play an active part in the management of the company – hence the term co-determination, that is, employees being involved in determining the future of the company. It is true, of course, that the number of employees of any particular company that get to sit on the supervisory board are only a very small minority of the employees of the company.

Because of their familiarity with this role, it is not unusual to find that the employee members of EWCs from these jurisdictions, very often attempt to influence the workings of the EWC to act more like a Supervisory Board. Where this happens, these individuals take the view that the EWC or Forum should have a say in, and be party to approving, management decisions of a transnational nature. Such an attitude takes the consultation role of an EWC way beyond the limits set for such a body both by the Directive and by the view of most multinational managements. Also, such moves by EWC members from these jurisdictions do not go down well with the employee members from the other EU countries represented on the Council/Forum.

Confidentiality

The issue of confidentiality is perhaps the one that has concerned managements the most when entering the EWC arena for the first time. For many managements, establishing an EWC or Forum means having to deal at first hand with employees' representatives from, what are, after all, foreign jurisdictions with different cultures as well as different languages. In a competitive commercial environment, these facts alone spell the need for extreme caution in the minds of most management (see Chapter 7 by Mark Gilman and Paul Marginson for support of this proposition with regard to British companies).

Whilst it is true that both the Directive and the Member States' transposing laws all make provision for legal remedy in the event of unauthorised disclosure of confidential information, this is seen very much as a case of 'closing the stable door after the horse has bolted'. In other words, the damage will have been done.

There is also the very real fear of litigation by aggrieved shareholders if Stock Exchange Rules (particularly including the rules in the US, where many UK and other European companies have secondary listings) are violated. The potential damage and cost implications of such litigation are too horrendous for any responsible Board to risk. However, experience to date suggests that some of the fears expressed in the early stages of EWC development have been unfounded, but this of course is no proof that managements are operating as openly as they would if they had no fear at all that confidential information would be disclosed.

The other side of the confidentiality coin is the provisions that the Directive and the respective Member States' laws make, which allow a company not to disclose information nor enter into consultation on information that it considers would harm the business if it was disclosed. It is by no means clear the extent to which this provision is relied upon, nor by the very nature of the subject can it ever be, but an educated guess suggests it is used quite extensively to limit the amount of information that is disclosed to an EWC. By the same token, Member States are required by the Directive to provide legal procedures that enable employees' representatives to challenge the legitimacy of withholding information. To my knowledge, there have been no such challenges, certainly not in the UK since the Transnational Information and Consultation of Employees Regulations (1999) came into force on 15 December 2000. This is perhaps more explained by the truism that 'we don't know what we don't know' than it is by concluding that multinational companies are operating in an open consultative style.

Conclusion: the future of European Works Councils

It has been estimated that there are over 1,800 companies across Europe that are within the scope of the EWC Directive. It has also been estimated that over

700 EWCs have been established since September 1994 when the Directive was first adopted, 450 or so of these having been established as Article 13 agreements between September 1994 and September 1996. These brief statistics do not give the impression that the managements of multinational companies are falling over themselves to grab a slice of the EWC action or that they regard an EWC as the best thing since sliced bread.

As I have tried to indicate, like any institution, there is good and not so good in the concept of an EWC. For the good to be realised it will depend almost entirely on the flair and enthusiasm across the organisation of which it is an instrument. As with any other aspect of the people-management process, such enthusiasm for an EWC needs to reside with the Chief Executive and where it does, this will be reflected down through the management hierarchy, or not, as the case may be.

There are perhaps two significant issues above all others that will influence whether EWCs in general develop in the future into structures that add value to those organisations that have them. I referred earlier to my observation of a lack of match of the abilities of EWC representatives to the type of strategic issues they are required to discuss if the EWC is to justify its place at the level of the controlling undertaking.

At this level of an organization, it is the investment-type decisions that are the critical ones in terms of the future of jobs of an existing and future workforce. They are by definition, the decisions that change the course of a business.

These are macro issues that raise questions such as; 'What sort of business are we going to have to be to survive and prosper in the future?' 'What sort of changes will have to be made to achieve this?' 'What then, are the reasons for, and the consequences of, our investment decisions?'

These sorts of questions will have had the best brains in the company pondering over them, together with external strategic advisors, investment bankers and a panoply of top technical experts who will all have deliberated long and hard over such questions. And here we hit what I consider to be the crunch point of this issue: what role can the representatives of the workforce play in these matters? I have frequently heard calls from EWC members for more technical training especially in financial matters. But, quite frankly, unless they are brought up to something akin to an MBA level of education, it will be impossible for them to properly get to grips with the issues involved.

So the EWC 'industry' is faced with a dilemma. Either it seeks something of a voice in the key strategic decisions, or it confines its role to discussing the effects of the decisions on the workforce. Most EWC constitutions settle for the latter, but as I indicate later, there is a demand from some quarters, mostly from Brussels, for more involvement of employee representatives in the key decisions. For this to have any reasonable prospect of becoming a reality, the types of people who become members of EWCs will have to change. Employee representatives who come forward will need an educational background and level of experience that is adequate to address the issues, and to hold a meaningful dialogue with corporate management. It is certainly not enough to rely on external 'expert' advisors to the representatives. They could never enjoy the type of relationship with corporate management that is necessary for sustained value to be achieved by all concerned.

The other significant issue affecting the future of the EWC construct is the outcome of the review of the EWC Directive that is likely to take place in late 2003.

The Commission's Directorate General for Employment and Social Affairs has already been accused by some of pursuing the European Trades Union Confederation's agenda of trying to shift the EWC movement very much down the German-style co-determination route. The preamble or Recitals that precede the Articles in the recently adopted European framework Directive on information and consultation (Directive 2002/14/EC of 11 March 2002) include such references as:

> The existence of legal frameworks at national and community level intended to ensure that employees are involved in the affairs of the undertaking employing them and in the decisions which affect them, has not always prevented serious decisions affecting employees from being taken and made public without adequate procedures having been implemented beforehand to inform and consult them.
>
> (ibid.: Recital 6)

Another of the Recitals states that:

> The existing legal frameworks for employee information and consultation at Community and national level tend to adopt an excessively *a posteriori* approach to the process of change, neglect the economic aspects of decisions taken and do not contribute either to genuine anticipation of employment developments within the undertaking or to risk prevention.
>
> (ibid.: Recital 13)

Both these extracts give a very clear indication that the European Commission intends that there should be active employee involvement prior to decisions being taken. In other words, moving much more towards the co-decision end of the employee involvement spectrum than the straightforward information and consultation position favoured by most managements.

In addition to a revision of what constitutes consultation, the report of the European Parliament's Social Affairs Committee drawn up in September 2001 lists some nineteen other changes that the Parliament wants to see made to the Directive. Space does not allow these to be debated here but suffice to say if even a quarter of the suggested amendments found their way into a revised Directive it would kill stone dead any hope of EWCs developing into structures capable of delivering meaningful transnational information and consultation to the majority of an organisation's workforce.

But I am sure that the prospect of EWCs becoming moribund bodies as a result of new legislation that turned them into little more than potential power play forums will not come to pass. The recent spate of election victories across Europe for the center-right parties has given the Council, which is the EU Member State Governments, a very different make up to the overwhelmingly left of centre ones who have promoted successive and often repetitious pieces of social legislation since the days of Delors. Personally, I do not share the expectation of some people that EWCs are facing extermination in the new shape of Europe, but I do have hope that the Council will bring its influence to bear to help to shape them into rather more balanced bodies through which all the players – particularly including employers – can feel that they are getting value from EWCs in equal measure.

7 Negotiating European Works Councils

Contours of constrained choice

Mark Gilman and Paul Marginson

Introduction

Reflecting a more widespread development in European Union (EU) social policy, towards regulation through agreement 'under the shadow of the law' (Bercusson 1992) between the social partners, the EU's 1994 Directive on European Works Councils (EWCs) gives preference to arrangements negotiated between management and employee representatives over the statutory model specified in the Directive itself. At the time of the Directive's adoption, the scope for the negotiation of bespoke, enterprise-specific European-level information and consultation arrangements was seen to offer management and employee negotiators a considerable degree of flexibility (Gold and Hall 1994: 183). To date, agreements establishing over 700 EWCs in multinational companies (MNCs) within the European Economic Area (EEA) have been concluded, representing an unprecedented incidence of European-level negotiating activity. In practice, reports on the provisions of these agreements have pointed to the emergence of some marked similarities, as well as differences, between the results of these negotiations (Bonneton *et al.* 1996; Marginson *et al.* 1998; Carley and Marginson 2000). This chapter presents a systematic analysis of the factors influencing the nature of the 'constrained choices' being made by management and employee representatives in concluding agreements establishing EWCs. Four propositions are investigated:

- a 'statutory model effect', whereby scope for negotiation notwithstanding, agreements tend to conform with the provisions of the Directive's statutory model;
- a 'learning effect', under which innovatory features of earlier agreements are diffused to later agreements;
- a 'country effect', whereby, in their main features, EWCs resemble the national arrangements for employee information and consultation of the country in which an MNC is headquartered and;
- a 'sector effect', whereby in important respects EWCs within a given sector resemble each other, possibly through the impact of the respective European Industry Federations of trade unions.

To explore these four propositions, which are not necessarily exclusive of each other, the chapter presents a multi-variate analysis of the provisions of 344 EWC agreements drawn from the European Foundation's comprehensive database. In respect of the third and fourth propositions, the existence of bi-variate effects on the contents of EWC agreements, stemming from the country-of-origin and sector of operation of MNCs, has already been established (Marginson *et al.* 1998; Carley and Marginson 2000). The analysis presented here asks whether such bi-variate effects remain robust when taking account of possible interactions between country of origin, sector and type of agreement.

The scope, and therefore the limits, of the analysis need to be made clear at the outset. The propositions developed and the data relate to what is specified in the agreements negotiated between management and employee representatives and which establish EWCs. The actual practice of EWCs may, of course, be rather different from what is laid down in an agreement. Ramsay (1997: 316) makes a similar point in relation to studies of works councils. Nonetheless, it can be argued that there is a relationship between the provisions negotiated in an agreement and the practice that subsequently develops. Agreements can be more or less supportive of EWCs developing activity and influence: in certain respects they can seek to prohibit – approaching one-half of all agreements preclude the EWC from considering one or more specified matters (Carley and Marginson 2000: 24) – or in others to promote – two-thirds of agreements provide for the dissemination of the outcome of EWC meetings to national and local levels (ibid.: 50). The terms of agreements will configure but not determine the actual practice of EWCs.

The next section reviews debates on the factors which may influence the contents of EWC agreements and formulates the four propositions. The approach to testing these propositions is then outlined in the third section on 'Method of approach' and the data and estimation method are presented in the fourth section on 'Data and estimation'. The fifth section 'Results' reports results. These are discussed in the sixth section 'Discussion' before some conclusions are drawn.

Influences on agreements establishing European Works Councils

In negotiating EWC agreements, the literature suggests that there are likely to be several sources of influence operating on management and employee representative negotiators (Hall *et al.* 1995). The first are company-specific factors such as the nature of the business and industrial relations arrangements and traditions within the company, the second are the terms of the Directive itself, and the third, as more and more agreements are concluded, are the provisions of existing EWC agreements. The fourth factor is the influence of the different systems of industrial relations, and of employee information and consultation and employee representation arrangements in particular, found in the countries in which MNCs operating in the EEA are headquartered. The fifth is the sector in which the companies concerned are located. In contrast to the first factor, the other four influences are each likely to act as sources of constraint on the choices made by management and employee negotiators in concluding an EWC agreement. The notion of 'constrained choice', in which the choices of actors are constrained by a range of factors including existing transnational, national and sectoral structures and traditions, the influence of legislative provisions and normative influences associated with developments deemed to be 'good practice', is preferred to that of 'strategic choice' proposed by Kochan *et al.* (1986).

Our first proposition is that a 'statutory model effect' might be observed, according to which the terms of the Directive are likely to have had a greater influence on Article 6 than on Article 13 agreements, and amongst Article 13 agreements on those concluded after the adoption of the Directive in September 1994 than on those concluded beforehand (see Chapter 1 by Ian Fitzgerald for a discussion on different types of agreement). The reasoning is as follows. Although the provisions of the statutory fall-back model were a potential influence on management and employee representatives negotiating agreements under Article 13 post-September 1994, the prospect that these might be implemented was one step further removed than for negotiations under the special negotiating body (SNB) procedures governing Article 6 agreements. Failure to reach an agreement under Article 13 still left the option of trying anew under the SNB procedure. Whereas, failure to reach agreement under the SNB procedure could lead to the implementation of the statutory fall-back model as the next step. In addition, as noted earlier, the Directive makes it mandatory for Article 6 agreements to include provisions on certain specified matters. Concerning pre-September 1994 EWC agreements, these are the least likely to be influenced by the terms of the Directive since, as noted, only draft versions might have been available to negotiators.

Reviews of the provisions of agreements have, however, noted the spread of some provisions which are not specified either in the Directive itself or under its statutory fall-back model. For example, Miller and Stirling (1998) note that a 1996 review of 111 EWC agreements concluded under Article 13 found that only a minority made any provision for the training of employee representatives. Yet, a subsequent review covering Article 6 as well as Article 13 agreements, reports that a majority of agreements concluded since September 1996 contain some sort of provision on training (Carley and Marginson 2000). This suggests that on this and other aspects of EWC agreements a 'learning effect' may be in process, in which innovations in agreements which come to be regarded by one or both negotiating parties as good practice are subsequently generalised as further agreements are concluded, or existing ones revised or re-negotiated. The existence of such a 'learning effect' is our second proposition.

The 'country effect' suggests that industrial relations arrangements, and in particular those concerning employee information and consultation, in the European country in which an MNC is headquartered will influence the provisions of EWC agreements; whilst the 'sector effect' suggests that similarities in production methods, employment practice and industrial relations traditions within sectors which transcend national boundaries, together with trade union organisation at European sector level, will influence agreements. The relative importance of these 'country' and 'sector' effects has been the subject of debate. Streeck (1997 and 1998) has questioned the 'European' nature of EWCs, arguing that in respect of their structure and role 'one can expect European Works Councils to be heavily coloured by the national system of their company's country of origin' (ibid.: 331). This is because employee representatives of the MNC's home country workforce, by dint of their established relations with group management and their numerical dominance, are likely to play a dominant role in negotiations and thereby significantly influence the structure and role of the resulting EWC. 'In effect, ... European Works Councils will be *international extensions of national systems of workplace representation*, instead of European institutions in a strict sense.' (Streeck 1997: 331, italics in the original). In contrast, analysing the negotiation and content of fifty-nine early EWC agreements, Rivest (1996) found significant cross-country, sector-specific patterns of similarity over and above country-specific differences. She argued that these cross-country similarities could be attributed to the differing strategies adopted by the European Industry Federations (EIF) of trade unions. This is at odds with the contention that EWCs are primarily international extensions of national systems: European-level actors also appear to be influential in shaping their character and sector – as well as country-specific influences appear salient. Thus, 'EWCs represent an *intersection* of country-specific and transnational influences' (Marginson 2000: 27, italics in the original). Hence, our third and fourth propositions are that both country and sector effects are important influences on the provisions of EWC agreements.

Method of approach

Our approach is to explore the purchase of the four propositions about EWC agreements developed in the previous section by focusing on a range of key features that are likely to shape the functioning of EWCs. The features selected fall into three groups, reflecting whether they are more likely to be subject to, respectively, the statutory model effect, the learning effect or the country-of-origin or sector effects.

The first group is those which are potentially susceptible to the 'statutory model effect', and comprises provisions on six matters: whether the basis for the distribution of seats amongst employee representatives on the EWC is specified; provision for a preparatory meeting of employee representatives; whether the employee side has access to external experts; the existence of a smaller select or steering committee; provision for additional meetings in exceptional circumstances and; confidentiality requirements. Reference to each of these matters is made in the text of the Directive – either in the main text itself or in the Directive's Annexe which specifies the statutory model EWC that can be invoked in case of failure to conclude an agreement. Our earlier argument suggests that because they are addressed by the Directive each of these provisions can be expected to show a statutory model effect, comparing Article 6 with Article 13 agreements. In contrast, the Directive makes no reference to the second group of issues, which instead result from the initiative of the parties themselves in negotiating EWC agreements. The group comprises three matters: provision for a follow-up meeting of employee representatives; scope for the select or steering committee to receive information and consultation on an ongoing basis and; provision for training for employee representatives. Whilst the Directive's statutory model provides for employees to meet without management representatives present prior to the EWC meeting, no provision is made for employee representatives to meet subsequent to the main EWC meeting. The facility to convene a follow-up meeting is likely to strengthen the effectiveness of employee representatives to pursue issues with management, and to report back to national and local representatives. The possibility of the EWC establishing a select committee 'where (its) size so warrants' is foreseen under the statutory model, but its possible role and activities are not elaborated on. Reviewing the contents of Article 13 EWC agreements, Marginson *et al.* (1998) found that most agreements specified that select committees had co-ordination and administrative roles in relation to the EWC. A minority, however, had rights to receive information in extraordinary circumstances and/or to receive information on an ongoing basis from management. Such rights, it was argued, were important to underpinning an EWC characterised by ongoing activity, in contrast to a symbolic once a year meeting (Marginson *et al.* 1998: 76–7). The absence of any reference to the provision of training for employee representatives in the Directive has been described as an 'opportunity missed' (Miller and Stirling 1998: 48). Miller and Stirling (1998) argue that training for employee representatives on EWCs is essential to their effectiveness, and to the overall functioning and impact of EWCs (see Chapter 12 by John Stirling). In line with earlier argument, provisions on the matters in this second group have the potential to exhibit a 'learning effect' as voluntary good practice is progressively diffused.

The third group comprises four features which are potentially the most likely to be shaped by country-of-origin and/or sector influences: the constitution of the EWC as a joint management–employee or employee-side only body; likewise the constitution of the select committee; whether the agreement specifies that management may withhold potentially detrimental information and; whether the agreement states that a trade union official may be present at EWC meetings. Individual provisions in both of the first two groups may also in addition reflect country and/or sector influences.

Under the Annex to the Directive, a statutory EWC is constituted as an employee-side only structure which then meets with management. In practice, reviews of the provisions of EWC agreements have found that the majority of EWCs, concluded under either Article 13 or Article 6, are constituted as joint management–employee structures (Marginson *et al.* 1998; Carley and Marginson 2000). Moreover, the bi-variate analysis contained in these reviews has revealed strong associations between the constitution of the EWC and the country of origin of the multinational company concerned. Thus, agreements in French-based companies all follow the French model for national and local consultation within enterprises and establish a joint EWC arrangement, whereas a majority of agreements in companies headquartered in Germany follow the German works council model in establishing an employee-side only EWC. Agreements in the UK might be expected to be shaped by voluntary practice in the form of joint consultative committees, and so it proves (see also Chapter 6 by Richard Hume-Rothery). There are, however, no *à priori* expectations for any differences between sectors. Because the Directive's statutory model provides for an employee-side only EWC, the implication is that any select committee will be similarly constituted (although this is not directly addressed). Again, it might be expected that provisions in agreements might be shaped by national practice in terms of information and consultation structures. Again, there are no *à priori* expectations for any differences between sectors.

Whilst Article 8 of the Directive addresses confidentiality of information disclosed by management, some agreements go further in additionally, providing that management may withhold from the EWC information that is deemed to be potentially detrimental to the company's interests. Such clauses might be more likely to be found in agreements in UK- and US-based MNCs, because of concerns that disclosure of some types of information to employee representatives might infringe shareholders rights. They might also be expected to be more prevalent amongst agreements in the finance sector, since financial information is seen to be particularly sensitive.

The Directive makes no mention of trade unions, yet unions were signatories to a substantial minority of Article 13 EWC agreements and have continued to be so for a minority of agreements under Article 6 (Carley and Marginson 2000). The right of a trade union official to attend EWC meetings is an indicator of the extent to which EWC agreements provide an ongoing role for trade unions. The incidence of provision can be expected to vary according to both the country-of-origin and the sector. National information and consultation arrangements in France accord a formal role to trade union representatives, whilst in the Nordic countries they are trade union based. In Germany, by contrast, trade unions have no formal role in works councils. Provision for a formal trade union presence at the EWC might therefore be more likely under agreements concluded in French- and Swedish-based companies than those headquartered in Germany. Turning to sector, analysing the strategies of the EIFs towards EWCs, Rivest (1996) suggests that federations in three industries – food and drink, chemicals and construction – have placed emphasis on securing a formal trade union presence in the workings of EWCs.

A limitation of our approach is that a given provision may reflect both statutory model and learning effects, which reference to the timing of the agreement (whether it was concluded under Article 13 or Article 6 – see the next section) will not enable us to unravel. In particular, one matter from our first group of issues might, arguably, also be susceptible to a 'learning effect'. In addition to the influence of the terms of the Directive, the inclusion of provisions for convening meetings of EWCs in exceptional circumstances might also have become more widespread in the wake of Renault's much publicised decision in February 1997 to close its Vilvoorde plant in Belgium without first convening an extraordinary meeting of its EWC (EIRO 1997). Such a concern does not apply to the third group of features.

Data and estimation

In testing the propositions about EWC agreements developed earlier, we proceed in two steps. First, the propositions concerning the statutory model and learning effects are tested by regressing the first two groups of provisions on a variable which indicates whether a given agreement was concluded under Article 6, under Article 13 once the Directive had been adopted in September 1994 or was a 'pre-Directive agreement', that is concluded before the Directive was adopted. A potential complication in identifying a learning effect would arise if agreements concluded under Article 13 had already been subject to re-negotiation. This was indeed the case with a minority of the twenty-six 'pre-Directive' agreements. But in the case of all the 360 Article 13 agreements concluded after the Directive's adoption on September 1994 our analysis is based on original versions. The same holds for the Article 6 agreements. The learning effect comparing 'pre-Directive' with 'post-September 1994' Article 13 agreements is therefore likely to be less well specified than when comparing 'post-Directive' Article 13 agreements with Article 6 agreements.

Second, the propositions concerning the country and sector effects are tested by regressing the third group of provisions on variables which indicate the country of origin and the sector of the multinational company concluding the agreement. Recognising also that provisions in the first two groups may also be subject to country and sector influences, these two groups of variables are in addition regressed on the country-of-origin and sector variables together with the type of agreement variable.

A problem in identifying the influence of country-of-origin effects across all 464 EWC agreements in the European Foundation database is that for several countries, the number of companies concluding agreements is in single figures. This poses estimation problems, and in order to avoid these the analysis is confined to agreements in companies headquartered in the six countries which account for the largest numbers of companies involved: France, Germany, the Netherlands, Sweden, the UK and the US. Together, MNCs in these six countries account for almost three-quarters (74 per cent or 344) of the 464 agreements (a small number of agreements concluded by companies headquartered in two or more countries, such as Unilever and Eurocopter, were also excluded from the analysis). So as to avoid reducing the sample size even further, a slightly different approach was taken to categorising the companies involved by sector. As far as possible, companies were assigned to broad industrial categories corresponding to the reach of the EIFs. Where numbers of agreements were too small, as in most parts of the service sectors, larger aggregate groupings were created.

The definitions and mean values of the thirteen key features of EWC agreements, the type of agreement and the country-of-origin and sector of the multinational company concerned are given in Table 7.1.

As each of the key features of EWC agreements is defined as a dichotomous variable, logistic regression analysis was utilised to generate the estimates reported in the next section.

Table 7.1 Description and mean values of selected features of EWC agreements, agreement type, country-of-origin and sector

Label	Description	Mean value
SEATDIST	The basis for distribution of seats is specified	0.82
PREPMEET	There is provision for employee reps to hold a preparatory meeting	0.86
EXPERT	The employee side has access to external experts	0.80
SELECT	There is a select committee	0.65
EXTMEET	There is provision for extraordinary meetings	0.81
CONFID	The agreement contains a confidentiality clause	0.88
POSTMEET	There is provision for employee reps to hold a follow-up meeting	0.28
SCINFO	The select committee receive information and consultation on an ongoing basis	0.40
TRAIN	The agreement provides for management to meet the cost of training for employee reps	0.42
EWCCONST	The EWC is constituted as an employee-side only body	0.33
SCCONST	The select committee is constituted as an employee-side only structure (0.35 with no select committee)	0.49
WITHDET	Management can withhold potentially detrimental information	0.25
TUPRES	A trade union official can attend meetings by right or by invitation	0.38
GER	Germany (Reference category)	0.29
FRA	France	0.13
NETH	The Netherlands	0.06
SWE	Sweden	0.08
UK	UK	0.20
US	US	0.24
MET	Metalworking (Reference category)	0.33
OTHPRD	Other production	0.02
FOODT	Food, drink, tobacco	0.13
CHEM	Chemicals	0.18
TEXCF	Textile, clothing and footwear	0.04
OTHMAN	Other manufacturing	0.10
CONUTL	Construction/utilities	0.05
FINA	Finance	0.06
OTHSER	Other services	0.09
PREDIR	Pre-Directive agreement, concluded before 22 September 1994	0.07
ART13	Article 13 agreement (Reference category)	0.72
ART6	Article 6 agreement	0.19

Results

The results from a series of logistic regressions on the influence of type of agreement, country-of-origin of the company concerned and sector are presented in this section. In line with conventional practice, the reference category chosen for the three independent variables is in each case that with the largest number of observations: agreements concluded under Article 13 after September 1994 for the type of agreement; Germany for country-of-origin and; metalworking for sector. Missing observations mean that the number of cases included in each regression varies.

Table 7.2 presents the results of regressing the six features of EWC agreements expected to exhibit a statutory model effect on the type of agreement. Five of the regressions are significant at the 1 per cent level, as indicated by the χ^2 statistic, with the sixth – that for SEATDIST – attaining significance at the 5 per cent level. The signs on the coefficients are all as predicted: as suggested by our statutory model proposition, agreements concluded before September 1994 are less likely to have a given provision, whilst those concluded under Article 6 are more likely, as compared with the Article 13 reference category. In the cases of EXPERT, SELECT and EXTMEET both coefficients are also significant. In the case of SEATDIST and CONFID, only the coefficient on the pre-September 1994 variable attains significance, whilst in the case of PREPMEET the coefficient on neither variable is significant. Of particular note in the light of earlier argument is the insignificant effect of Article 6 agreements on SEATDIST, which is contrary to the effect expected.

The results from the regressions for the three specific provisions expected to capture the learning effect are reported in Table 7.3. Two of the regressions are well specified, as reflected in the χ^2 statistic, that relating to SCINFO slightly less so. The coefficient on the Article 6 variable has the expected sign and is significant in all three regressions. The coefficient on the pre-September 1994 variable has the expected sign in two of the three regressions, but only attains significance in

Table 7.2 Estimates of potential 'statutory model' features of EWC agreements

	SEATDIST	PREPMEET	EXPERT	SELECT	EXTMEET	CONFID
Constant	1.642[a]	1.663[a]	1.278[a]	0.463[a]	1.381[a]	2.281[a]
	(0.168)	(0.172)	(0.151)	(0.127)	(0.155)	(0.214)
PREDIR	−1.200[a]	−0.682	−1.095[b]	−0.726[c]	−0.939[b]	−2.194[a]
	(0.459)	(0.508)	(0.456)	(0.439)	(0.454)	(0.469)
ART6	0.006	7.539	1.699[a]	1.595[a]	1.595[a]	0.152
	(0.384)	(12.654)	(0.610)	(0.420)	(0.611)	(0.513)
N	344	335	341	344	344	344
-2 Log-likelihood	315.170	245.977	323.905	420.699	314.575	226.489
χ^2	6.342[b]	22.061[a]	19.684[a]	24.247[a]	15.968[a]	20.809[a]

Notes
Standard errors in parentheses; a, b, c denote significance at 1%, 5% and 10% levels, respectively.

Table 7.3 Estimates of potential 'learning' features of EWC agreements

	POSTMEET	SCINFO	TRAIN
Constant	−1.142[a]	−0.617[a]	−0.476[a]
	(0.148)	(0.167)	(0.130)
PREDIR	−1.899[c]	0.212	−0.686
	(1.033)	(0.666)	(0.528)
ART6	1.208[a]	0.799[b]	1.145[a]
	(0.297)	(0.318)	(0.298)
N	330	222	331
-2 Log-likelihood	365.684	292.611	432.545
χ^2	24.907[a]	6.367[b]	19.038[a]

Notes
Standard errors in parentheses; a, b, c denote significance at 1%, 5% and 10% levels, respectively.

one (that relating to follow-up meetings). The results are consistent with the existence of a learning effect amongst agreements concluded under Article 6 when compared with their Article 13 counterparts.

Turning to the potential influence of the country-of-origin and the sector of the companies concerned, results from the four features considered to be most likely to be susceptible to these influences are reported in Table 7.4. The left-hand differs from the right-hand panel in that the agreement type variables are included in the estimates in the latter. The χ^2 statistic indicates that each of the regressions is well specified. As expected, country-of-origin influences on EWCCONST are strong. France, the UK and the US all attract large negative coefficients, indicating that they are markedly more likely to establish joint management–employee structures than the reference category of Germany. The effect is highly significant in the case of the UK and the US, but not so for France (where the large standard error probably reflects a specification problem arising out of the fact that no agreements concluded by French-based companies provide for an employee-side only structure). In addition to the country-of-origin effects, distinct sector effects are also evident. Agreements in the food and drink, chemicals and other service sectors are all significantly more likely to establish a joint management–employee structure than those in the reference metalworking sector, whereas those in the other manufacturing sector are significantly less likely to do so. Turning to the right-hand panel, of further note is that, controlling for country-of-origin and sector, agreements concluded under Article 6 are significantly more likely to establish an employee-side only structure. Some, but not all, of the country-of-origin and sector effects carry over into the results for SCCONST. Of the country-of-origin effects, that for the UK remains large and significant: select committees in UK-based companies are more likely to be constituted as joint bodies than those in German-based companies. Sector effects of similar distinctiveness continue to be evident, with jointly constituted select committees significantly more likely to be found in, again, food and drink, and chemicals as compared with metalworking. Again, too, the right-hand panel shows that select committees established under Article 6 agreements are more likely to be employee-side only.

The expected country-of-origin effects on WITHDET come through, with agreements not only in UK- and US-, but also Dutch-based MNCs being significantly more likely to include a clause, enabling management to withhold potentially detrimental information. Consistent with prior expectations there is also a significant finance sector effect.

Significant country-of-origin effects are evident on TUPRES, but they are not particularly in accord with the expectations developed earlier. Contrary to expectations, agreements in French- and UK-based companies are not significantly more likely to provide for a trade union official to attend the EWC than those in German-based companies. Yet, those in Dutch- and US-based companies are significantly less likely than agreements in their German-based counterparts to formally provide for a trade union presence. Distinct sector effects are evident: agreements in each of six sectors are significantly more likely to provide for a trade union official to attend EWCs than is the case in the metalworking reference category.

In the previous section, we noted that the nine features selected because they were expected to be susceptible to one or other of the conformity and learning effects might also be subject to country-of-origin and/or sector influences. Accordingly, Table 7.5 reports findings from regressions which include the variables representing these additional influences. The left-hand panel refers to the six 'statutory model' provisions, whilst the right-hand panel refers to the three 'learning' provisions. The likelihood ratio tests indicate that the inclusion of the country-of-origin and sector influences improves the explanatory power in six of the nine regressions. The three where this is not so are the regressions concerning PREPMEET, EXTMEET and POSTMEET. For the four 'statutory model' provisions for which the overall explanatory power is improved, both significant country-of-origin and significant sector effects are evident. Amongst the country-of-origin effects, those relating to agreements concluded by companies based in the two countries, the UK and Sweden, stand out. Agreements in UK-based MNCs are significantly more likely than the German reference category to include provisions on confidentiality, but significantly less likely to specify the distribution of seats on the EWC. Agreements in Swedish-based companies are significantly more likely to include a provision for access to external experts and to establish a select committee, but are significantly less likely to contain a confidentiality provision. Amongst the sector effects, those in other services (in effect the service sector other than finance) are the most distinctive. As compared to the metalworking reference category, these are significantly less likely to provide for access to experts, to establish a select committee or to contain confidentiality provisions.

In the right-hand panel of Table 7.5, the χ^2 statistic for the POSTMEET regression indicates that the addition of the country-of-origin and sector variables was not jointly significant. Significant country-of-origin influences are evident for both SCINFO and TRAIN but there are, however, no significant sector influences. Amongst the country-of-origin effects, those relating to agreements in Dutch- and Swedish-based companies are most prominent. These are significantly more likely

Table 7.4 Estimates of potential 'country-of-origin and sector' features of EWC agreements

	EWCCONST	SCCONST	WITHDET	TUPRES	EWCCONST	SCCQNST	WITHDET	TUPRES
Constant	0.799ᵃ	2.075ᵃ	−3.289ᵃ	−0.915ᵃ	0.774ᵇ	2.000ᵃ	−3.205ᵃ	−0.879ᵃ
	(0.289)	(0.467)	(0.563)	(0.276)	(0.307)	(0.477)	(0.563)	(0.281)
FRA	−9.783	0.195	−0.858	0.022	−9.968	−0.005	−0.721	0.056
	(14.435)	(0.642)	(1.152)	(0.388)	(14.353)	(0.671)	(1.157)	(0.395)
NETH	0.337	0.603	3.097ᵃ	−1.355ᵇ	0.122	0.323	−2.932ᵃ	−1.303ᵇ
	(0.556)	(0.897)	(0.687)	(0.589)	(0.584)	(0.915)	(0.692)	(0.593)
SWE	−0.343	−0.494	1.078	−0.144	−0.661	−0.746	0.966	−0.080
	(0.470)	(0.645)	(0.806)	(0.456)	(0.485)	(0.670)	(0.814)	(0.460)
UK	−3.369ᵃ	−1.534ᵃ	2.603ᵃ	−0.064	−3.744ᵃ	−1.835ᵃ	2.477ᵃ	−0.029
	(0.619)	(0.517)	(0.592)	(0.349)	(0.654)	(0.556)	(0.596)	(0.353)
US	−1.775ᵃ	−0.070	3.368ᵃ	−0.733ᵇ	−2.142ᵃ	−0.201	3.210ᵃ	−0.697ᵇ
	(0.379)	(0.534)	(0.575)	(0.349)	(0.420)	(0.555)	(0.578)	(0.354)
OTHPRD	0.029	−0.573	−7.099	0.447	0.238	−1.311	−7.873	0.412
	(0.907)	(1.287)	(17.657)	(0.751)	(0.947)	(1.324)	(28.762)	(0.752)
FOODT	−1.857ᵃ	−1.615ᵃ	−0.090	1.380ᵃ	−2.022ᵃ	−1.636ᵃ	−0.096	1.394ᵃ
	(0.625)	(0.555)	(0.429)	(0.395)	(0.684)	(0.566)	(0.429)	(0.397)
CHEM	−1.060ᵃ	−0.911ᵇ	0.210	0.688ᵇ	−1.272ᵃ	−1.132ᵇ	0.226	0.714ᵇ
	(0.408)	(0.474)	(0.432)	(0.346)	(0.425)	(0.501)	(0.438)	(0.349)
TEXCF	−0.207	0.466	0.503	2.535ᵃ	−0.233	0.456	0.478	2.538ᵃ
	(0.863)	(1.150)	(0.708)	(0.707)	(0.862)	(1.160)	(0.707)	(0.708)
OTHMAN	0.931ᶜ	0.696	0.012	0.712ᶜ	1.033ᶜ	0.874	−0.001	0.709ᵇ
	(0.559)	(0.728)	(0.557)	(0.426)	(0.575)	(0.738)	(0.558)	(0.426)

	(1)	(2)	(3)	(4)	(5)	(6)	(7)	(8)
CONUTL	0.384	−0.014	0.534	0.231	0.177	−0.2446	0.302	0.320
	(0.746)	(1.120)	(0.981)	(0.595)	(0.771)	(1.145)	(1.007)	(0.606)
FINA	−0.325	−1.035	1.170[c]	1.189[b]	−0.407	−0.972	1.176[c]	1.186[b]
	(0.826)	(0.742)	(0.672)	(0.528)	(0.847)	(0.783)	(0.675)	(0.530)
OTHSER	−1.030[c]	−0.940	−0.002	1.173[a]	−1.033[c]	−1.026	0.018	1.186[a]
	(0.557)	(0.695)	(0.593)	(0.441)	(0.565)	(0.717)	(0.599)	(0.442)
PREDIR					0.101	7.428	−6.374	−0.043
					(0.676)	(17.759)	(19.563)	(0.478)
ART6					1.381[a]	1.119[b]	0.334	−0.314
					(0.421)	(0.473)	(0.362)	(0.326)
N	336	221	344	344	336	221	344	344
−2 Log-likelihood	278.866	209.100	284.303	421.197	267.655	197.752	280.693	420.254
χ^2	143.111[a]	29.670[a]	102.584[a]	36.912[a]	154.321[a]	41.018[a]	106.194[a]	37.855[a]
Likelihood ratio test for inclusion of agre'nt date $\chi^2(2)$					22.422[a]	22.696[a]	7.22[b]	1.886

Notes
Standard errors in parentheses; a, b, c denote significance at 1%, 5% and 10% levels, respectively.

Table 7.5 Estimates of country-of-origin and sector influences on potential 'statutory model' and 'learning' features of EWC agreements

	SEATDIST	PREPMEET	EXPERT	SELECT	EXTMEET	CONFID	POSTMEET	SCINFO	TRAIN
Constant	2.495[a]	1.073a	1.409[a]	0.722[a]	1.548[a]	2.266[a]	−1.713[a]	0.0013	−0.916[a]
	(0.4423)	(0.331)	(0.330)	(0.290)	(0.340)	(0.434)	(0.337)	(0.337)	(0.291)
FRA	−0.268	0.538	−0.350	0.579	0.016	−0.422	−0.598	−0.726	0.880[b]
	(0.510)	(0.519)	(0.442)	(0.413)	(0.494)	(0.495)	(0.537)	(0.515)	(0.415)
NETH	−0.537	8.855	6.951	0.389	1.441	8.143	0.934[c]	0.425	1.787[a]
	(0.636)	(35.773)	(12.423)	(0.550)	(1.079)	(33.306)	(0.588)	(0.625)	(0.565)
SWE	0.425	1.476[c]	1.506[c]	2.341[a]	0.022	−0.927[b]	0.763[c]	−0.558	1.558[a]
	(0.719)	(0.804)	(0.805)	(0.808)	(0.584)	(0.543)	(0.202)	(0.527)	(0.496)
UK	−0.934[b]	1.355[b]	0.586	0.060	−0.506	1.302[c]	0.388	−2.331[a]	0.188
	(0.439)	(0.556)	(0.439)	(0.360)	(0.414)	(0.690)	(0.403)	(0.601)	(0.372)
US	0.118	0.926[b]	0.025	0.209	0.252	8.212	0.330	−0.185	0.344
	(0.503)	(0.478)	(0.394)	(0.344)	(0.442)	(17.849)	(0.387)	(0.418)	(0.350)
OTHPRD	−0.807	0.546	−1.502[b]	−0.587	5.896	−0.433	1.632[b]	2.064	−0.628
	(0.944)	(1.107)	(0.724)	(0.723)	(11.896)	(1.165)	(0.745)	(1.332)	(0.846)
FOODT	−1.288[b]	−0.308	−0.435	−0.770[b]	−0.379	0.306	0.294	−0.206	−0.437
	(0.479)	(0.602)	(0.503)	(0.406)	(0.489)	(1.131)	(0.432)	(0.504)	(0.404)
CHEM	0.090	−0.118	−0.256	−0.530	−0.368	−0.902[c]	0.042	−0.199	0.142
	(0.530)	(0.467)	(0.423)	(0.362)	(0.414)	(0.528)	(0.412)	(0.428)	(0.357)
TEXCF	−1.157[c]	0.593	−0.904	−0.803	−1.083[c]	−1.294	0.133	−0.404	−0.267
	(0.696)	(1.104)	(0.684)	(0.608)	(0.648)	(0.930)	(0.744)	(0.799)	(0.624)

OTHMAN	−1.155[b]	−0.213	−0.736	−0.438	0.303	−0.227	0.761[c]	−0.426	0.370
	(0.518)	(0.594)	(0.521)	(0.463)	(0.503)	(0.684)	(0.460)	(0.591)	(0.438)
CONUTL	−0.783	−0.161	0.1.121	−1.638[b]	−0.005	−0.636	0.409	−0.1.003	−0.898
	(0.757)	(0.884)	(1.106)	(0.631)	(0.848)	(0.797)	(0.684)	(0.792)	(0.660)
FINA	−0.034	0.947	−0.218	−0.684	0.751	8.102	1.241[b]	−0.605	−0.512
	(0.733)	(1.101)	(0.678)	(0.544)	(0.823)	(32.806)	(0.587)	(0.728)	(0.565)
OTHSER	−0.829	−0.727	−0.925[c]	−1.399[a]	−0.108	−1.228[b]	0.336	−0.317	0.469
	(0.575)	(0.614)	(0.546)	(0.480)	(0.576)	(0.624)	(0.509)	(0.634)	(0.455)
PREDIR	−1.695[a]	−0.519	−1.002[b]	−1.037[b]	−1.069[b]	−1.814[a]	−1.682	0.030	−0.896
	(0.531)	(0.561)	(0.501)	(0.492)	(0.508)	(0.537)	(1.064)	(0.714)	(0.574)
ART6	0.031	8.348	1.576[b]	1.655[a]	1.658[b]	0.280	1.239[a]	1.147[a]	1.143[a]
	(0.413)	(20.050)	(0.628)	(0.433)	(0.627)	(0.624)	(0.323)	(0.013)	(0.324)
N	344	335	341	344	344	344	330	222	331
-2 Log-likelihood	287.243	227.742	297.866	393.612	297.669	177.045	347.766	260.203	401.388
χ^2	33.766[b]	40.295[a]	45.605[a]	51.334[a]	32.874[a]	70.253[a]	42.825[a]	38.775[a]	50.195[a]
Likelihood ratio test for inclusion of country and sector $\chi^2(13)$	27.424[b]	18.235	26.011[b]	27.087[b]	16.906	49.444[a]	17.918	32.408[a]	31.157[a]

Notes

Standard errors in parentheses; a, b, c denote significance at 1%, 5% and 10% levels, respectively.

than their counterparts in German-based companies to provide for a follow-up meeting and training for employee representatives.

With two exceptions, the signs on the individual coefficients on the agreement-type variables remain the same when comparing the relevant columns in Table 7.5 with their counterparts in Tables 7.2 and 7.3, respectively. The same kind of comparison reveals that the magnitude of the coefficients changes in most cases, but not greatly, and that levels of significance remain unchanged. Thus, the statutory model effects shown in Table 7.2 and the learning effects of Table 7.3 are robust to the inclusion of country-of-origin and sector effects.

Discussion

The results provide evidence to support each of the four propositions about the influences shaping the provisions of EWC agreements. As underlined at the outset, the propositions are not exclusive of each other and the results show that each operates as an identifiable influence on the provisions of EWC agreements.

There is strong evidence for the effect of the statutory model: provisions which are specified either in the text of the Directive itself, or in the model EWC elaborated in the Annex, are in general more likely to be found in Article 6 than Article 13 agreements, and in both of these as compared with pre-Directive agreements. There are, however, exceptions. No statutory model effect was evident in the case of PREPMEET, probably because the practice was already widespread under pre-Directive agreements. It has been argued that these pioneering agreements exercised an influence on the drafting of the Directive (Gold and Hall 1994), and an interpretation consistent with our results would be that in respect of employee preparatory meetings the provision in the Directive was shaped by already existing practice. Also the specific requirement that agreements under Article 6 specify the distribution of seats amongst employee representatives was not reflected in any noticeable difference between these and their Article 13 predecessors. However, one further piece of evidence for the 'statutory model effect' was also evident: agreements under Article 6 are more likely to establish an employee-side only EWC, in line with the requirements of the Directive's Annex, than were Article 13 agreements.

The results are consistent with the operation of a learning effect when comparing the provisions of Article 6 with Article 13 agreements. Article 6 agreements are more likely than earlier agreements to provide for follow-up meetings for employee representatives, for select committees to receive information and consultation on an ongoing basis and for training for employee representatives. In each instance, the effect is robust to the inclusion of variables capturing country-of-origin and sector influences. Although practice cannot be read off from the provisions of agreements, the effects of such learning are resulting in an increasing proportion of agreements whose provisions facilitate the development of an 'active EWC', in which there is ongoing activity on the employee-side and liaison with management, as distinct from a 'symbolic EWC' whose existence is confined to the formalities of a once a year meeting (Marginson *et al.* 1998: 76–7). In particular, the 'opportunity missed' by the Directive, and by many early agreements, to make explicit provision for the training of employee representatives (Miller and Stirling 1998), is now being addressed on a more widespread basis in Article 6 agreements. Again, however, caution is in order in inferring anything about the extent and nature of the training provided.

Crucially, the scope for such 'learning' is not confined to new agreements: many agreements specify the duration after which they are open to review and re-negotiation. This presents management and employee representatives with an opportunity to incorporate innovatory provisions adopted in agreements concluded subsequent to their own, or to formalise emergent practice. The fact that some 'pre-Directive' agreements had been re-negotiated may explain the lack of evidence for a learning effect between these and 'post-September 1994' Article 13 agreements. Unfortunately, no systematic data yet exist which would allow a longitudinal comparison of the terms of given EWC agreements as they undergo the process of review and re-negotiation.

The country-of-origin effects revealed by our results on the constitution of EWCs as joint or employee-side only structures are consistent with arguments that EWCs will resemble the structures of information and consultation which prevail under the national system of the country in which a given multinational company is headquartered (Streeck 1997 and 1998). For the constitution of the select committee, this influence is more muted, although still significant when comparing agreements in UK with those in German-based MNCs. The greater incidence of more restrictive clauses dealing with disclosure of information amongst agreements in UK- and US-based companies is consistent with earlier arguments about shareholder prerogatives under the Anglo-Saxon system of corporate governance. The effects on TUPRES were not, however, those expected. The role accorded to trade unions in the French and British models of consultation notwithstanding, agreements in French- and UK-based companies were not more likely than those in German-based organisations to provide that a trade union official could attend EWC meetings. Agreements in Dutch MNCs are, however, less likely to provide for a trade union presence than those in their German counterparts, even though works councils structure in neither country provides for a formal trade union role. The surprise here is the higher than expected incidence with which agreements in German-based MNCs are providing for a trade union presence. The absence of provision for a trade union presence amongst US-based MNCs might reflect the extent of non-unionism amongst these.

Further country-of-origin contrasts were revealed by the results on the 'statutory model effect' variables. The greater tendency for agreements in UK-based companies to contain a confidentiality clause probably also reflects sensitivities about protecting the privileged position of the shareholder, but if so a similar effect might have been expected amongst agreements in US-based MNCs (see Chapter 6 by Richard Hume-Rothery). The finding that agreements in Sweden are more likely to provide for access to experts reflects long-established national practice (Knudsen and Bruun 1998). The 'country-of-origin' effects which were significant influences on the 'learning effect' variables, suggest that agreements in companies headquartered in the Netherlands and Sweden are the most, and those in UK-based companies the least, likely to contain provisions which facilitate the development of an 'active' as compared with a 'symbolic' EWC. In the case of the Swedish-based companies, this assessment does not entirely accord with Knudsen and Bruun's (1998) review of agreements in companies based in the Nordic countries. Their focus, however, was confined to Article 13 agreements. In the case of UK-based companies, this might be because neither management nor employee representatives in the UK has previous experience of local works councils practice.

Significant sector influences on the provisions of agreements are evident when the country-of-origin of the multinational company concerned is also controlled for, something which could not be confirmed in earlier reports which relied on bi-variate analysis (Marginson *et al.* 1998; Carley and Marginson 2000). Clear sector effects are evident where it was anticipated, on TUPRES and in respect of the finance sector on WITHDET, but also on several other provisions about which we had no *à priori* expectations. Agreements in the metalworking sector are significantly less likely to provide for a trade union official to participate in EWC meetings than those in six of the other eight sectors. Rivest's (1996) conclusion that in negotiations to establish EWCs some EIFs have emphasised securing a trade union presence continues to hold good for food and drink and chemicals, but not any longer for construction. Sector influences are also evident on the constitution of EWCs, and of select committees, as joint or employee-side structures. In both instances, agreements in the food and drink, and chemicals sectors are more likely to establish joint structures than those in metalworking. The same is the case for the constitution of EWCs in the non-finance service sectors. These sector differences may reflect differing strategies by the EIFs, but they may also stem from differing industrial relations traditions. For instance, joint arrangements have traditionally been more extensive and employer–trade union relations more co-operative in chemicals than in metalworking.

Sector differences might have been expected on the three 'learning effect' variables, on the grounds that the incidence of the provisions concerned might reflect differences in approach between the EIFs in their attempts to shape the outcomes of negotiations. The absence of any significant sector differences on TRAIN is perhaps surprising, and indicates that this matter is not accorded greater emphasis in some sectors than in others.

Conclusion

The operation of a clear 'statutory model effect' indicates how when 'bargaining under the shadow of the law' (Bercusson 1992) the choices made by management and employee representatives over the provisions of EWC agreements tend to be constrained. But the provisions of the statutory model EWC specified in the Directive are not the only factor influencing the way in which choice has been exercised by the negotiating parties: the chapter also finds tangible evidence of 'country' and 'sector' effects on the provisions of EWC agreements. This simultaneously shows that the scope for choice offered by the EWCs Directive can and has been exercised by management and employee representatives in concluding agreements, whilst also suggesting that existing country and sector-specific industrial relations structures and traditions have constrained the way in which such choice has been exercised.

The uncovering of a 'learning effect' reveals that a different kind of dynamic is also in play: as a result of the negotiating process the parties are developing a momentum of their own, in which good practice progressively evolves. Periodic review and re-negotiation of agreements means that the scope for learning is ongoing. The scope and nature, but also the limits, of such learning is likely to be a consideration in the European Commission's decision about the possible revision of the EWC's Directive, deferred in the outcome of its recent review to an unspecified date in the future (Hall 2000). A particular issue raised by trade unions in the review process has been the absence of any reference in the Directive to the need for information and consultation to be in good time (EIRO 2000). A little over one-quarter of Article 6 agreements specifically address the timing of information and consultation (Carley and Marginson 2000: 28), but no comparative information is available for Article 13 agreements and hence it has not been possible to investigate whether any learning effect is in operation on this crucial matter. Identifying the sources of such learning has also been beyond the scope of this chapter. Potentially important are the roles played by the relatively small number of management consultants advising the management during negotiations to establish EWCs and the strategies of national- and European-level trade union organisations.

Finally, the salience of both country and sector influences on the provisions of EWC agreements places a question mark against the perspective that sees EWCs as primarily international extensions of national structures of information and consultation. The influence of national systems of industrial relations on the provisions of EWC agreements is important, but the similarities within particular sectors, which cross national borders, reflects a more general process of 'converging divergences' (Katz and Darbishire 2000) under which growing divergence in industrial relations arrangements and practice within national systems is occurring alongside increased cross-border convergence of practices within given sectors.

Acknowledgements

The data are drawn from the European Foundation for the Improvement of Living and Working Conditions' database on EWC agreements. The chapter has benefited from earlier work with Hubert Krieger, Otto Jacobi and Mark Carley. Helpful comments have been provided by the two referees, Mark Hall, Aline Hoffman, Torsten Müller, Tony Edwards and participants at the annual BUIRA conference, July 2000.

References

Bercusson, B. (1992) 'Maastricht: A Fundamental Change in European Labour Law', *Industrial Relations Journal*, 23(3): 177–90.

Bonneton, P., Carley, M., Hall, M. and Krieger, H. (1996) 'Agreements on Information and Consultation in European Multinationals', *Social Europe* Supplement 5/95, Luxembourg: Office for Official Publications of the European Communities.

Carley, M. and Marginson, P. (2000) *Negotiating EWCs: A Comparative Study of Article 6 and Article 13 Agreements*, Luxembourg: Office for Official Publications of the European Communities.

EIRO (1997) 'The Renault Affair and the Future of Social Europe', *European Industrial Relations Observatory Update*, 2/97: 2.

EIRO (2000) 'EWC Adopts Resolution on EWCs Directive', *European Industrial Relations Observatory*, Ref: EU0001221N (January).

Gold, M. and Hall, M. (1994) 'Statutory European Works Councils: The Final Countdown?' *Industrial Relations Journal*, 25(3): 177–86.

Hall, M. (2000) 'Commission Reports on Implementation of the European Works Council Directive', *European Industrial Relations Observatory*, Ref: 0005248F (May).

Hall, M., Carley, M., Gold, M., Marginson, P. and Sisson, K. (1995) *European Works Councils: Planning for the Directive*, London: Eclipse.

Katz, H. and Darbishire, O. (2000) *Converging Divergencies*, Ithaca, NY: ILR Press.

Kochan, T., Katz, H. and McKersie, R. (1986) *The Transformation of American Industrial Relations*, New York: Basic Books.

Knudsen, H. and Bruun, N. (1998) 'European Works Councils in the Nordic Countries', *European Journal of Industrial Relations*, 4(2): 131–55.

Marginson, P. (2000) 'The Eurocompany and Euro Industrial Relations', *European Journal of Industrial Relations*, 6(1): 9–34.

Marginson, P., Gilman, M., Krieger, H. and Jacboi, O. (1998) *Negotiating European Works Councils: An Analysis of Agreements under Article 13*, Luxembourg: Office for Official Publications of the European Communities.

Miller, D. and Stirling, J. (1998) 'European Works Council Training: An Opportunity Missed?', *European Journal of Industrial Relations*, 4(1): 35–56.

Ramsay, H. (1997) 'Fool's Gold? European Works Councils and Workplace Democracy', *Industrial Relations Journal*, 28(4): 314–22.

Rivest, C. (1996) 'Voluntary European Works Councils', *European Journal of Industrial Relations*, 2(2): 235–53.

Streeck, W. (1997) 'Neither European Nor Works Councils: A Reply to Paul Knutsen', *Economic and Industrial Democracy*, 18(2): 325–37.

Streeck, W. (1998) 'The Internationalization of Industrial Relations in Europe: Prospects and Problems', *Politics and Society*, 26(4): 429–59.

Part III

European Works Councils

Management views and representatives' experiences

This part provides a view from the two main sides of the European Works Council (EWC) table. It has three case studies, viewed from very different perspectives and in very different ways, and a survey of the EWCs of multinationals headquartered outside and inside the European Economic Area (EEA). The first two chapters offer a management perspective of the EWC experience through, first, an in-depth case study by one of the senior managers at the EWC, and, second, through the results of two main surveys of the managers at EWCs. The third and fourth chapters again use case study data, the first to explore the experience of trade union EWC delegates analysing the impact that membership has had on their national trade union roles. The second as evidence of the need for language and cultural training if EWCs are to function effectively.

Management views

Chapter 8 by Antonia S. McAlindin provides a case study of the EWC at Scottish and Newcastle (S&N) from the perspective of a practitioner with intimate knowledge. She gives a historical account of the factors that initially led to the composition of an information Forum in the 1970s, which in the 1990s was reorganised to form the EWC. The account gives an insight into the factors that influenced, not only the setting up of the Forum but also its subsequent development. McAlindin begins by identifying the early Bullock proposals for employee participation in the 1970s as a trigger for not only the S&N development but also for many other participation procedures. When the Forum was re-negotiated in 1996 a similar approach was taken and she emphasises that the bodies were and are organised along the lines of a management communication channel rather than a body where negotiations could develop. As with Hume-Rothery, of importance to her is that the Forum does not undermine management prerogatives.

Recent research has found that the Forum is dormant between meetings with no international networking or little impact on lower level industrial relations (Marginson *et al.* 2001). An important reason for this is the British dominance of the Forum (see Chapter 11 by Barbara Tully), although the recent acquisitions of major European brewers will challenge not only this dominance but could prove a trigger for international networking with the introduction of representatives who have a tradition of participation in decision making. The representatives' role in decision making, either involvement when decisions are formulated (participation) or when the effects are experienced (information) is one of the key issues of concern for both sides of industry.

Chapter 9 by Satoshi Nakano uses two main sources of data for its management view of EWCs introducing the views of senior managers in multinationals based within and outside the EEA. The data is organised into three main categories; 'main functions' which are factors relating closely to the Directive, 'secondary effects' which include corporate governance, industrial relations and cost and benefit factors, and 'institutional characteristics' which relate to the structure of an EWC. Interestingly, as with McAlindin, the majority of managers perceived their EWC as being a useful tool for the communication of information. However, in contrast to the example given by Hume-Rothery they did not believe that it would be useful at times of restructuring. Further when cost was considered the majority, perhaps not surprisingly, found EWCs a problem, a similar view expressed by Hume-Rothery and hinted at by McAlindin. He also reports that some senior managers believed that a European tradition of consultation could go beyond the EEA, an issue discussed in the final part of the book.

Representatives' experiences

Rachel Annand uses her case study of the Compass EWC to investigate the connections between the trade union delegates' European and national roles. Chapter 10 builds a picture of the EWC representatives through two main sources of information; questionnaire data obtained from an EWC employee-side meeting in 2002, and telephone interviews with a cross section of delegates. The EWC is dominated by female delegates who made up over 80 per cent of representatives at the 2002 meeting and Annand discusses whether this influences the issues that are discussed. The body of the chapter, though, concerns itself with how membership of the EWC has improved delegates' bargaining position and their personal ability to carry out their national union roles.

Annand concludes that close connections do exist between the representatives' roles on the EWC and their national union work. She also argues that EWC representatives' concerns are generally similar across national boundaries, asking if this will be 'the glue' that helps bind their potentially divisive language, cultural and industrial relations backgrounds. The most interesting facet of the chapter is the brief glimpse it gives of the lives of the women, who even though they come from these very different cultural backgrounds have had similar problems to overcome, both of a personal and union nature.

Barbara Tully in Chapter 11 discusses the importance of language and intercultural communication for the successful functioning of an EWC. It draws on three sources of data: an analysis of the ETUI database of EWC agreements;

a series of interviews with EWC representatives; and a case study of the Kværner EWC. The recurring theme of the chapter is the dominance of the English language, not only with regard to its overwhelming choice as a working language for EWCs but also when spoken by native speakers whose idiomatic and regional accents can prove an obstacle to effective communication with non-native speakers.

She develops this theme with regard to the organisation of an effectively functioning EWC communications network, arguing that the two main challenges to success are representatives' access to technology and the barrier of language. She believes that the main way to overcome these is through adequate training for representatives, allowing them to operate information and communication technologies (ICT) and communicate in a way that builds a united EWC. The case study is used as evidence of a successful EWC communications network, built on access to ICT and language training, which proved sustainable even when business restructuring caused a number of EWC members to be transferred to employment in other multinationals. In these cases representatives used the skills they had learnt to begin new networks that in some cases stretched beyond the boundaries of Europe.

8 Putting the European Works Council Directive into practice

Antonia S. McAlindin

Introduction

This chapter provides a case study of the Scottish and Newcastle (S&N) European Forum. S&N today comprises a number of diverse businesses that employ a workforce of over 40,000 with a plc group head office based in Edinburgh. It is the leading brewer in Britain and one of the largest in Europe with a portfolio of well-known brands. The brewing division of S&N, Scottish Courage, employs 6,000 staff and was formed in 1995 following the acquisition by S&N of the Courage business. In addition to the UK operations, the company owns Beamish and Crawford in Ireland and has an importing company in the USA. The Retail Division, S&N Retail Ltd owns around 1,500 managed public houses and 1,000 leased public houses across the UK employing 30,000 employees.

S&N has always been committed to the principles of employee involvement and operates a wide range of briefing, consultation and bargaining arrangements throughout its operations. This includes domestic works councils where applicable, recognised trade unions, and a European Works Council (EWC), known as the Forum. During the history of the Forum, the Company also owned a leisure division consisting of Center Parcs and Pontin's Holiday Club which employed approximately 10,500 staff at the time the divisions were disposed of in 2001 and 2000, respectively. As will be discussed, the acquisition of the leisure division took S&N into other European Union (EU) Member States necessitating the establishment of an EWC. Although the leisure division is no longer part of the Group, when the Company sold the division it acquired an international beer division established in France and Belgium which necessitated the continuance of an EWC.

The next section charts the history of the original S&N consultative committee which evolved into the present EWC and discusses the decision to enter into an Article 13 agreement. The section on 'Aim, Composition and procedures of the Company Forum' describes the aims, composition and procedures of the Forum and the final section discusses the issues that have arisen as the EWC Forum has grown. This final section uses research undertaken by Warwick University that analysed aspects of the S&N Forum and ends by looking at recent acquisitions and the future of the Forum.

The original chairman's Forum

In the mid-1970s, there was considerable debate and interest in the principles of industrial democracy. The UK had joined the European Community where most of the then members operated a works council system and at a time when there was widespread discussion of European Commission proposals (see Chapter 1 by Ian Fitzgerald). The Labour Government of 1974 set up a committee under Lord Bullock to establish some form of industrial democracy. They were greatly influenced by the 1974 Trades Union Congress (TUC) paper on industrial democracy. The terms of reference for Bullock were not about whether to have such a democracy but how a system which involved workers representatives could work in the UK.

Two contrasting reports were published in 1977 which demonstrated the gap between employers and unions on this issue and because of its opposition to Bullock, the CBI advocated a system of participation agreements to be achieved voluntarily within organisations. Fear of Bullock led to many such agreements being established and to the popularity of joint consultative committees. Although the Bullock proposals fell with the advent of a Conservative administration in 1979, by then many such agreements had been established.

It was against this background that S&N decided to establish its own system of participation. In 1978 it set-up the Chairman's Forum in advance of any legal compulsion and in order to improve industrial relations during difficult and changing times. Although Bullock fell, the company kept the Forum because it provided an opportunity for a wide range of employees and trade union representatives who might otherwise not have met, to come together twice a year to meet the full Board of directors. The Chairman at that time, Peter Balfour, saw the Forum as a means of promoting the development of good employee relations. Central management saw it as a method of communicating to employees what was happening within the company, the way in which decisions were taken and allowing employees the opportunity to question these issues.

The objectives of the Forum were to communicate the progress of the Group, the activities of the various operating divisions and businesses, to discuss matters of Group concern and interest, and to allow management, employees and unions to meet together in a non-negotiating environment of mutual interest. Its membership consisted of the main board of directors, the Chairman and secretary of each of the recognised trade unions, lay delegates from each of the trade union groups, personnel directors of local operating companies, Group Personnel and Industrial Relations departments and management representatives within the Group as a whole. Over time, this was adapted to cover non-union areas and involvement was therefore directly through the trade unions or by appointment by management.

At that time the total workforce of S&N was in the region of 7,000 and the organisation was structured as one single entity plus a hotel group known as Thistle Hotels. Term of office of non-union members was two years and the Forum met twice a year in Edinburgh. The format of the day was presentation by the management of company performance, future strategy, financial situation and a number of presentations relating to different parts of the organisation.

Representatives were able to ask questions at any stage of the proceedings. The Forum was specifically started to be a communication channel and not a place for negotiation.

As it had grown, membership of the Forum had adapted to represent the various parts of the business including Pontins and Center Parcs and latterly the acquisition of Courage. However, given the size and spread of the organisation, it was not possible to include a representative from every area and so the Head of the Central Works Council in Center Parcs was included but not every country in Center Parcs was covered. It was clear that with the arrival of the European legislation that this situation would have to change.

By 1995, when it became obvious that there would be European legislation on EWCs, S&N was a totally different organisation with a different organisational structure to that which had served the previous Chairman's Forum. A decision had to be taken on whether to adapt this Forum to changing legislation or to set up a Forum for Center Parcs employees separate from the Chairman's Forum.

The European Works Council Directive's impact on Scottish and Newcastle

S&N had sufficient employees in more than one Member State other than the UK, to make the establishment of an EWC for those employees inevitable. The countries covered included the Netherlands, France, Germany and Belgium, all countries with established works council machinery and Ireland, which was similar to the UK. In all of these countries except Ireland the employees worked for Center Parcs. In Ireland, there was Beamish and Crawford a brewery, and a site at Trebolgan which was a chalet holiday centre for Pontins. Any EWC would therefore be heavily biased towards Center Parcs.

S&N was opposed to the legislation but decided along with other UK employers to take a pragmatic approach (see Chapter 6 by Richard Hume-Rothery). It accepted the likelihood of a change of Government in the near future with the then adoption of the legislation and it was not clear whether the Article 13 option would still be available. Against this, there was a need to set up an EWC in the non-UK countries. What would happen to UK employees in such a case, in particular those in Center Parcs UK? In addition, S&N already had the Chairman's Forum, which appeared in broad outline to be very similar to the proposed EWC. The Forum was well established, well respected and more or less representative. Discussions therefore ensued on how to progress the move from the existing Forum to what would comply with the Directive.

The Forum was perceived to have a number of advantages over the Directive. It was bigger, allowing better representation. It included full-time trade union officials who were regarded as making a positive and knowledgeable contribution. It met twice per annum and covered local as well as transnational issues. At the very least, it complied with the spirit of the Directive and could be adapted. On the down side, it was not representative enough in its coverage, for example, including all countries, it would have to involve representatives more in setting the agenda, feedback would have to be more organised and it would have to move from a heavy emphasis on information giving to consultation. In order to ensure that the new Forum would comply with the Directive and not be challenged, it was imperative to get the agreement of the whole workforce to the proposed way forward.

Moving forward

Because the UK was not covered by the legislation at that time, there was no legal system in the UK to underpin what would effectively be a voluntary agreement. It was unclear whether this would suffice, even a collective agreement in the sense given to it by UK legislation, that is, with a recognised trade union, is not regarded as binding unlike many other EU countries.

In addition, the umbrella trade union organisation in Europe that dealt with the food and drinks industry had its own agenda. S&N had to be sure that everyone was on board with the proposals and that genuine agreement was reached. Since it is believed that the Forum was better than the Directive in its scope and membership, any challenge to the S&N proposals could only result in a diminution of coverage for employees, that is, the minimum required by the Directive, which would mean a predominantly Center Parcs forum. In any case, the eventual Constitution provided that the new Forum could be ended by either side giving notice and included a provision to re-negotiate the Forum at regular intervals. This was felt to give adequate protection to the representatives should they feel that the Forum did not meet the objectives of the Directive. Indeed as the Forum includes full-time officials who might otherwise be excluded by the Directive (unless they qualify as experts) then it is not surprising that Brian Revell, the National Secretary from the Transport and General stated at the time of signing the Agreement:

> This is a good agreement which reflects the positive industrial relations within the company. Other employers should note that S&N have welcomed trade union involvement, whereas some employers continue to endeavour to marginalise trade unions from European Works Councils.

In deciding to move forward, S&N had a number of options. It could ascertain whether there was support for setting up a Special Negotiating Body as described in the Directive. However, S&N is a complex structure with different divisions in different countries with different bargaining and consultative structures, Works Councils in Europe, unions and non-union representatives in the UK including village councils in Center Parcs UK and various consultative bodies in Retail. It was difficult to envisage how to set up such a body and how individuals would be nominated to take part.

The Company therefore announced at the Chairman's Forum the intention to move towards a Forum that would comply with the Directive. Discussion was to take place with employees on moving the existing Forum to this position. Forum members were asked for their views and within each division discussion took place through the normal consultative channels, that is, works councils and trade unions plus any other formal consultative processes that existed. In addition, each division decided on direct communication to employees. In Beer, Retail, Group Head Office and Pontins each employee was sent a letter explaining the intention to change the previous Forum to a new format. Individuals were asked for their views and given contact points and articles appeared in various internal Company newspapers. Within Beer, discussion took place with full-time trade union officials on a number of occasions. A similar process took place within Retail and members of central management also went to the Netherlands to meet the representatives of various works councils plus the umbrella trade union organisation for the food and drink industry.

In addition, the Company drew up a draft constitution based on the existing Forum and the Directive. Where the existing Forum was an improvement on the Directive it remained, where the Directive was better it was changed. For example, existing numbers were broadly in line with the Directive as they had increased as the Company had acquired different companies, however, there were insufficient individuals from overseas. There had previously been no pre-meeting and the Company was not entirely convinced that such a meeting could be productive. It was also recognised that any new Forum had to have the opportunity for consultation as well as information giving.

The Constitution document was intended as an initial discussion document not as a final document and individuals were invited to make comments and criticisms. Indeed the meeting in the Netherlands provided many constructive comments particularly in relation to some of the newer areas such as pre-meeting, training of representatives, election, term of office, etc. The experience of European employees who were works council representatives was useful and an indication of their familiarity with the subject matter. A vast amount of literature on experiences of European and domestic works councils was studied as well as making direct contact with other companies who were going through or had gone through a similar process.

The process of agreement was not easy. How can you be sure that more than 45,000 individuals agree? In many cases, an assumption had to be made that the various representatives had the power to make such a decision on individuals' behalf. This was easier to assume where there were elected unions or works councils but less so for non-elected individuals. In order to comply with an Article 13 agreement, it was necessary to demonstrate agreement of the whole workforce otherwise the agreement could fold. It was also imperative to have the backing of the European trade union movement and this was achieved.

Issues to be addressed included frequency of meetings (two per annum plus pre-meetings), content, contribution to the agenda (drawn up by management and distributed for comment and contribution six weeks before the Forum), feedback (newsletter drawn up after each forum), confidentiality, term of office (two year initially but under review). Membership, once numbers were ascertained, was left to each division and legal structure but each country and each level of job was to be included. Management grade representation posed a problem as in the UK there was no consultative process that covered them. In contrast to this in some European countries, management could be elected members of works councils. In the UK, some unions were uncomfortable having discussions with management. The Directive envisaged a membership of thirty but Article 13 allowed more flexibility. The opportunity was therefore taken to have an increased membership including full-time officials of recognised trade unions.

Agreement was eventually reached in July 1996 to commence the new Forum in October 1996. The agreement was signed by representative members of the works councils, representatives of recognised unions including the umbrella union, members of central management and the Executive and was communicated to employees. The Agreement was attached to the Constitution and provided that the Agreement would last initially for three years but could be ended by either party by giving notice, that the Constitution would be reviewed after one year and that major changes could only be made by the Forum as a whole or via any members elected for that sole purpose. It acknowledged that it was not a legally binding agreement under UK law nor was it part of any individual contract of employment.

Aims, composition and procedures of the Company Forum

The principal aims of the Forum are contained in the Constitution, for example:

> [the Forum] provides an opportunity for all grade and levels of employee to be informed and consulted about business activities of Company significance and to have the opportunity to communicate their own opinions and views to the appropriate levels of management.
>
> (S&N 1999: 1)

It goes on to state the belief that the agreement complies with the Directive, as agreed with all employees. That the Forum is not a negotiating body, nor is it intended to be utilised as an advanced communication vehicle for future changes which are confidential, nor as yet announced to affected employees, price sensitive or better dealt with on a local as opposed to transnational basis (this is confirmed in the representative guidelines). However, under the Constitution representatives may raise questions on local issues.

It is intended that dialogue in the Forum takes place in a spirit of trust and mutual respect and that management continue to maintain managerial prerogative for managing Company affairs. Obviously, there will be differences in perception and objectives of management and representatives but it is hoped that the spirit of trust ensures that these differences do not destroy the foundations of the Forum.

As is required by Article 13 of the Directive, the S&N voluntary agreement covers the entire workforce of the Company. It consists of the Chairman, Chief Executive, executive directors, members of management, employee representatives from all sectors of the workforce and recognised full-time trade union officials. It is clearly noted in representative's guidelines that representatives are not expected to represent the views of other employees in their own job category. They are representatives from, rather than for, the workforce, similar to Members of Parliament elected to represent their constituents but not to canvass their views on every single subject. With the size of S&N, it was felt that this would be too cumbersome a task.

The numbers of Forum members at that time were roughly proportionate to the divisions of S&N, for example 15 members from the Beer division, 12 from Retail, 10 from Center Parcs including at least one from each country, three from Pontins, two from Group Head Office and up to seven full-time officials from amongst the trade unions recognised by the Company, overall there were originally 53 members on the Forum. There were too many recognised unions to give a place to each union so these rotate. In addition, by agreement internal or external participants could be invited to attend.

It was impractical to have representation for each Company location or subsidiary which would have made the Forum unmanageable. It was intended that the opportunity would be taken to cover new locations when a term of office has expired, however, it is feared there may be little rotation of certain members. For instance, the members from outside the UK were keen to reflect the term of membership on their domestic works council, which might in some cases be six years. Shop stewards in the UK are elected and it may be that the same stewards are re-elected on more than one occasion. There are pros and cons of change of membership, experience dictates that it can take some time before individuals feel able to participate fully in the Forum – there is a learning curve. Too short a membership can mean individuals learning the ropes and then leaving. But if membership is too long, then individuals may not only become stale, but the perception of the wider workforce is that it becomes an elitist establishment. Clearly, trade unions prefer to keep the same membership as they become better accustomed to the Forum and its members.

Each division of S&N is responsible for the allocation of places with the appropriate employee representatives. Where there are recognised trade unions or works councils this is usually straightforward and accords with the need in the Directive to accord with local laws or practice. Where no such structures exist, individuals are elected either through putting themselves forward and being endorsed by others or in the case of management by nomination (this has had to change).

Employees are expected to have had one complete year of service with S&N before being nominated as a representative. They are elected to serve on the Forum for two years, that is, four meetings. The Forum meets every April and October in Edinburgh. It is permitted for representatives to be re-elected provided their membership does not exceed six years, full-time officials can obviously serve longer.

The meeting is normally opened by a presentation from the Chief Executive followed by a number of presentations on issues of general interest. This is normally a presentation by a senior manager or director from a part of the business (this rotates over the year so that Beer, Retail and the two leisure divisions each have a slot) and individuals can ask questions at the end of each presentation. The last slot is an open forum where representatives can ask questions about any matter of interest, although, generally issues tend to be of local interest. Attempts are made to encourage more consultation as opposed to information giving.

In exceptional circumstances, the Forum can meet more than twice per year. It would be difficult to extend the number of meetings per year on a permanent basis as it is a large exercise organising the Forum and bringing together all the members of the Board of Directors with employee representatives.

The representatives' guidelines

Initially one thing that became clear at the Forum was that representatives were often confused as to what their role was and what was expected from them. For this reason, a training session was set up prior to the pre-meeting in October and guidelines for representatives were drawn up.

These guidelines provided some background to S&N itself, describing the main parts of the business. They also describe the setting up of the Forum from the previous Chairman's Forum, in the light of the then pending European legislation. The principles from the Constitution are set out including a statement that the Forum is not a negotiating body nor appropriate for discussing terms and conditions of employment, nor an advanced communication vehicle, nor a replacement for local communication channels.

They further set out how representatives are elected, their term of office, training, travel, etc. They also explain the operation of the Forum, the pre-meeting, the role of representatives before the meeting, at the meeting and in relation to feedback.

Pre-meeting

Forum employee representatives are entitled to meet on the afternoon preceding the Forum. They are responsible for its working arrangements and organise the designation of a chairperson, agendas, feedback, etc. In addition to this, an informal meeting normally takes place between representatives and some members of senior management the evening before the Forum.

Not surprisingly, the organisation of the pre-meetings has been a somewhat difficult affair. To put a mixed group of employees together with no framework obviously led to initial confusion. Many representatives were unsure of their role. However, the group soon organised themselves with a Chair, Vice-chair, Secretary and three deputies. In this way they have been able to communicate between meetings and to organise the actual meetings. The sub-group is now a formal Liaison Committee which may meet with senior management between Forum meetings to progress and review the workings of the Forum.

When the mandatory review of the Forum was undertaken after one year, the Liaison Committee assisted in organising the training of representatives and providing language facilities at the Forum including the pre-meeting. The Forum's official language is English which has become an issue as, although most of the original non-UK employees (Center Parcs) spoke very good English, they were not always able to follow the speed of discussions or the various dialects. The new representatives from Kronenbourg and Alken-Maes (see p. 129) do not in general speak English and this has led to some slight problems.

Agenda

All representatives are asked to comment on the agenda, add to it, or suggest items in advance of the Forum and of recent years this has become more common. Representatives are also asked at that stage to identify any questions which they would like answered if they are able to do so at that time. This enables a considered response if further information is sought. However, this does not preclude any questions from the floor on the day or via the pre-meeting. As part of the review of the Forum, agenda distribution was altered to involve the Liaison Committee commenting on it prior to general distribution, suggesting speakers or topics. A final agenda is sent out three weeks prior to the Forum.

Confidentiality

Information discussed at the Forum is generally regarded as confidential. Representatives are entitled to discuss and pass on such information to employees within the Company but are asked not to discuss any information outside the Company that could be sensitive or advantageous to competitors. On certain occasions, representatives may be expressly told that information is confidential and should not be discussed outside the Company Forum with anybody, as is permitted by the Directive.

Feedback

It is important that the results of the Forum meetings are communicated back to employees in general. This is no easy task with over 40,000 employees spread over a wide area. Surveys of employees' views on feedback indicate a mixed response. Some want more general Company information but many want more local information. Most employees know about the Forum but are unclear about what it does. Many show little interest in information outside their own division. Feedback is via 'News and Qs' which summarises the meeting of the Forum and the questions asked. This goes to each representative, each department head and to each public house. Discussions are taking place about presentation of the feedback document and the extent of distribution. However, any increase in distribution or improvement in format will have implications for cost. Representatives, in addition, may use existing mechanisms to 'spread the word'. This may be via union meetings, works councils, notice boards, local company magazines, etc. The names and telephone numbers of Forum representatives and contacts are also published in Company literature and the feedback documents from the Forum. Employees are free to contact an appropriate representative or the personnel department if they require any information.

Discussion

To a certain extent, S&N was less affected by the new legislation because of its existing Forum. It had been normal for the Executive to meet representatives of employees throughout the year. Initially the changes which had to be made were relatively cosmetic, that is, increasing numbers of employees, providing for a pre-meeting and more formalised feedback. However, with each meeting there have been gradual changes not only in the working of the Forum but in the under-standing of its function and the attitudes and behaviours of its participants. There is a learning curve and it has not yet reached its conclusion.

The old Forum would have evolved in any case but not so rapidly – it has effec-tively been deepened and widened. Representatives have become more confident and more prepared to ask for changes to enable them to carry out their functions more effectively. Pre-meetings have become more challenging and a recent survey of representatives (undertaken by EWC representatives) indicates that the pre-meeting provides a very valuable opportunity to meet people from other parts of the business and from other countries and cultures.

However, there are still areas of uncertainty as many representatives are not entirely sure just what is expected of them, that is, are they expected to canvass other employees' views, raise topics, feedback information. The whole area of 'transnational information' is contentious – what is included? The survey demon-strates that individuals want local knowledge for the most part and whilst wanting the organisation to be successful do not necessarily want to know the 'master plan'. Some representatives feel that they should be the focal point for major announce-ments whereas the Company view has always been that consultation on such issues would be at a local level. A major issue is how to move from information giving and asking of questions to genuine consultation and how to make it work with a group which meets twice per annum.

However, it has become clear with each meeting that both central management and representatives are moving towards a democratic body. Issues addressed over the years have included feedback, training, language facilities, term of office and of course the eventual UK legislation. It was not felt that this would have a major impact on S&N as the present arrangement is better than the mandatory provisions of the Directive and the Forum has been agreed.

However, the Company took the opportunity to review the Forum, initially after one year in accordance with the Agreement and again after three years when UK legislation was imminent. The latter review confirmed an Article 13 agree-ment as there was a great deal of confusion as to the status of existing Article 13 agreements under the Directive, that is, where the UK had not been covered. Changes were also made to the Forum name so it more closely resembled an EWC and new organisational aspects were added. It was accepted that transla-tion facilities were imperative, that there should be pre- and post-meetings, that the Liaison Committee be used as the appropriate vehicle for communication in between meetings, to provide annual training for both new and existing representatives and to extend the period of office. The most important of these was the need for training and the term of office of representatives. It was agreed that there should be training run by a specialist outside agency, Northumbria University was chosen and a training needs analysis carried out by the TUC. The training subsequently took place at the Forum in April 2000 and was extremely well received. It highlighted the fact that many of the misunderstandings on the operation of the Forum could be alleviated by good training which has been continued (see Chapter 12 by John Stirling).

Warwick University research

Shortly before the sale of Center Parcs, the Company took part in research conducted by Warwick University (Marginson *et al.* 2001) to determine the impact of an EWC on management decision making. Eight companies were analysed in-depth. The research acknowledged that there might be differences between Anglo-Saxon economies and other European countries, and even US companies based in Europe where in the main European management prevailed. In Anglo-Saxon economies there is no domestic tradition of statutory procedures for ongoing employee information and consultation, and whose 'outsider' systems of corporate governance emphasise shareholder value above all else and do not embrace the interests of employees as stakeholders. There is also less likely to be a system of industry-wide collective agreements. These remarks are very pertinent to the S&N situation both with and since Center Parcs.

The research indicated that S&N was an organisation where the EWC was largely dormant between meetings with little or no international contact amongst representatives in the interim and with little impact on industrial relations at lower levels.

Many of the observations related to the UK system of industrial relations where the UK was the home country for the EWC, for example, management were identified as being cautious and restrictive in their approach to EWCs, seeking to maintain managerial control of the process and its impact. Furthermore, the upward effect of UK traditions of employee representation, where the home workforce is generally diffuse, reflected the absence of strong information and consultation institutions in the UK. In addition, there is an unfamiliarity in the case of UK employee representatives with works council structures and group-level consultation processes. These factors as well as, their limited resources relative to those enjoyed by senior employee representatives in some other countries has led UK employee representatives to concede the leadership role in the EWC to 'better placed' representatives from countries with more established traditions of representative participation.

The results of the Warwick research at S&N concluded that the range and intensity of changes introduced as a result of the EWC activity was closely correlated to the fit of the EWC with existing management decision-making structures.

Where there was little or no managerial co-ordination at European group level and where key decisions are taken either at the national or at the global level, there is little with which the EWC can engage. National industrial relations structures are still relied upon as the primary arena, while decisions taken at the global level remain out of reach of the EWC.

S&N took part in the research during the time when its then leisure division was run as a separate division to the Beer and Retail divisions. Much of what is said above would therefore apply, as management structures were not integrated and it was difficult to find transnational topics which were relevant to two quite distinct businesses. Added to this, the dominant grouping in the EWC were the British constituting the bulk of the workforce, part of which was unionised. The conclusions of the research are therefore relevant to the UK and it is doubtful whether the research would have come to a different conclusion even in the new structure today.

Business restructuring

Since the review of the Constitution in 1999, two major changes have occurred in S&N. The first is the sale of Center Parcs and the second the acquisition of Kronenbourg. Both of these are transnational issues and both have had implications for the future of the Forum. Parts of the Constitution have had to be reviewed, for example, membership profile and this took place over the 2000/2001 period.

It was unfortunate that the first organised training took place at a time when Center Parcs had been told that they were to be sold. Therefore, the first training in April 2000 consisted mainly of UK Beer division employees. Clearly, this was not the most efficient use of training in transnational issues. However, employees were aware of the acquisition of Kronenbourg, based in Strasbourg, Elidis the distribution network and Alken-Maes brewing based in Belgium. Individuals from these parts of the Company attended their first meeting in October 2000. There are five members from Kronenbourg, three members from Alken-Maes, and three members from Elidis. Members of management visited each of these locations to explain the background to the Forum, the reason for the distribution of seats, the structure of the Company and the future operation.

A number of things quickly became apparent. These were individuals from a highly unionised background with sophisticated works councils. They were comfortable challenging management and were well informed on a number of organisational issues. There was strong pressure to increase the number of seats to each of these areas, although, that would have been numerically unrepresentative. In addition, these were parts of the organisation involved in brewing and distribution similar to the UK and therefore the subject matter discussed would have more 'transnational' relevance. There was strong pressure from amongst these groups to renegotiate the Constitution and representatives' guidelines.

Since October 2000, they have been part of the Forum and the first meeting in October 2000 was a 'getting acquainted' meeting. However, the French and

Belgium representatives asked the majority of challenging questions on the day and had strong views on whether the Forum matched their views of an EWC.

At the April 2001 meeting, a French trade union representative was elected as Chair of the Liaison Committee (consistent with the Warwick findings). The previous chair and secretary had been full-time officials and it was felt to be time for employees to take over this role. This has proved an interesting turn of events as the individual does not speak English with obvious implications for communication. However, it has also become obvious that there are cultural differences between the different countries that affect how information is presented and received. Some of the annual training is attempting to help representatives understand such cultural differences. There is strong pressure from the French to make the Forum much more like domestic French works councils and it can be difficult to persuade representatives that this is not the intention of the Forum.

Representatives' training has continued developing in areas such as 'organisational understanding' and 'understanding of finance'. The French and Belgian representatives have sought large amounts of information on organisational structure, background, distribution of locations, employee numbers, branded goods, capacity, etc. and this has been provided. A recent report (Stirling and Tully 2002) on training has identified some of the issues raised by representatives as issues in taking the Forum forward, for example, language training, better use of technology, better communication to managers.

What next?

The organisation has changed dramatically over recent years. Since the acquisition of Kronenbourg and Alken-Maes, the Company has also taken significant stakes in a number of organisations:

- The Boutari Group; where S&N has agreed in principle to enter into a partnership with the Greek listed beverage business involving an investment in their brewing subsidiary Mythos Breweries SA. S&N will have a 46 per cent stake in the Greek beer business which is number two in the market.
- United Breweries; where an agreement has been reached in principle to form a strategic partnership with this leading Indian Brewer. S&N will invest in a new joint venture that will develop and acquire brewing businesses.
- Central De Cereveja; S&N has entered into a joint venture to run the Portuguese brewer and distributor Central De Cervejas (Centralcer).

In addition, it has recently acquired Hartwall, which is Finland's leading beer and soft drinks company. Hartwall owns 50 per cent of BBH, which is a 50:50 joint venture with Carlsberg breweries. Only in the latter will there be an impact on the Forum necessitating possibly three more representatives. This means that total numbers attending the Forum can be around sixty plus translators, technicians etc. and this constant growth may make the future running of the Forum unsustainable. Whilst there were no substantial costs in establishing the new Forum because the previous Forum was still in existence it is now more representative and covers a greater geographical area. Therefore, more representatives mean more travel and accommodation in addition to time off work and hospitality.

In addition to this, the divisions are changing and there will be EU legislation on national information and consultation that is bound to have implications for the overall Forum. From the organisation's point of view the costs and practicalities of continuing to expand the Forum may require a review. Size will also have implications for the representatives and the reality of dealing in a meaningful way with issues. An obligation at national level may lead, in particular, to the UK having to develop some sort of structure at divisional level and, in such a case, there will be questions as to the overlap between the two. A constant problem for representatives is their desire to bring local issues to the Forum rather than using local structures, which may be altered by the addition of a national structure. The first consultative document on the new legislation will help the Company decide how to begin discussions on implementation but it is inevitable that this will eventually impact on the running of the Forum.

Conclusion

The above is a description of the setting up of the European Employee Forum in the UK and is not intended as an analysis of its effectiveness. The Warwick research summarised in general the impact of UK-based EWCs on decision making and this was an accurate reflection of the situation in S&N for many of the reasons described. It is clear that it has been difficult to find subjects that are transnational in order to make discussion realistic.

From the representative perspective, many different views emerge. For those with a European background, there is a sense of frustration that the EWC does not more closely resemble domestic works councils that are more prescriptive and in some cases give quite wide rights to representatives. For UK representatives, views depend in part on whether the individual is union or non-union. Although the numbers are relatively well balanced, in reality non-union representatives are often more reluctant to speak and ask questions and comments have been expressed about union domination. In reality, union representatives are not only better equipped to participate due to their union duties, but also have a union structure for onward communication.

Increasingly the subject matter of the Forum has hinged on domestic issues. Although individuals are encouraged to ask questions on any subject, the Forum is not intended to deal with issues best dealt with at another level. In recent years, however, the quality of questions on the business as a whole, its direction, strategy, marketing plans, international mobility, etc. have become more marked and this is likely to increase as familiarity, increased access to documentation and training continues.

It is clear that the Forum is a journey, it will change along the way as the organisation changes and we are not yet at any final destination.

References

Marginson, P., Hall, M., Hoffmann, A. and Müller, T. (2001) *The Impact of European Works Councils on Management Decision-Making in Anglo-Saxon Multinationals: A Case Study Comparison*, Industrial Relations Research Unit: University of Warwick.

Scottish and Newcastle (1999) *European Works Council Constitution*, Edinburgh: Scottish and Newcastle.

Stirling, J. and Tully, B. (2002) *Developing European Forum Training at Scottish and Newcastle*, unpublished, Work and Employment Research Centre: Northumbria University.

9 Managing European Works Councils from outside Europe

Satoshi Nakano

Introduction

As yet there has been little research on management views of functioning European Works Councils (EWCs). This chapter therefore attempts to help fill the gap, and has three objectives. The first is to suggest hypotheses concerning the factors likely to affect management evaluation of EWCs, mainly on the basis of previous surveys. The second is to offer empirical evidence on the views of senior managers in multinationals, using data collected from multinationals mainly outside Europe, which is then compared with that of a European Economic Area (EEA) sample. Third, a more detailed analysis of the findings is presented.

The EWC Directive covers multinational companies with headquarters outside the EEA if their employment within the EEA is above the threshold. The number of EWCs established in such companies is considerable, comprising 186 (about 24 per cent) of some 770 agreements listed in the European Trade Union Institute (ETUI) database (Kerckhofs and Pas 2001). Most of these firms are based in countries that lack a system of national works councils, and this might be expected to affect management evaluation of the compulsory procedure for information and consultation.

The majority of non-EEA companies covered by the Directive are based in North America, where the industrial relations system is characterised by 'adversarialism'. Management policy has been a major cause of declining private-sector unionisation in the US, and employers there 'show great reluctance to embark on any system or adventure which might either renew interest in the union movement or give the unions a new tool to work with' (Heenan 1998: 159). Labour policies in Japanese big business are sometimes termed 'bureaucratic paternalism'. Management have some reluctance to lay off employees, and the relative insulation from the external labour market creates a form of enterprise unionism. Joint consultation committees at various levels are prevalent, covering approximately 80 per cent of unionised and 40 per cent non-unionised establishments in 1989, but they are not mandatory and the distinction between collective bargaining and consultation has become increasingly unclear in the unionised sector.

Factors affecting management views of European Works Councils

Management evaluation of EWCs may be considered as a function of their perceived costs and benefits (Freeman and Rogers 1993: 51). Possible costs and benefits of the system are identified from existing surveys as well as employers' documents and classified under the following categories: the perceived main functions of EWCs; their secondary effects; and their institutional characteristics (Nakano 1999):

Main Functions   The first group of factors are those relating closely to the legislative objective of the Directive. They may include such functions of the institution as simultaneous information and communication, facilitation of the processes of restructuring and improvement in the quality of decision making (Freeman and Rogers 1993; Pedersini 1998).

Secondary Effects   Those factors that do not relate directly to the main functions are classified as secondary effects. They relate mainly to corporate governance and industrial relations, and also entail costs and benefits. Possible costs include delay in corporate decision making, erosion of managerial prerogatives, direct and indirect financial expenditure, increases in bureaucracy, influences on employee expectations and possible effects on European trade unionism and collective bargaining (Gold and Hall 1992; Hall *et al.* 1992; Kerckhofs 1996; Wills 2000). Possible benefits include the development of a sense of involvement among employees, corporate culture formation, new relations with trade unions and/or works councils, and information dissemination among managers (Pedersini 1998; Wills 2000).

Institutional Characteristics   The third category of factors that could affect management views of EWCs are their institutional characteristics. Employers' criticism of EWCs, for example, has particularly been focused on the consistency between a centralised system of information disclosure and decentralised structure of corporate governance (see Chapter 4 by Sjef Stoop for a discussion of multinational influences on EWC structure). Branches and affiliates of some companies function as autonomous profit centres and this is especially true where there is a local shareholding (UNICE 1991). A mandated requirement to inform and consult at a level where business decisions are not routinely taken is 'at best a waste of resources, and at worst necessitates the creation of parallel and irrelevant organisation' (Multinational Business Forum 1993). Other factors may include both the quasi-mandatory nature of works councils and legislative flexibility allowed in the processes of establishment (Daly 1996: 4).

To these factors may be added the industrial relations climate of the respective multinationals and the subjective orientation of their managers. The former may be a prerequisite for a proper functioning of the institution and studies demonstrate that managers' experience can be very diverse (Gold and Hall 1992: 52; Daly 1996: 9). Employer evaluation of EWCs is also likely to be influenced by the subjective orientations of the managers themselves. The classic dichotomy of 'unitarist' and 'pluralist' may be utilised as frames of reference (Gospel and Palmer

1993: 63). Given the limitations of this dichotomy (e.g. employers are generally 'unitarist' to varying degrees), other subjective indicators such as the extent of principled acceptance of information and consultation rights are also relevant.

Research method

The data presented in this chapter is derived from successive empirical studies carried out in the winter of 1998 and spring of 1999 (Nakano 1999 and 2000). The former is a complete survey of thirty-five Japanese multinationals listed in the ETUI database as covered by EWC agreements (ETUI 1998). Questionnaires mainly in English were sent to 'those who take charge of personnel or who participate in the EWC meetings as a delegate of the management at the head office in Europe'; a limit of six weeks was set for replies. In the latter study, 100 multinationals covered by the Directive were randomly sampled from the same database. The sample excluded those covered by the former survey and fifty were taken from the multinationals with headquarters outside the EEA.

The questionnaire used in these studies was identical except for a few details and was composed of a main and a supplementary section. In the main section, an overall evaluation of the EWCs as well as some twenty-five more detailed questions concerning their costs and benefits were sought. These questions related to the functions of EWCs specified above and, for each of them, there was a seven-point interval scale to measure the strength of the opinion expressed. There were also questions on issues, which closely relate to the evaluation of the EWC, such as problems related to its establishment and administration, and experience of transfers, mergers or closures of undertakings. In the supplementary questionnaire, the respondents were asked to state major characteristics of their agreement when it had not been covered by the European Foundation's periodic analysis.

Apart from these two studies, Oguri carried out in the summer of 2000 a questionnaire survey on management views of voluntary EWCs in German, Swedish, French and British multinationals (Oguri 2000). Although the analytical framework used in his study differs from the one by the author, the thirteen items in his questionnaire were formulated largely in the same style so that the results could be examined in a comparative way.

Just over half the companies replied in Nakano (1999) and fourteen (40 per cent) provided usable responses. The nationalities of the respondents were: five Japanese, four Belgian, two French, one each British, Dutch and German. Respondents were mainly personnel managers at European headquarters, but also included a president, a legal officer and managers in other sections. Three companies declined to participate and another three replied that the Directive did not cover them. Twenty-five responded in Nakano (2000) of which seventeen were usable. Six declined to participate and two replied that the Directive did not cover them. Respondents included managers of personnel and administration departments, vice presidents and a group secretary. Eight companies were headquartered in the US, two each in Germany, the Netherlands, Sweden and the UK, and one in a non-EEA country. The nationalities of the respondents were: nine British, three

German, two Dutch, two Swedish and one French. Respondents of the US companies were British (five), German (two) and French (one). Supplementary interviews were mostly conducted at headquarters in Europe.

Establishing and managing the European Works Councils

In the former sample, all the companies except three had 'Article 13' voluntary agreements. One car manufacturer had concluded an 'Article 6' agreement in the summer of 1998. The two remaining multinationals had not yet set up EWCs, but one was planning an 'Article 6' agreement and the other an application of the subsidiary requirements of the Directive. In the latter, there were ten 'Article 13' and three 'Article 6' agreements, one of which was re-negotiated after a take-over. Among the remaining companies, one had been involved in an acquisition and another was in the process of making an 'Article 6' agreement. Some of those without EWCs pointed to a lack of interest among (or applications from) the workforce.

Out of twenty-one managers who referred to the reasons of their choice of 'Article 13' agreement, sixteen pointed out its flexibility on such matters as selection of members, agenda setting and devising a cost-efficient structure, although one added that a very good relationship with the works councils was obviously a precondition (Deere, USA). For some a social dialogue structure in Europe was more a 'fact of life' and passive acceptance on the part of employers may be more prevalent among recent or future agreements. In two other cases, however, managers stressed the necessity of an effective consultation procedure. For one manager, Europeanisation of the market as well as organisation, particularly in the sales area, was prominent and the EWC was perceived as a means to 'give this message to the employees, too' (Pioneer, Japan). As mentioned later, another company devised an innovative system where business group directors utilise the existing site works councils for multinational information and consultation, but this was an 'Article 6' agreement (DSM, the Netherlands).

Among the thirty-one companies, seven noted problems in establishing their EWCs, these related to the number and composition of employee representatives (three companies), relations with trade unions (two), conditions to invite external specialists and consistency between the terms of European and local works councils (one each). Interviewees were asked specifically about trade union involvement in the processes of establishing the EWCs. Aware of the adverse publicity of the early agreement of, for example, Honda, two managers said that they were open to holding meetings with European trade union representatives.[1]

Several respondents also pointed out problems of administration, some of which were technical (e.g. translation at meetings or information feedback to the workforce), whereas others related to the nature of the EWCs (e.g. the extent of information disclosed, blurred distinction between local and European matters and frictions or disturbance of an operations information disclosure on restructuring). The characteristics of the sample agreements did not differ largely from those

Table 9.1 The characteristics of sample agreements

Characteristics of the EWCs	Number of sample agreements
Legislation applied (if any)	Belgium 4/ Germany, Luxembourg, the Netherlands, Sweden 2 each/ Others 3/ Not specified or not known 16
Choice of legislation	Location of management 7/ Largest establishment 4/ Content of legislation 0/ Others 1/ Not specified or not known 19
Structure	Single European council 21/ Councils for business divisions 3/ Others 1/ Not known 6
Composition	French (joint) style 17/ German style (employees only) 6/ Others 1/ Not known 7
Selection of representatives[a]	Local law and practice 15/ Appointment by works councils 6/ Appointment by trade unions 2/ Election 2/ Others 1
Agenda setting	Jointly 22/ Management side 3/ Not known 6
Extraordinary meetings	Existence of provision 18/ Non-existence of provision 7/ Not known 6
External experts in EWCs	Under certain conditions 18/ Not allowed 6/ Full member 1/ Others 2/ Not known 4
Feedback of information[a]	Minutes 17/ Joint communiqué 10/ Representatives 5/ Others 3

Note
a All relevant items.

in the EEA (Table 9.1); as in the fall-back provisions in the Annex of the Directive, they predominantly (84 per cent) have the form of a works council at European level, and the issues dealt with generally follow those outlined in Article 2, covering transfers, mergers and closures of undertakings, substantial changes of organisation and working methods and collective redundancies (Marginson *et al.* 1998).

However, unlike the Annex, the French practice of a joint committee of management and employee representatives is prevalent (71 per cent). The number of representatives on the EWCs varied from one to 34 on the management side and eight to 47 on the employee side, the latter of which exceeds the standard provision of 30. Most of them have some provisions for external participants, but only one permits their participation as a full member of the EWC. Agenda setting is mostly (87 per cent) a joint process with somewhat varying procedures. The proportion with provisions for extraordinary meetings in exceptional circumstances (72 per cent) is lower than the general European average (81 per cent).

European industrial relations and global companies

Overall evaluation

The results of the main questionnaire are summarised in Table 9.2. The first figures in the table show the responses of the Japanese multinationals and the second in the

Table 9.2 Management views of the EWCs

		Positive (1–3)%	Neutral (4)%	Negative (5–7)%	Mean	Mode	SD
1	Overall evaluation	71(53)	21(29)	7(18)	2.86(3.53)	2(3)	1.10(1.55)
	Main functions						
2	Improve information for employees	93(65)	7(18)	0(18)	2.64(3.47)	3(3)	0.74(1.62)
3	Improve information for managers	79(65)	21(6)	0(29)	2.86(3.47)	3(3)	0.77(1.77)
4	Facilitate exchange of opinions	93(76)	0(6)	7(18)	2.64(3.24)	3(3)	0.93(1.52)
5	Alleviate problems during restructuring	29(29)	57(29)	14(41)	3.79(4.41)	4(4)	0.80(1.66)
6	Promote spirit of co-operation	93(71)	7(12)	0(18)	2.79(3.29)	3(3)	0.89(1.57)
	Secondary effects						
7	Delay decision making[a]	57(24)	14(35)	29(41)	3.64(4.06)	2(4)	1.78(1.89)
8	Undermine right to manage[a]	79(53)	14(35)	7(12)	2.79(3.29)	2(3)	1.05(1.65)
9	Require considerable expense[a]	29(0)	14(0)	57(100)	4.36(5.82)	5(5)	1.60(0.81)
10	Increase bureaucracy[a]	43(12)	21(12)	36(76)	4.00(5.24)	5(5)	1.41(1.44)
11	Create inequalities between companies[a]	57(24)	14(47)	29(29)	3.21(4.00)	2(4)	1.76(1.41)
12	Disseminate information among managers	50(24)	29(47)	21(29)	3.71(4.29)	3(4)	1.27(1.69)
13	Help develop corporate culture	93(59)	0(18)	7(24)	2.86(3.71)	3(3)	1.10(1.57)
14	Enhance labour productivity	21(12)	36(29)	43(59)	4.64(4.94)	4(4)	1.55(1.39)
15	Help develop a sense of involvement	86(65)	14(12)	0(24)	2.93(3.65)	3(3)	0.62(1.58)
16	Help develop relations with unions etc.	64(65)	29(18)	7(18)	3.21(3.59)	3(3)	0.89(1.54)
17	Raise employees' expectations[a]	0(12)	29(35)	71(53)	5.00(4.88)	5(6)	0.78(1.36)
18	Bring about Euro-bargaining[a]	36(24)	50(29)	14(47)	3.64(4.18)	4(5)	1.39(1.67)
19	Bring about Euro-unionism[a]	43(24)	21(29)	36(47)	3.93(5.12)	3(6)	1.33(1.58)
	Institutional characteristics						
20	Mismatch with corporate structure[a]	36(18)	14(18)	50(65)	4.43(5.06)	3(7)	1.28(1.82)
21	Create unnecessary duplication[a]	64(12)	7(24)	29(65)	3.50(5.12)	3(7)	1.45(1.50)
22	Flexibility in formulation	71(82)	21(6)	7(12)	2.86(2.82)	3(3)	1.35(1.13)
23	Legislation required for works councils	43(35)	21(29)	36(35)	4.07(4.18)	3(4)	1.90(2.07)
	Industrial relations climate						
24	Have good employee relations climate	79(100)	14(0)	7(0)	2.43(1.88)	2(2)	1.22(0.70)

(Continued)

Table 9.2 (Continued)

		Positive (1–3)%	Neutral (4)%	Negative (5–7)%	Mean	Mode	SD
	Subjective orientations						
25	Unitarist ideology	93	7	0	2.14	2	0.77
26	Accept information in principle	93(82)	7(6)	0(12)	2.43(2.71)	3(2)	0.85(1.79)
27	Accept participation in principle	79(47)	14(12)	7(41)	3.07(4.24)	3(3)	1.38(1.68)
	Total	62(44)	19(21)	19(36)			

Notes
Japanese multinationals $N = 14$ (Sample multinationals $N = 17$).
a Reversed for presentation.

parentheses those of the sample multinationals. Overall evaluation of the former sample was fairly favourable and scored 2.86 on the seven-point scale, against a possible optimum score of 1.00. One manager strongly agreed with the statement 'overall, the European Works Council is good for the firm', whereas five agreed and one disagreed. Japanese respondents were, though, less enthusiastic than their European counterparts: their average score was 3.33, still significantly better than neutral. The average of overall evaluation among the latter sample was 3.53. The respondents perceived the net benefits, but were close to neutral. Confined to those multinationals whose headquarters are located on the Continent, this figure became 3.1 and the UK average was 4.00. This may be biased by non-responses: it is likely that those who completed the questionnaire would be more open in their approach to public and human relations matters than those who did not.

Main functions

Items 2–6 in Table 9.2 relate to the main functions of the EWCs. Despite the differences in the extent of evaluation between the two samples, opinions about the individual functions of the EWCs were similar; they were judged as a fairly effective tool, particularly for dissemination of managerial information among employees (average score of 2.64/3.47), bi-directional communication (2.64/3.24) and co-operation (2.79/3.29), whereas a majority doubt if it would alleviate employment problems at times of restructuring. The data of thirteen items were then broken down into the country of ownership and the non-EU average was re-calculated. The results are shown in Table 9.3, together with the results of the survey on European multinationals (Oguri 2000).[2] In these categories, too, the patterns of responses were similar and, except for some items on the side-effects of the EWCs, the country of ownership did not seem to bring about discernible differences of management evaluations.

Hence, 'it is much appreciated by the employee representatives because it gives them a better understanding of what is going on in Europe' (Pioneer, Japan). But for

Table 9.3 Breakdown by country of ownership (mean)

		Japan	*US*	*Non-EU*	*France*	*Germany*	*Sweden*	*UK*	*EU*
2	Improve information for employees	2.6	3.0	2.8	2.9	3.1	3.0	3.1	3.0
3	Improve information for managers	2.9	3.3	3.0	3.7	3.4	3.7	3.6	3.5
5	Alleviate problems during restructuring	3.8	4.5	4.1	3.6	4.2	3.7	3.6	3.9
6	Promote spirit of co-operation	2.8	2.9	2.9	3.2	3.5	3.2	3.4	3.4
7	Delay decision making[a]	3.6	4.1	3.9	3.3	2.7	3.0	2.9	2.9
8	Undermine right to manage[a]	2.8	3.4	3.0	2.8	2.7	2.5	2.5	2.6
9	Require considerable expense[a]	4.4	5.5	4.8	4.5	3.5	4.7	4.0	4.0
11	Create inequalities between companies[a]	3.2	3.9	3.6	2.9	3.2	2.7	3.0	3.0
14	Enhance labour productivity	4.6	5.1	4.8	4.7	4.8	4.5	4.9	4.8
15	Help develop a sense of involvement	2.9	3.5	3.1	4.0	3.8	3.8	3.6	3.8
17	Raise employees' expectations[a]	5.0	4.6	4.9	3.5	3.1	3.5	3.0	3.2
20	Mismatch with corporate structure[a]	4.4	4.5	4.6	4.0	3.3	3.7	3.4	3.5
21	Create unnecessary duplication[a]	3.5	4.5	4.0	4.4	3.2	3.7	3.3	3.5
	N	14	8	23	10	18	6	14	48

Note

a Reversed for presentation. Data for EU countries derived from Oguri (2000).

management, too, 'in principle, it has some positive points such as improved dialogue and involvement of employees and their representatives' (Panasonic, Japan). For another manager, it is 'one more opportunity for top-level management to meet face to face with employees of each level and each country' (Nissan, Japan). Average scores of about 3.00 and relatively low standard deviations, particularly among the former sample, indicate the existence of a general consensus on these points.

Nevertheless, some qualitative reservation was also expressed. As categorised by Lecher and Rüb (1999) and Marginson (1999) EWCs often start as a formal or symbolic forum for information, extending national systems of industrial relations. The management in one multinational found 'the actual impact of the EWC was lower than expected, due to the very broad and general nature of the information and issues discussed' at this level (Bridgestone, Japan). Admitting that it would allow for bi-directional communication which other methods of information dissemination lack, another interviewee doubted if a small number of EWC members could adequately represent employees' interests in diverse business units; 'in the UK, we have some one thousand people and would probably end up with two representatives on the works council. It would be very difficult for them to obtain the views of the workforce and it is very often their own views that they are expressing' (Sealed Air, USA).

However, he did not deny the possibility that this might change. French representatives have a different cultural background and were 'far more confrontational and serious about works councils', whereas in the UK, they were learning the system. It was not that the latter was more or less co-operative, but 'they are less confident and, once they gain experience, they will use the works council effectively'.

The respondent's judgement's were much less optimistic on whether EWCs would alleviate employment problems at times of organisational change and restructuring. How can this result be interpreted? The questionnaire included separate questions on the experience of transfers, mergers or closures of undertakings and the effectiveness of the EWCs in settling employment problems on such occasions. Three in the former and five in the latter sample replied that they had experienced such organisational changes. Responses on the latter point were thus largely speculative, and showed a division of opinion: six respondents in the former and four in the latter thought the EWC would be effective, five and ten ineffective, respectively, and the others failed to answer this specific question.

Opinions seemed to converge on two points; the unpredictable outcome of the information and consultation procedure and the 'dualist' nature of the present system. Some interviewees stated that the EWC might make it easier to deliver information, but it is unlikely to make the processes of redundancy smoother. As the Renault Vilvoorde case illustrated, *ex post facto* disclosure of such information is illegal, but the friction caused by the prior release of information could make mergers, relocations and redundancies impossible, or give rise to strong resistance (Fuji Photo Film, Japan; Pioneer, Japan).

There is also an inevitable separation between the information and consultation procedure, on the one hand, and local negotiation processes, on the other. Although EWCs were introduced to ensure that 'the employees of Community-scale undertakings are properly informed and consulted when decisions which affect them are taken in a Member State other than that in which they are employed' (Preamble of the EWC Directive), many pointed out that, if there were redundancies, such issues would be predominantly dealt with at a local level. Among them, three managers referred to the importance of both national and European processes being run through cumulatively (Bridgestone, Japan; Svenska Cellulosa, Sweden). Since the functions of the EWCs are limited to information and consultation, management is required to negotiate with local works councils or trade unions after the multinational meetings have taken place. The real interests of employee EWC representatives may be tied to the employment position of their individual workplaces rather than company employees in Europe as a whole. European collective bargaining would obviously change the situation, but some consider it unlikely in the near future and others point out that it would provoke other problems such as role demarcation between European and local trade unions.

In spite of such scepticism, some interviewees did point to a role that EWCs can take in reorganisations. In one leading multinational company, the EWC provides a framework for restructuring and functions with local works councils or their equivalents. For example, the company experienced a period of heavy restructuring in the 1990s, which attracted mass-media coverage. At this time a managerial consensus was formed between a company chairman and a Business Group president on a transfer of production facilities between two north European countries, the information was given to local management and works councils. At the same time, management held meetings with the select committee of the EWC, including employee representatives from the affected areas. During the process, the EWC proposed an alternative with some reduction of personnel and the acceptance of lower wages, instead of a full closure of a factory. This alternative was then re-examined and management decided to close it on the grounds of capacity utilisation, decrepitude and pollution problems. The tight labour market was claimed to have helped implementation of a social policy.

Despite the quantitatively similar results of the questionnaire surveys, interviewees did give an impression that confidence with the social dialogue structure was naturally more prevalent among those multinationals in the Germanic–Dutch and north European traditions of industrial relations (Marginson *et al.* 1998), where the EWCs were often positively designated as a 'preventive system' or as 'negotiating partners'. Although employee representatives on an EWC might have the impression that a decision had already been taken before the procedure took place, such a decision was often based on a thorough analysis of alternatives. Management would not dare to go to the EWC with proposals that were not sound and safe. If they did, their corporate reputation would be at risk. It might slow down corporate decision making, but as far as the quality of the decision is concerned, it is more positive. 'The sheer fact that the EWC exists has a preventive value' (anonymous company) for management.

Hence, for a Dutch manager, French or south European works councils with strong trade union influences were perceived as another type of consultation system. An EWC that embraces different cultures was thus 'like Babylon, not only in languages, but in understanding what we were talking about'. At a meeting, representatives from Italy and Spain remained passive recipients of information and the management started up a training process 'to enhance dialogue, rather than just monologue' (DSM, the Netherlands).

Secondary effects

Items 7–11 and 17–19 in Table 9.2 relate to possible costs of the EWC institution. In both surveys, the majority of the respondents replied that the EWCs were unlikely to undermine the right to manage, but do involve considerable financial expense. They did not always endorse the assertion by the European employers' federation that they would obstruct or delay managerial decision making (3.64/4.06). Nevertheless, the high standard deviation of this variable shows that opinions were divided on the matter. A similar pattern can be seen with the alleged negative effect on the competitive position of companies obliged to establish a council. In the former sample 71 per cent and in the latter 53 per cent indicated apprehension for the effects on employees' expectations and demands (5.00/4.88).

A comparison with the EU sample shows that such apprehension on decision making and employees' expectations was less salient among European multinationals.[3]

Financial expenditure, referred to by an interviewee as a 'tax on business in Europe', related particularly to translation, which might also be required for frequently held select committees (Deere, USA; Pioneer, Japan). The actual amount paid for the EWCs largely differs among companies and, according to Oguri (2000), 20 multinationals (55.6 per cent) out of 36 estimated that approximate annual expenditure per employee covered by the EWC agreement was less than €10, which is close to European Commission's original estimate (Kerckhofs 1996), whereas four spent between €10–19, four between €20–49 and eight more than €50 (Oguri 2000). Opinions on expense may reflect the ways in which the EWCs are organised, the financial situation of an enterprise or a manager's attitude.[4]

As for the 'negative' effects of fostering European bargaining and transnational trade unionism, patterns of responses differed slightly. In the former sample, half were relatively neutral on bargaining, whereas opinions were polarised on unionism. In the latter, 47 per cent replied that these would be the case. One interviewee stated that, since the establishment of an EWC in 1996, 'trade unions are working more and more together in a European way'. Another said that 'trade unions ... see this as an excellent alibi. And they are right, as more and more corporate decisions have a European dimension'. Some conjectured that, because of persistent national differences of work rules, salary levels, working time and work organisation, comprehensive labour market integration in Europe is unlikely in the near future, making it difficult for unions to change EWCs from a mechanism of information to negotiation.

The opinions expressed in the survey may also reflect respondents' experience of, or attitudes towards, trade unionism. Some at the core of management expressed apprehension that unions had gained too much influence over employees, or even that cross-national solidarity among employees would be dangerous, whereas another respondent perceived no such problems. It should be noted that despite the apprehension shown by some managers towards trade unions, the industrial relations climate in their companies was generally favourable.

Items 12–16 in the questionnaire relate to positive secondary effects of EWCs. The majority regarded that the EWCs influenced the formation of corporate culture (2.86/3.71), employee involvement (2.93/3.65) and the development of relationships with works councils and trade unions (3.21/3.59). Such expectations were more widely and strongly shown in the Japanese multinationals; 93 per cent in the former referred to the effect on corporate culture formation, whereas 59 per cent in the latter did so, and 86 per cent in the former pointed to a sense of involvement, whereas this was limited to 65 per cent in the latter. The socio-cultural background of management might influence the functions of the institution.

Institutional characteristics

The institutional characteristics, items 20–3, of EWCs were not generally regarded as a problem, since most managers appreciated that they had flexibility in shaping them (2.86/2.82). On the other hand, there was substantial disagreement whether their establishment should have been made a legal obligation. Half the respondents agreed with UNICE that there was an institutional mismatch with decentralised corporate decision-making structures (4.43/5.06), although this does not apply to the EU sample. One interviewee stated that his was not a company but a collection of companies, in that each establishment was independent in implementing its budget, although budget meetings are held and overall investment plans are made by central management. By contrast, national works council structures fit such an organisation well.

However, another respondent noted a re-centralisation in the European industries and the role EWCs would play in such a structure (Deere, US). Some also emphasised that the centralised council was particularly useful as an information mechanism in a decentralised corporate structure (Pioneer, Japan). They tried to ensure that employee representatives feedback information to employees, as they need to know what is going on in other production and sales centres.

In the latter survey, one interviewee stated that establishing plural EWCs at a business group level was an alternative, and installing working parties at that level was the third option proposed by employee representatives. The principal reason why they did not take these options was the cost required for the piled-up systems. The evaluations on depth and extent of information and consultation were also important, as management did not think a detailed discussion at this level was either necessary or adequate. The company has a decentralised structure and the closure of a factory is within the responsibility of each company chairmen to whom the factory belongs, although business groups may analyse a situation by benchmarking factories at European level. Thus, in the current system, central management gives managerial information of other relevant levels and the interviewee did not find any problem in relation to the higher-level substitution.

Some explicitly developed alternative systems. For example, at a multinational in the latter sample, multinational information and consultation are carried out annually by business group directors at the level of site works councils (DSM, the Netherlands). Alternatively, when a planned decision has significant consequences for employees, the consultative bodies have a right to ask business group directors to discuss the matter or to consult with equivalent bodies in other countries. A supervisory committee composed of board members and employee representatives is set up and, if a conflict arises in a process of consultation, this committee is called in to mediate. Thus, since the enforcement of the 'Article 6' agreement, site works councils for local information and consultation, which are dealt with by site managers, have also been presided over by business group directors for the decentralised EWC.

The interviewee stressed the merits of such a model. First, the company has a decentralised structure built around business groups that are empowered to carry out all business functions, although their strategies require approval of, and their performance is monitored by, the board. In order not to make the EWC a 'system without a content', consultation should take place with those who initiate changes. Second, it enables direct and extensive consultation with works council representatives and their equivalents. Third, in the Annex model of a maximum of thirty people, some companies pursuing different businesses in the Netherlands, for example, might not be represented. By utilising the existing channels of consultation, this problem of under-representation can be avoided. The interviewee emphasised that the company was one of those which helped develop the 'Dutch model' of social policies, based upon the system of works councils and the ideology of consensus formation.

A system tailored for such needs might entail some consequences. The agreement, established with the co-operation of Dutch unions and against the European unionists who preferred implementation of the Annex, is akin to the model of 'national parent company dominance' (Lecher and Rüb 1999). The system is also less likely to provide the scope for a collective identity to develop. Nevertheless, what has been sought is to establish in industries the social right to information and consultation for workers and citizens. It still remains to be seen if the varying EWC institutions can effectively achieve this aim.

Conclusion

In times of global competition, labour market de-regulation, persistent unemployment and the ebbing strength of trade unions in some countries, the adoption of the EWC Directive was seen as a 'miracle' (Blanpain and Windey 1996). It was a miracle only achieved after thirty years of trial and error, through which the initial attempt by legislature of upward harmonisation was replaced by a voluntaristic effort of co-ordination of national industrial relations systems (Streeck 1997). Nevertheless, the development of European social policy based upon social dialogue since the mid-1980s reminds us of the tradition of the corporatist or integrated welfare state (Mishra 1984). We are yet to see if this 'modernised' approach will be a harbinger of the social economy and a new paradigm of democracy in Europe (Wills 1997).[5]

In this chapter, management views of EWCs were assessed in terms of their overall evaluation and some twenty-seven individual functions, particularly focusing upon multinationals with headquarters outside the EEA. Seventy one per cent of managers of the Japanese and 53 per cent of the sample multinationals found net benefits in the EWCs and the overall evaluation scored averages of 2.86 and 3.53 on the seven-item scale. They were perceived as a tool of information, co-operation, involvement and formation of corporate identity. However a majority considered that the EWCs adversely affected employees' expectations, that the financial expenses were a burden for the companies and that they involved a mismatch with decentralised corporate structure. Many doubted if they alleviated employment problems during restructuring.

On the other hand, a majority did not think that it would seriously obstruct corporate decision making or affect the competitive edge of multinationals. Judgements on other aspects of the institution showed no clear balance of opinion. A comparison with some EU multinationals suggested that such views were unlikely to relate to prior experience, or lack of it, of national works councils, whereas apprehension about some negative effects of the EWCs was less conspicuous in the European sample.

One thing that is clear is that the EWCs are valued for both practical and normative reasons. Although expressing reservations concerning co-determination systems, some respondents stated that the European tradition of consultation could spread to Asia and North America in the future. Though 'unitarist' in their outlook, 93 per cent in the former and 82 per cent in the latter thought that, in principle, information and consultation with employees should be improved. A majority would accept that disclosure of corporate information should become something akin to a societal rule. Such a general consensus may indicate that at least those who participated in this survey see in the institution something beyond perfunctory fulfilment of legislative requirements.

Acknowledgements

This research could not have been carried out without the co-operation of those busy senior managers who kindly spared time for the questionnaires and/or interviews. Useful comments were given by Richard Hyman, Peter Kerckhofs, Richard Nicole and the original anonymous referees. Fukashi Oguri kindly provided the author with the original data he collected for his research.

Notes

1 Some early agreements, such as that to set-up the 'Honda Communication and Consultation Group' in December 1994, excluded trade unions on the grounds that the EWC was an internal organisation of company management and employees (EWCB 1997). Izawa (1996) reported that some managers from Japan, accustomed to dealing with company unions in their home country, seemed to have had misgivings about the involvement of industrial unions unfamiliar with the particular situation of the enterprise.
2 Data for the EU countries were re-calculated from the questionnaire Oguri used in his research. Some of the questions were formulated slightly differently; for example, the description of item two was 'it improves the understanding of managerial information among employees' and the extent of agreement or disagreement was asked in Nakano (1999 and 2000) whereas Oguri (2000) asked the question 'do you think the EWC has improved the understanding of the international business situation and management views among employees?'. In Oguri's survey, opinions 'during the establishing stage of the EWC' and 'after experiencing the EWCs several times' were separately asked. The latter showed slightly favourable responses in some cases (positive opinions on item two were 69 and 81 per cent, on item three 60 and 60 per cent and on item five 38 and 41 per cent, respectively) and it is these that are shown here.
3 The differences are statistically significant at the 5 per cent level.
4 In Oguri's survey, the sample multinationals were divided into two; one with annual expenditure less than €20 and the other over €20. A comparison showed that management's evaluation of the EWCs was more favourable among over €20 group.
5 Allan Larsson of the European Commission has written; 'The EWC directive has important implications for the modernization of the European social model. . . . We have moved from social conflict to social dialogue and we have to relate that social dialogue to social reality' (ETUI 1996: 55).

References

Blanpain, R. and Windey, P. (1996) *European Works Councils: Information and Consultation of Employees in Multinational Enterprises in Europe*, Leuven: Peeters.

Daly, J. (1996) *The Emerging Shape of the Irish Transposition Legislation*, conference report by the Department of Enterprise and Employment.

European Trade Union Institute (ETUI) (1996) *European Works Councils and the Europeanisation of Industrial Relations*, Brussels: ETUI.

European Trade Union Institute (ETUI) (1998) *Multinationals Database: Inventory of Companies Affected by the EWC Directive*, Brussels: ETUI.

EWCB (1997) 'European Metal Workers' Strategy for EWCs', *European Works Councils Bulletin*, 8: 4–7.

Freeman, R.B. and Rogers, J. (1993) 'Who Speaks for Us? Employee Representation in a Nonunion Labor Market', in B. Kaufman and M.M. Kleiner (eds) *Employee Representation: Alternatives and Future Directions*, Madison: IRRA.

Gold, M. and Hall, M. (1992) *Report on European-level Information and Consultation in Multinational Companies: An Evaluation of Practice*, Dublin: European Foundation.

Gospel, H.S. and Palmer, G. (1993) *British Industrial Relations*, London: Routledge.

Hall, M., Marginson, P. and Sisson, K. (1992) 'The European Works Council: Setting the Research Agenda', *Warwick Papers in Industrial Relations*, 41.

Heenan, R.L. (1998) 'The North American Point of View', in R. Blanpain (ed.) *Labour Law and Industrial Relations in the European Union*, The Hague: Kluwer.

Izawa, A. (1996) *Oushu Roushi-kyougikai heno Chousen*, Tokyo: Japan Institute of Labour.

Kerckhofs, P. (1996) 'La revendication syndicale des comités d'entreprise européens et sa traduction dans la directive 94/45/CE', mimeo, Université Catholique de Louvain.

Kerckhofs, P. and Pas, I. (2001) *European Works Councils: Full Text Database*, Brussels: ETUI.

Lecher, W. and Rüb, S. (1999) 'The Constitution of European Works Councils: From Information Forum to Social Actor?' *European Journal of Industrial Relations*, 5(1): 7–25.

Marginson, P. (1999) 'EWC Agreements under Review: Arrangements in Companies based in Four Countries Compared', *Transfer*, 5(3): 256–77.

Marginson, P., Gilman, M., Jacobi, O. and Krieger, H. (1998) *Negotiating European Works Councils: An Analysis of Agreements under Article 13*, Luxembourg: OOPEC.

Mishra, R. (1984) *The Welfare State in Crisis*, Sussex: Harvester Press.

Multinational Business Forum (1993) *Thriving on Diversity (Diversité et Prospérité): Informing and Consulting Employees in Multinational Enterprises*, MBF.

Nakano, S. (1999) 'Management Views of European Works Councils: A Preliminary Survey of Japanese Multinationals', *European Journal of Industrial Relations*, 5(3): 307–26.

Nakano, S. (2000) 'Management Views of European Works Councils: A Survey of Sample Multinationals', *Shakai-seisaku Gakkai Shi (The Journal of Social Policy and Labor Studies, Japan)*, 5: 219–38.

Oguri, F. (2000) 'Management Views of Voluntary European Works Councils: Questionnaire Survey of German, Swedish French and British multinational companies', unpublished MA thesis, University of Warwick.

Pedersini, R. (1998) 'The Impact of European Works Councils', Eironline, online. Available HTTP: http://eiro.eurofound.ie/1998/07/study/TN9807201S.html (accessed 30 December 2002).

Streeck, W. (1997) 'Industrial Citizenship under Regime Competition: The Case of the European Works Councils', *Journal of European Public Policy*, 4(4): 643–64.

UNICE (1991) 'Position Paper on Information and Consultation' (March).

Wills, J. (1997) 'Harbingers of a Social Economy in Europe?', Working Paper No. 2, University of Southampton.

Wills, J. (2000) 'Great expectations: Three Years in the Life of a European Works Council', *European Journal of Industrial Relations*, 6(1): 85–107.

10 Bringing it all back home
Trade unions and the Compass Group

Rachel Annand

Introduction

This chapter addresses the difficulties facing trade unions organising in Compass, and looks at the ways in which the union representatives on the European Works Council (EWC) integrate their experience of the EWC into their union work. Wills argues that 'without close connections between local, national and European levels of representation, EWCs are likely to be seen as remote institutions, with little influence or relevance for those employed on the ground' (Wills 1999: 32), a view widely supported (Martinez Lucio and Weston 2000; Stirling and Fitzgerald 2001; Waddington 2001). The relationship of this international layer of activity to the local, regional or national consultative mechanisms in the countries of the EWC affects the co-ordination of trade union activity. This, in turn, affects the representativeness of shop stewards or their equivalents on the EWC, and their links with their respective workforces. This study seeks to illustrate the dilemmas that this additional representational activity can pose for representatives in three countries, the UK, France and Sweden, in a company whose composition presents a number of challenges for the unions, in a sector which is widely regarded as difficult to organise.

The case study gives a brief description of Compass and of the nature of its workforce, before describing the construction and composition of its EWC. The members of the EWC are then described (those present at the 2002 meeting of the EWC), identifying their union roles and length of service as trade union and as EWC representatives. It is argued that 'longer spells (of participation) help representatives to build up relationships with other delegates, to become accustomed to the workings of the council and generally to become more effective in their role' (IDS 2002: 8). Material from more detailed interviews with individual representatives is then presented, to examine the ways in which they became involved in trade union activism, and the route by which this led them to a seat on the EWC.

This leads to a short discussion of the feminine nature of the participation in this particular EWC, and the effects of the high proportion of women delegates on the functioning and agenda of the EWC – in other words, the ways in which the women's (diverse) experiences as representatives affect the form and function of the

EWC, and vice versa. The outcomes of the EWC process are then addressed, from the point of view of the local representatives in their everyday trade union lives. This includes the determination of issues to place on the agenda, the variety of reporting-back mechanisms, and the support given to delegates by their unions. The ways in which the EWC relates, or fails to relate to local bargaining issues, to union organisation and development is then covered. Finally, the study addresses the impact of the EWC on the development of the union representatives themselves, an issue highlighted by most of them as very, or extremely important.

Research methods

This case study was conducted using a number of different methods. The three countries, the UK, France and Sweden, were selected in order to reflect the very different industrial relations models of the countries of the EWC (Ferner and Hyman 1992), as well as for pragmatic reasons of language. Interviews took place, mainly by telephone, with full-time officials in the UK (from UNISON and from the TGWU), France (CFDT) and Sweden (HRF). These gave background information, and are not generally reported.

Permission was obtained to attend the employee-side meeting of the EWC in June 2002. Notes of this meeting were taken, and during the meeting, permission was given for a questionnaire to all the delegates to be presented, using the simultaneous translation facilities of the meeting. The questionnaire was distributed to delegates in the English version, which was then replicated on OHP slides which were immediately translated orally into the delegates' working languages and all delegates completed the questionnaire.

Whilst this method would appear reasonably robust, errors of interpretation may have affected the results. In addition, while attempts were made to design questions which would withstand the differences in national trade union form and function, this was not foolproof: the Danish delegate, for example, explained that his election method (by the workers of two different companies) was not covered. A five-point response scale was used where relevant, and a star rating system was used instead of the conventional category headings: the importance of factors from 'no importance' to 'extremely important' was rated from no stars to four stars (see Table 10.3). This attempt to 'culture-proof' the form has the advantage of being linguistically neutral, but the disadvantage of being open to possible misunderstanding. However, the interviews with delegates revealed no substantial problems with the questionnaire data.

At the EWC meeting, appointments were made with the targeted delegates for telephone interviews at mutually convenient dates. Of the seven UK reps, six were asked for interviews: the TGWU had two seats, and only one of the delegates was interviewed. Overall, the UK representatives came from UNISON, the GMB, PCS, USDAW and the CWU. No one refused, and all but one of the interviews was completed. French delegates came from CFDT and FO affiliates and were interviewed in French, which was later translated by the author. The Swedish delegate was from the HRF and was interviewed in English.

The company and its European Works Council

Compass is amongst the largest catering companies in the world. It has little if any involvement in manufacturing, and its core business is the cooking and serving of meals. It operates in the school meals service, and in other public sector environments where meals are provided to service users. It is also involved in the running of company canteens, in both public and private enterprises. It provides meals for travellers in trains and planes, and operates restaurant chains for road travellers. In the company's words:

> Our agreed objectives for the year 2000 are to...build a dominant market share in our targeted geographic markets in foodservice, initially for Healthcare, Education, Business and Industry – through effective, sector-focussed teams... to establish a profitable concession business in identified geographic markets where commercially viable...
>
> (Compass 1998: 4)

Its vision is 'to be the highest quality and most profitable owner and operator of the world's top foodservice businesses' (ibid.: 2).

The company originated as a management buyout in 1986, and has expanded by 'a combination of organic growth and acquisition' (IDS 2002: 23) and now employs 300,000 people altogether, with 100,000 in the UK and some 60,000 in mainland Europe (ibid.).

The sector of operation is characterised by low pay, a high percentage of women in the workplace (Lindley 1994: 23–4), reportedly high labour turnover (from the interview material), and a high incidence of part-time working, and occupational segregation by gender. The relatively small, scattered workplaces, which characterise contract catering, create problems of union organisation. Many catering staff are 'employed in small work groups even where the employing organisation is large, for example as...canteen staff in a large factory...' (Munro 1999: 13).

Originally established in September 1996 as one of the 400 'voluntary' Article 13 agreements covering UK workers (Marginson *et al.* 1998: 2), the EWC was re-negotiated after a major company merger in 2002, and currently has 29 seats, covering 17 countries, plus 2 permanent employer representatives (IDS 2002: 24). The UK and Germany lost seats in this arrangement, in favour of the smaller countries of operation. The method of selection has also changed in the UK, from an electoral-college system covering unit-based non-management staff, and unit-based management and office-based administrative staff (Joint Trade Union 1996; UNISON 1996). The selection method in the UK is now by trade union nomination.

The actors

Table 10.1 lists the employee representatives present at the June 2002 meeting, and is drawn from responses to the questionnaire. All the delegates but the two

Table 10.1 Characteristics of the EWC members present at the employee-side meeting, June 2002[a]

Country	Union	Union posts held	Years EWC	Years Union	How many represented
Denmark	RBF	Workplace combined union members' representative	5	15	1,250
France	FO-FGTA	Délégué sydicale centrale	4	20	18,000
France	CFDT-FdS	Délégué sydicale centrale	4	22	South West region
France	CFDT-Cadres (substitute)	Titulaire, comité d'entreprise	1	1	
Germany	NGG	None	3	8	9,000
Germany	NGG	Collective bargaining committee	New	5	9,000
Ireland	SIPTU	National women's committee	2	25	40/1,600[b]
Italy	CGIL	Trade union representative	2	20	1,700
The Netherlands	None	(Chair, works council)	6	—	6,500
The Netherlands	None	(Secretary, works council)	2	—	6,500
Norway	HRAF	Convenor	5	14	2,500
Portugal	Sind Hotelaria do norte	Union leader	1	1	—
Portugal	Sind Hotelaria	Union leader	2	5	—
Spain	UGT	Branch executive committee	2	14	All in Spain
Spain	CC.OO	Union delegate	6	8	All in Spain
Sweden	HRF	Regional representative	1	20	150/3,000[b]
UK	TGWU (1)	Shop steward; Regional and National levels sector committee and women's committee	2	20	20/thousands[b]
UK	TGWU (2)	Senior steward	2	8	—
UK	UNISON	Convenor, Vice Chair women's network	6	10	All UNISON in the UK
UK	GMB	Convenor: Regional and National Equal Rights committee: Regional council and committee: branch secretary	3	14	All GMB England
UK	CWU	None	2	2	All CWU/BT in Scotland
UK	USDAW	Union representative	2	15	28
UK	PCS	Union representative	6	7	16

Notes

$n = 23$.

a Delegates from Belgium, Switzerland, Austria, Luxembourg, Greece and Finland were not present.

b The first figure is workplace level, second is on EWC.

from the Netherlands are trade union representatives, and the average length of trade union service is 12 years. This covers a length of service amongst the union representatives ranging from one to 25 years, with six delegates claiming 20 or more years' experience, and 12 (just over half) with 10 years' or more. It is therefore clear that there is a considerable wealth of experience assembled in the EWC. Only one (German) delegate holds no other union posts, for everyone else one or more trade union posts are held. It is impossible to compare the seniority of these posts across the union structures of the 11 countries represented, but it is clear that some of the delegates are holding posts of considerable status in their national union structures, whilst others are operating at local level.

Despite the transnational context, this finding reflects that of Upchurch *et al.* (2002) in their study of three unions in the southwest of England, where they found that 42 per cent of union workplace representatives (UWRs) had been representing the union for more than seven years. They note that the transparent stability of the UWRs within the organisation is likely to have both positive and negative implications. On the one hand, 'it would enable a degree of trust to develop...in order to represent member interests effectively...some potentially negative implications may flow from long tenure, such as a process of slow bureaucratisation of the stewards...' (ibid. 2002: 130).

The EWC was set up in 1996, and first met in Paris in 1997 (Compass 1997). The longest period of service on the EWC is therefore six years, and four of the 22 delegates have been there since the start, including one of the non-union representatives. This is important for the stability of the body, and for the transfer of learning within it. But in some respects, the length of service on the EWC is an artefact of the investment and disinvestment strategies of Compass rather than a reflection of the trade union lives of the delegates. It is no surprise to find that there is no real difference in length of trade union experience between this 'founding' group and the more recent arrivals: there is on average eight years' excess of union over EWC experience for the 'founders', and nine years for the group as a whole.

The numbers of workers represented at the EWC by the delegates is hugely variable, and reflects national representative patterns and structures, as well as varying concepts of 'mandate'. Two of the British representatives regard themselves as representing directly the people in their workplace: the Spanish delegates see their constituency as 'the whole of Spain', covering all Compass workers regardless of their location in Spain, or of which subsidiary they work for. The idea of 'constituency' is therefore highly varied, and the concepts of representativity and of mandate, as varied as the constituencies.

Table 10.2 shows the ways in which the representatives were selected for the EWC, according to their replies to the questionnaire. The overwhelming way of getting on this works council is through union nomination: only the two non-union representatives and the Danish delegate are elected by workplace elections. The second most frequently selected category is that of indirect election or nomination, and this has produced unclear results: this category covers both indirect elections and (mainly) nomination by the unions from amongst their representatives on other bodies.

Table 10.2 Patterns of nomination

Nominated by my union	14
Elected or nominated from another body	6
(e.g. national level works council)	
Elected by the union members in the workplace/s	—
Elected by a vote of everyone in the workplace	3[a]
Selected by the management	—
Any other way	—

Note

a In the Danish case, this means election by the workers of two companies.

Table 10.3 The most important things that membership of the EWC brings for your union (identified by 'star' rating)

	****	***	**	*	
It improves the negotiating relationship with the local/national management	7	6	1	3	1
It brings more members into activity in the union	4	3	6	2	3
It helps to inform members about the union's activities	3	13	2		1
It has contributed to my personal learning and development	14	6	2		
It helps in organising members in our company	5	5	4	2	4
It gives the union a propaganda advantage	5	3	5	5	1

The third set of questions on the questionnaire concerned the use that delegates make of their EWC involvement, and the results are presented in Table 10.3. It is evident that representatives feel that their participation in the EWC improves several aspects of their work as representatives in their own countries, but the highest rating goes to the contribution that the EWC participation makes to their personal learning and development. Of the 22, 20 union representatives (and one of the non-union representatives) ticked the two highest categories on this question.

Delegates are firmly, but less strongly of the opinion that EWC membership improves local or national negotiating relationships (13 out of 21 in the top two categories). Out of 21, 16 feel that it helps with informing members, but few responses fall in the top box here. For the remaining questions, the positive response tails off, and it is noticeable from the interview data that there are, in some cases specific reasons for the response, relating to a particular occurrence: for example, Margarette (see Table 10.4) relates an initial recruitment effect caused by EWC membership to the contested environment in the early days of privatisation.

It would be inadvisable to attempt a further analysis of this data: it is multinational and cross-cultural, and cannot be regarded as sufficiently robust to analyse in greater depth. The most interesting findings are those reported – the importance attached to training and development, and positively but less strongly, to local or national negotiation, and to membership information. These two latter points suggest a positive articulation of the EWC with other national and local union activities. The interview data also reveal that in several cases, the training effect is one of improving bargaining information, contacts or knowledge that helps the local representative to carry out their bargaining activities.

This finding gives some support to Streek's view that 'in firms to which it applies, the Directive creates a *dualism* of representative bodies, by *adding* a European Works Council to existing national councils' (Streek 1997: 654; emphasis added), although no national councils exist in the UK, and the relationship is to other negotiating levels. It will be seen in the following section that there is not consistent evidence of a structured, formalised relationship between the EWC and the national or local levels of activism in terms of bringing items to the EWC, or the reporting back of its outcomes, but there is a relationship expressed through the practice of the shop stewards who participate in this additional piece of representative machinery.

The actors – becoming a representative and a European Works Council representative

This section of the case study is based on the material from the individual interviews. All the interviewees were asked permission to use their names, and all agreed. Their first names and representative details are listed in Table 10.4. All were asked why (or how) they became a union representative, and for most, it was

Table 10.4 Case study interviewees

Name	Country	Union	Union posts held	Years EWC	Years Union	How many represented
Claire	France	CFDT-FdS	Délégué sydicale centrale	4	22	South West region
Elisabeth	France	CFDT-Cadres (substitute)	Titulaire, comité d'entreprise	1	1	
Patricia	France	FO-FGTA	Délégué sydicale centrale	4	20	18,000
Junice	Sweden	HRF	Regional representative	1	20	150/3,000[a]
Ann	UK	USDAW	Union representative	2	15	28
Dawn	UK	TGWU	Senior steward	2	8	—
Margarette	UK	UNISON	Convenor, Vice Chair-women's network	6	10	All UNISON in the UK
Pauline	UK	PCS	Union representative	6	7	16
Thomas	UK	CWU	None	2	2	All CWU/BT in Scotland

Note
a The first figure is workplace level, second is on EWC.

more or less accidental. Pauline relates her experience:

> The union rep from PCS approached me from the union office over there, from DVLA, and said would I like to do it, so I said 'yes, OK, let me have a word with my boss first'. I said [to him] 'if I get nominated do you mind', and he said 'no, it's up to you', so that's what I did. No one else seemed interested. . . .

Elisabeth's experience is similar:

> Well, really it was just that they needed someone and the person who did it before me was someone I really admired, the person who had left the union post. That was why really, and also to help all the people at work.

Junice, Patricia and Dawn were more proactive. Dawn has a family history of activism: the other two sought out the union. Junice says:

> When I started to work where I'm working now . . . I immediately became a member of this union. I was active in that I was beginning to have opinions about things, so they asked me if I would like to join the local club, that's how it's built in Sweden, with clubs at the workplace. And there it started, and it has become more and more jobs for the union.

Patricia's involvement was sought out, she says 'you could say it's a little bit like entry into a religious order when you want to, when you get involved in trade unionism: it's as though you make an offering, it's something which is so engrossing'.

   There is no discernible country effect in these stories: the experience of volunteering, one way or another, and then being sucked into the union, appears to transcend national boundaries. For the EWC, the representatives were invited or selected to take their union's seat on the EWC. Dawn says:

> I was recommended by the union, by . . . the National Officer. They rang up first, and they said, 'before you say yes, you'd better have a word with your husband', I said, 'what for?' and he said, 'just to make sure, because it could take up a lot of your time', I said 'right, fine'. As it was, Mike was on holiday, and I said, 'they want me to go to a meeting in Holland, but I've got a meeting in the UK first, so can I go?' . . . He said, 'what are you asking me for?', I said, 'well, they told me I've got to ask you' and he started laughing, and said 'well, that's a first'.

Margarette had been involved with the Compass EWC since the beginning, and was involved in the pre-meetings. She got on the EWC by election in the first place:

> when the final results came out . . . it was two UNISON people at the top of the ballot. So we were very, very pleased . . . we were actually at National Conference and it came out over the PA system, please could we go to the

desk. Well, neither of us knew what was going on, and we didn't know each other either. We met and we found out and it was very good. The meeting was just the following week, we had literally a week to get sorted out.

Patricia has a depth of experience in her union. She explains how the decision was made in the European and national union levels:

the EWC agreement...is signed by EFFAT, which has its headquarters in Brussels, and only two unions are members of it, FO and CFDT. It's at that level that the designations are made, so our federal secretary for the FO food workers union, M. Raphael Nedzinsky, designated us. He asked the secretary of the FO (Compass) branch to choose somebody, so he chose me, because I am perhaps the most experienced.

The understanding of the trade union context shown here reflects a point made by Wills:

It is...clear that the French representatives have more experience in the works council arena. As they already hold national meetings with senior managers and are used to dealing with questions of corporate strategy and decision making at this level...Without a national works council, the British trade union representatives do not have an overview of the situation in the UK nor do they have the opportunity to meet each other before they attend the EWC.

(Wills 2000: 96)

This is also true of Junice, who is a worker director in her company. She says:

I got no training before I went...The first time I went to the EWC I wasn't quite sure what sort of things we were supposed to talk about, but I felt prepared even though I didn't have any training. I'm used to talking with the company, so it was rather the same.

For most of the representatives, the experience of being 'dropped on', often at short notice, is more common than the experience of engagement in a union plan or strategy, even for experienced, nationally active trade unionists such as Dawn. For Anne, the consequences were enormous:

I rung the Manchester office up and asked them what it entailed, and I was the only one that had even asked about it. So with me being the only one, they said that I could represent USDAW, so that was how I came to be involved in it...there wasn't a lot of time really. I had no passport, I had to quickly get myself a passport and everything...The first meeting was Amsterdam, I met with one of the other ladies that's on the committee, Dawn...It was the first time I'd ever been abroad, the first time in my life.

The actors: women on the European Works Council

Eighteen of the EWC representatives present in June 2002 were women, and all but one of those interviewed were female. An immediate question of participation is raised: childcare is an issue, which has been acknowledged since the 1960s at least:

> Trade union work is satisfying but it consumes time and it is ... partly because of their domestic responsibilities that so few women act in a representative capacity for their unions in the wider Movement ... But at shop floor level, there are hundreds of women serving as shop stewards ...
>
> (Hughes 1968: 29)

Most of the women either had no children (in one case), or had grown-up children. For the four who had young children now, or at earlier stages of their union careers, there is appreciation of the husbands and ex-husbands, who look after the children. Dawn offers praise:

> I've been blessed really, I've got a really good husband, I don't tell him often enough that I appreciate what he does. But he's brilliant with the kids, if I didn't have his support there I wouldn't be able to do what I do, he's fantastic with the kids.

Claire's children are grown up, but she too expresses a sense of good fortune in having a supportive husband:

> I'm lucky to have a conciliatory husband, since I spend as much time out as in the house. So I'm lucky that my husband ... can come home at lunchtime, and see to the children's homework, it's him that saw to them more than me ... He's not an activist, he's not a trade unionist, he always tells me that I'm taking the place of the many. But he's not against it.

There is little evidence from the women interviewed of any significant impact of women's groups in the unions on their decisions to get or stay involved, with one exception, Margarette. For her, the women's group was crucial:

> The shop steward who had recruited me ... he said to me, 'would you like to go to the women's meeting on a weekend?' ... So I went to the women's meeting, and after that I went to all their meetings. I am vice chair now, and I've been on National Women's Committee and been very involved with the women's group. I look round at [meetings], and I see women who came in like myself, who knew nothing and had done nothing and they all came up through our women's group ...

Equally, there is little evidence of a classic 'women's agenda' appearing on the EWC agenda. As Colgan and Ledwith (2002) note, 'Women are not a homogenous group...it is not realistic to see women as a single interest group when it comes to "women's concerns" ...' (ibid.: 270). Munro points out that the range of issues and problems raised by the women NHS cleaners she studied could be seen as 'narrow, mostly relating to having to do more work in less time and having inadequate materials... [but] these issues...actually related to wider problems of work, intensification and restructuring' (Munro 2001: 466). Some of the examples of the problems raised by the EWC delegates do appear concrete and narrow at first sight: there is a lot of concern with packaging, for example, but this apparently mundane item reflects serious and daily problems with getting the job done, and done safely, as Pauline explains:

> There's a lot of packaging waste. We have portions of milk come in, to go with the coffee. They come in boxes of 400 jiggers, and they're wrapped up again, with cling-film or poly-film over the top, you have a heck of a job to break into them. You can cut yourself on the cardboard, easily. Cans are another issue, they come in from Coca Cola, you should see the way they're wrapped up. Loads of cling-film round them.

The amount of packaging slows them down, causes health hazards, and on some sites, creates a problem of disposal. However, whilst this is a major issue, and recognised as such by the establishment of an environmental working party as a sub-group of the EWC, it is not evident that this is an issue relating to the female nature of the workforce: it appears more likely to be a factor deriving from the type of work performed in this industry. Thomas, the one man on the UK group, raises similar issues: the works canteen he works in is on the ninth floor, exacerbating the waste problem.

The outputs: putting items on the European Works Council agenda, and reporting back

There is enormous variation between the delegates in the way in which linkages operate between their local and national institutions, or workplace groups and the EWC. Thomas is trying to get an improvement in paternity leave:

> Last year I had an item on the agenda, it was paternity leave. Everybody was kind of taken aback you know, but there's equal opportunities for fathers actually. We need three days...the ladies on the UK forum, they're going to back me up on that one.

Pauline is pursuing the issue of waste and wastage, and Junice is currently involved in trying to get an issue on the agenda:

> This year, I took an item to the EWC, I'm not sure it was translated correctly, as I had no response at all. I was asking if the members of the meeting could join together to make a programme for what we call in Sweden 'the worker's

environment' and that includes all kind of things, like the lighting is correct, the noise levels are correct and to check that machinery is not broken: all these things that makes it possible for us to work in the place . . . But nobody really took notice of it, so I decided to write it down and send it [to the trade union side co-ordinator] . . . It was my own initiative in the beginning, then I discussed it with the workers of my workplace and with my union.

She also has a reporting structure, 'when I come back from the EWC, I make a report. I send it to the head office [of the union] in Stockholm, and I hope to get it in the union newspaper'.

Patricia makes formal and informal reports:

I did a report to my *Comité d'Entreprise* about what was said, and about the positions that I took in the meeting. So it's clear that there is a direct connection between the two . . . I think it's very important to give a report to your colleagues. If you don't, then it really isn't any use for anything . . . I speak to lots of people, for them it's a completely 'foreign' world: they ask, 'what do the English think of this? We're in an English company, so what do the English think of this, that and the other?'

For the other French titular representative, Claire, the report-back to the union is unproblematic: the connection to the membership is less evident:

I represent a lot of things, I'm not there for myself, I represent all the employees in general in Compass in France . . . I've started to write my report, [which will go to the CFDT] and there are several people who have asked to see the report . . . I talk a lot about the EWC to those around me. I explain what the EWC is, and what happened, and a bit about the problems of the countries who were represented, and also about what the senior managers who were there were thinking about our problems in France. There's no connection between the employees in France and the EWC, they don't care about it. They've got their own problems.

For the UK reps, without a national structure, reporting back causes serious problems. Margarette reports to her women's committee, but does not regard that as the correct forum. Her previous union reporting structure has changed, and she currently is unable to find out where to send her report. She also has problems contacting her 'constituency', which is all the UNISON members in Compass, nationwide. Thomas reports to the BT convenor, even though he and the catering staff are not BT employees. He also reports informally to his work colleagues:

As soon as I come back, they're asking what did you do, what were you talking about, they are really interested in it. I'm actually finding people are approaching me, they didn't used to at all, but now they know I'm on this Works Council and involved with the union, they'll come to me.

Pauline's experience is different. She has no formal reporting structure, and the shift patterns in her workplace make it impossible to get a meeting organised to report back:

> Someone said, 'you should sit us down and we should have a meeting about it', and I said, 'OK, two o'clock then', and they said, 'Oh no, I can't stay then.' Oh, great, so when? I too have work to do, and they want to go home.

The pattern of responses confirms the observation of Stirling and Fitzgerald, that 'there was considerable variation in the range and effectiveness of systems for reporting back' (Stirling and Fitzgerald 2001: 19). There are clearly factors here relating to national trade union and industrial relations systems. The UK representatives are very conscious of their lack of national consultative structures. They currently meet each other twice a year, and are expecting to agree a national consultative committee shortly, in advance of the impending implementation of the National Information and Consultation Directive. Margarette explains:

> We said look, we're coming in here cold, the Germans and the French they've had their national works councils, and they know what they're going to ask. They know what's going on and how they feel about things, and we knew nothing. So we kept asking for a meeting and the last two years we have had a pre-meeting...And that has been very helpful, we've got to know each other, we've also got to know the company and we are able to iron out any little problems we've had. All sorts of things that we want brought up at the meeting, and sort it out between all of us and get some decisions made before we actually go into the Works Council meeting...We really notice the difference; the German delegates come and they used to say, 'what you doing about the environment?' And 'what are you doing about...' They're so far ahead of us, but now I think we're catching up.

Bringing it all back home: using the European Works Council outcomes

For almost all the representatives interviewed, the EWC was experienced as beneficial. Their responses fell in three major categories, shaped by the questionnaire reported above:

- Improvements to the bargaining relationship.
- Improvements to the union's organising activities (recruiting, organising, retaining members).
- Improvements to the representatives' capacities to carry out their jobs.

The bargaining relationship

Not all of the EWC delegates are involved in formalised collective bargaining, but all of them are involved in representational activities that involve negotiations on behalf of others. Dawn and Thomas identified an advantage in the increased bargaining power that came with increased respect by their local managers. Thomas, whose building is being sold off, and whose future employment is as uncertain as that of his co-workers, says:

> I get more respect because I am on the International Council. You're getting told about things before your bosses … It's a bit of what you know and who you know, it's a bit of both. It's not a power thing or an ego thing, it helps to represent your members.

Dawn agrees, and explains how contact with the Group head office helps her to resolve local problems:

> My manager speaks to me a lot better, he treats me a lot differently than he did. He's not as rude and arrogant as he was, because he knows that any problems I have, if I'm not getting the answers I need, I'll ring up and say 'hang on, I've got a problem with this, how would I go about it?' If I put a call in to somebody outside of my subsidiary, then obviously Compass will get in touch with my bosses and say 'why is Dawn upset? Can we do something to sort it out?' From my own perspective it's made it a lot better because people treat me differently, and they don't treat me as though I'm stupid, which is how I was treated a lot of the time before.

Claire points out the difficulties associated with closer contact with the Group senior managers, and the risks of co-option:

> It can also be a handicap, I negotiate on wages, and at the EWC I see all the reasons why there won't be a pay rise. I see all the problems about qualification, about training, and the attempts of the company to value the employees. It can hold me back in negotiating, as I know the position of the managers.

Junice has additional layers of trade union concertation to deal with. As well as her role of worker director, she needs to work within the Nordic group of unions:

> We had a meeting in Copenhagen, the Norwegian and the Danish representatives with the Chairman of the Board, to be prepared for this European Works Council. There I got a lot of information that was useful for my understanding of the construction of the company, both in Sweden and in other northern countries, which is a bit different from what the company is in England and in the rest of the world. That is useful for me, for the next time I go to the Board meeting, but that is only twice a year. So I can make links between the Board and the EWC.

For most of the delegates, the information they obtained at the EWC allowed them to make the link between company policy and workplace practice: if

Company initiatives are, or are not reaching their workplace, they know about it, and can take action. Ann says:

> I've only just seen about this new training package, they've got a new induction now ... I noticed when I was going home on Tuesday morning, the lady who's doing the training now, she was doing some inductions, she had all this new stuff in her hand. When I go back I must know how they've got on with this new stuff.

Claire reports her fellow workers as more sceptical:

> When the questionnaire [on employee satisfaction] arrived, the employees didn't want to answer it, they thought it was a lot of paper for nothing. They wanted something concrete, and there wasn't enough. They said, 'too many words and not enough action'. ... The purchases that the Compass group has made abroad, the employees don't understand this: they say that if Compass has money to spend on buying other companies, then 'why do we have such poverty wages?' It's not everyone who says that of course, I'm speaking relatively here.

The importance of these points made by the EWC delegates is that they reveal that it is extremely difficult to make a clear estimate of the ways in which the new institution, the EWC, relates to the older industrial relations institutions. Many of the ways in which delegates report using the EWC outcomes are not obvious, are localised and are not easily researched by quantitative methods. Whilst the interview method used here indicates some of the connections being made with the EWC, it does not give a picture of spread, or of robustness: there is no evidence on how far this effect spreads beyond the practice of the individual representatives. Where reports are made to the union there is no evidence as to the consequences, if any, of that reporting. What is evident is that there *are* connections, and that there is an integration of the EWC experience into local and national trade union practice.

Improvements to union organising activities

None of the respondents reported a systematic improvement in organising activity as a result of the EWC, but most of them were able to identify particular moments where the EWC had made a difference. Although this question has a positive response from the questionnaire results, and from the interviews, the effect appears weak, and is not fully reported here.

Improvements to the representatives' capacities to carry out their jobs

This is the category of the questionnaire that received the most enthusiastic endorsement, and this is generally reflected in the interviews. The nature of the learning is varied: it can be about the Company, about its policies, about its senior managers, or about the situation of fellow delegates, at home or abroad. Elisabeth, a new union representative attending the EWC for the first time as a substitute, talked about what she had learned about the company:

> At the EWC, I learnt a lot more about the group. At the company level we don't know everything, we don't know what's going on in the UK, or in the other countries. We don't hear anything about the problems that they have there. We learnt quite a lot in the meeting, the problem is how to bring this into operation – what can we do with this information.

Thomas's response emphasises his learning about comparative working practices and standards:

> It's opened my eyes a lot. From our working conditions up here, how it differs … If I know that other people are not being asked to do the things that we're being asked to do, I can say well the other people down in England don't put up with that, so why should we. It helps that way, it just shows you how workers are getting treated, not even just in Britain, all over. You don't want to go too far below the line, below that standard. OK, you need to work and you need to do the job, but you don't need to bend over backwards.

Pauline agrees with Thomas: 'It just gives me a broader outlook into what other countries are up to, and what we could be doing, what we should be doing, and what we aren't doing.' Rather than coercive comparison by the company (though this may exist through benchmarking, despite the limitations imposed by a service that cannot be relocated, as it consists of local service), there is evidence of comparisons being made by the representatives, who are seeking upward movements not reductions (Streek 1997; Weston and Martinez Lucio 1998).

Dawn talks of improvements to her confidence, and says she has gained more understanding of the union itself and the union movement. Whilst Patricia talks of the career path that she's abandoned in favour of trade union involvement, but of the personal satisfactions from union work: 'It's really brought me so much in terms of personal enrichment: this is a bit egocentric, but it has allowed me to know myself better.'

Conclusion

This chapter has investigated the ways in which the union representatives on the Compass EWC integrate their experience of the EWC into their union work, looking for the presence or absence of the close connections that must be essential if these remote bodies are to have relevance or usefulness for unions locally, and for their stewards and members. This case study suggests strongly that such connections do exist, but not always in ways that are visible from the outside. Representatives on this service-sector EWC report a variety of ways in which membership of the EWC has impacted on their personal and trade union lives, with the most important aspects being on their bargaining practices, and on their development as workplace representatives. How far that transfers into the unions as a whole is unclear from this study, but there is an evident relationship between the denser institutional structures of France and Sweden, and the degree of articulation between EWC representatives and their unions. It will be interesting to follow the arrival of the UK-level machinery in this case. Apart from this issue, the concerns expressed by the EWC representatives were generally similar across national boundaries, suggesting a commonality of union experience at workplace level. This may just be the glue that binds these diverse trade union lives into common enterprise, and makes the EWC into a living part of the industrial relations machinery.

References

Colgan, F. and Ledwith, S. (2002) 'Gender and Diversity: Reshaping Union Democracy', *Employee Relations*, 24(2): 167–89.

Compass (1997) 'Minutes', from the first annual meeting: Paris, 20 June 1997.

Compass (1998) *Our Future*, Internal Publication.

Ferner, A. and Hyman, R. (eds) (1992) *Industrial Relations in the New Europe*, Oxford: Blackwell.

Hughes, J. (1968) *Trade Union Structure and Government: Membership Participation and Trade Union Government*, Research Paper No. 5, Part 2, Royal Commission on Trade Unions and Employers' Associations, London: HMSO.

IDS (Incomes Data Service) (2002) 'Comparing EWCs in Practice', *IDS Study*, 722.

Joint Trade Unions (1996) (CWU, GMB, PTC, RMT, TGWU, UNISON and USDAW) *Compass European Council – A Message to all Trade Union Members in Compass Group and its Subsidiaries*, Circular to members eligible to vote in the CEC election.

Lindley, R. (ed.) (1994) *Labour Market Structures and Prospects for Women*, Manchester: Equal Opportunities Commission.

Marginson, P., Gilman, M., Krieger, H. and Jacobi, O. (1998) *Negotiating European Works Councils: An Analysis of Agreements under Article 13*, Luxembourg: Office for Official Publications of the European Communities.

Martinez Lucio, M. and Weston, S. (2000) 'European Works Councils and "Flexible Regulation": The Politics of Intervention', *European Journal of Industrial Relations*, 6(2): 203–16.

Munro, A. (1999) *Women, Work and Trade Unions*, London: Mansell.

Munro, A. (2001) 'A Feminist Trade Union Agenda? The Continued Significance of Class, Gender and Race', *Gender, Work and Organisation*, 8(4): 454–71.

Stirling, J. and Fitzgerald, I. (2001) 'European Works Councils: Representing Workers on the Periphery', *Employee Relations*, 23(1): 13–25.

Streek, W. (1997) 'Industrial Citizenship under Regime Competition: The Case of the European Works Councils', *Journal of European Public Policy*, 4(4): 643–64.

UNISON (1996) *Compass Group European Forum: Election of Representatives in the UK*, Statement of Principles: Internal Circular.

Upchurch, M., Danford, A. and Richardson, M. (2002) 'Research Note: Profiles of Union Workplace Representatives: Evidence from Three Unions in Southwest England', *Industrial Relations Journal*, 33(2): 127–40.

Waddington, J. (2001) 'Articulating Trade Union Organisation for the New Europe?', *Industrial Relations Journal*, 32(5): 449–63.

Weston, S. and Martinez Lucio, M. (1998) 'In and Beyond European Works Councils: Limits and Possibilities for Trade Union Influence', *Employee Relations*, 20(6): 551–64.

Wills, J. (1999) 'European Works Councils in British Firms', *Human Resource Management Journal*, 9(4): 19–38.

Wills, J. (2000) 'Great Expectations: Three Years in the Life of a European Works Council', *European Journal of Industrial Relations*, 6(1): 85–107.

11 Organising across borders

Developing trade union networks

Barbara Tully

Introduction

Whilst multinational companies have long since been aware of the benefits of effective international communication, workforces within these companies have largely tended to be organised in local and national settings. However, the establishment of European Works Councils (EWCs) has led employee representatives to recognise that they too must improve their international communication networks and move towards cross-border co-operation and organisation. Within this new forum of representation the issues of language and intercultural communication therefore assume a much greater importance than before.

Language is often considered a soft issue in employment relations (Miller *et al.* 2000) and frequently as a local and an individual issue by multinational management (Marshan-Piekkari *et al.* 1999). This chapter will argue that language and intercultural communication are central issues to address if EWCs are to function successfully as transnational bodies. Effective communication relies on transmitting information about each other's systems and cultures as well as developing social links. This communication process requires language as its main communication tool and it is only when language is treated as a core issue and given the support and focus that it deserves that it will become an effective political tool in the development of EWCs.

The chapter draws on quantitative data from an analysis of 475 EWC agreements (Miller *et al.* 2000) to contextualise the language issue and then on qualitative data from twenty-eight interviews with EWC representatives from Italy, France, Belgium, Norway, Sweden, Spain, Denmark, Finland, Germany, Austria and the UK all of whom represent a different multinational company. Finally, it will present a case study of an EWC, which has attempted a systematic approach to the development of language and communication. It also draws on observations made during training programmes, which have been run together with a colleague for the EWCs of several different multinationals.

Background: language, culture and power

If language is considered to be the main communication tool in such cross-border forums, what social and political issues are embedded in the language debate?

First, there is the question of choice of language. Whilst it seems that English is the common choice of a working language in most EWCs (in our analysis of the ETUI database of 243 agreements where a working language is identified, 198 – 81 per cent – specified English, Miller *et al.* 2000), there are examples of EWCs which are operating multilingually, using all the languages of their representatives. One EWC representative who was interviewed noted such a language policy and argued that this was the only way to be truly democratic at their EWC. He admitted, however, that in reality communication was extremely difficult, particularly between meetings when representatives had to rely on colleagues at work to translate messages coming in and going out. The tendency was to limit communication to an absolute minimum.

Of those who nominate English as their working EWC language, it is overwhelmingly the case that those representatives using English will, in the main, be non-native speakers. Crystal (1997) claims that over 80 per cent of English which is spoken in the world is between non-native speakers. It is true to say, however, that the level of competency in a language will be reflected in the degree of power and control the speaker can exert in a situation. Thus, undoubtedly, the native speaker will have an advantage over all but the most fluent speakers. Crystal also charts the development of an emerging world standard of spoken English (EWSSE) that would avoid varieties, idiomatic and colloquial terms and strong regional accents with the implication that power relations would be more equitable. However, in our experience of EWCs, it is often the native speaker who is least aware of how to standardise speech and therefore will retain control to a large extent. Pennycock (1994) in his work on the cultural politics of English goes so far as to say that international English, rather than being some fixed linguistic system, should be viewed as a system of power/knowledge relationships which produce an outcome of understanding. This is particularly pertinent to inter-group relations within a transnational body such as an EWC, which has the potential to fracture easily given the fact that it may house a divergent set of individuals, representing a range of employees, political views, social and cultural identities against a background of constant flux due to organisational change and a certain sense of insecurity and clarity as to the extent of their power.

Crystal also argues that as well as intelligibility, language carries with it identity and as such, identity is a more emotive and powerful concept than the former, carrying with it social and political values. An awareness of these values would seem to be important if the EWC were to begin to function as a transnational entity since they carry with them a map of national structures, organisations and a diversity of social and cultural information. An inability to communicate such differences may lead to isolation and exclusivity.

This leads us to the question of how to define the word 'culture'. Often we refer to culture as values, traditions, customs and above all nationality. Blommaert (1997) point out that nationality is a bad index of culture since it disregards multi-ethnic societies and makes assumptions that there is a sharedness of culture or a cultural 'norm'. Resorting to national stereotypes can be counterproductive unless they are seen as a starting point to deconstruct and deepen understanding of attitudes; for example, attitudes towards management or styles of communication in meetings. Blommaert and Verschueren (1998) highlight the idea that culture is often seen as fixed, unchanging, set-in-stone, when in reality, it is constantly changing and being re-invented. The fact that we frequently 'create' new cultures may be an important issue to explore in an EWC. It may be beneficial to spend time establishing a group cultural identity that is not seen to be dominated by any one specific interest group and allows for a 'new' group culture to emerge.

But even more crucial to the issue of culture is that language carries with it a value; that there is a difference of power and authority in any interaction and that we are continually adapting our style to respond to different situations of power. Hymes (1974) argues that it is these intuitive laws, established socially, which can have an effect on intercultural communication and degrees of tolerance and acceptance of 'the other'. As a positive approach, Rampton (1999) suggests that the key to this issue is flexibility; his research has shown that we assume many identities and often incorporate identities which are not our own. Such ideas may be important to discuss in the context of the successful functioning of a transnational body such as an EWC. By creating a new group identity which accepts power diversity and is flexible and generous in giving and receiving verbal and non-verbal messages, it may be possible to create a culture of unity out of cultural and linguistic diversity. By acknowledging differences and being open and honest about the effects of these differences on the EWC a sense of trust and solidarity can be engendered and communication will inevitably improve.

After running an intercultural awareness training session with the EWC of a large multinational that had just announced large job losses, representatives were asked for feedback on this type of training. Rather than commenting that time spent on such 'peripheral' issues was detracting from more urgent issues, respondents stated that the training had created a sense of openness and trust which had prepared them well for their meeting with management and helped them to function more effectively as a body. They felt that this was time well spent and that they were able to see tangible benefits of allowing time to understand each other better.

Building a network

The challenges

The qualitative data identified two key issues that have to be faced in order to construct an effective communications network. Importantly these issues were central in the challenge to establish an effective EWC at the case study multinational Kværner.

Access to technology

The expansion of the Internet has provided a powerful tool for international communication and it is clear that EWCs need to utilise this tool to maintain and develop communication. In many cases, full EWC meetings are only held annually and thus the ability to use information and communication technologies (ICTs) effectively between meetings is paramount. Whilst for most white-collar representatives using e-mail is part of their daily routine, for many blue-collar workers the Internet is not accessible at the workplace. Indeed the interviews identified that some representatives still have difficulties in gaining access to even a fax machine.

For some workers, access to e-mail is not the only hurdle. Some need training to use e-mail and to be able to access company information via the Internet. 'Access to technology', was highlighted as a problem in several of our interviews and often seems to be dependent on the attitude of local managers who may be unaware of, slow, or even reluctant to implement what may be central company policy. In many cases financial arguments had been used to deny access, as had been reluctance on the part of local managers that the EWC representative may have access to more information than themselves. In one EWC, the chair of the Liaison Committee did not have an e-mail address, which made it extremely difficult for the committee to function, especially since using the phone was not a viable alternative as there was also a language problem.

Language

Language was identified as the most important barrier to communication in his or her EWC by every interviewee. A French Select Committee member noted:

> My EWC has solved many problems but the main one is language. We have agreement in the Select Committee that all can use their own language. When we phone each other, we have a trade union worker who takes the calls. But it's not always possible, it's a real problem ... especially outside of the meetings. In the meetings we have translation and it's no problem for translation of documents. Outside we use what we can but it is very difficult.

Most stated that the main difficulties occurred outside of the meetings during opportunities for social networking and between meetings using the phone or e-mail. Some EWCs had requested interpreting facilities in the evenings but had been refused on financial grounds.

A Belgian representative stated, 'we have asked for to [*sic*] have an interpreter outside of the meeting but they won't. It's too expensive'. A Danish Select Committee member said, 'one evening we dine with management and we have interpreters. We all try to use English but not everyone can'.

Language training was seen as the solution to this problem in all cases. However, in an analysis of 475 agreements in the ETUI database, of the 365 (77 per cent) which contain explicit provisions referring to language, only 25 per cent mention language as a training topic (Miller *et al.* 2000). Most of the language references are to interpreting and translating and as these represent one of the highest and recurrent costs of running an EWC (ECOTEC 1999) companies can trade off language training against interpreting facilities. Siemens, for example, make this explicit in their agreement, 'individual EWC members shall be provided with language training provided this results in an actual reduction in translation costs'.

Where training is provided, responsibility is often placed either on the individual to recognise their language training needs or on the EWC itself, in most cases, to come up with a training request. Many substantiated the point made earlier that language was not prioritised as a central training issue by the company and that when it was viewed as a local issue – as was largely the case by management – it became much more difficult to address. As a Finnish representative said, 'Management won't pay for 30 members to do language training...only for the Select Committee. Local management must pay and then it is very difficult because all systems are different.' A Danish representative added, 'Our CEO says that its (language) every country's problem' (i.e. not a central problem). Marshan-Piekkari *et al.* (1999) suggest that one way ahead would be for companies to appoint a Language Officer 'to co-ordinate and develop language policies (at all levels in the company), to oversee their implementation and assist in the auditing of current and future language needs' (ibid.: 383).

Those who had received training agreed that communications had improved – especially in social relations in the group. Their training took different forms: some had intensive blocks of language study and others weekly classes, either in a small group or on a one-to-one basis. All language training had been outsourced and some interviewees commented that it was often too general and not focused on the specific needs of an EWC representative.

A further problem identified was that despite studying another language (in most cases English) the fact that meetings were only held annually meant that there was little opportunity to practice their newly acquired language skills in an authentic context. An Austrian Select Committee member commented, 'I have unlimited training but it is difficult for me to use English once a year.'

There was a common observation that 'Southern European' representatives generally had more language difficulties. Many of them did not speak any other language. In the words of a Norwegian representative, 'We always have problems with south [*sic*] countries in Europe...there are language problems. They stay alone after the meetings because they cannot talk another language. It's difficult for the group.'

Although, a Spanish representative responded, 'Spain, Portugal, Italy have more difficulties learning languages. Less contact in Europe. We have the sea, unlike central Europe. It's difficult for England too. They only speak English but that's OK.'

It is clear from these comments that such issues must be discussed in the group and that a group decision should be taken on how best to support colleagues to develop language skills.

One language issue which was not always clearly identified but emerged from observations of EWCs in action was the communication difficulties imposed on the group by native speakers of the working language – in most cases English. Whilst discussing EWSSE Crystal (1997) notes that it is not owned by any one group or nation but is a standardised version of English without regional dialectical differences. This is witnessed to some extent already in 'Brussels-speak'. This may be in its infancy, if yet born at all, but one Norwegian Select Committee representative can appreciate the need for such a variety in this comment:

> When a not-so-good foreign speaker…communicates in English by phone or face-to-face, and he understands a not-so-good German better than the English guy, well the main problem is with the English guy, not the not-so-good speaker. Because the English guy is not able to talk in a way that makes the other person understand.

This problem is often noticeable in a transnational setting. Native speakers are frequently unaware of the complexities of the language they are using, of their speed of delivery, of the strength of their local accent and of the idiomatic phrases and colloquialism used. Idiomatic English and quick repartee are often used by native speakers with the best intentions as a way of diffusing tension, of informalising a situation and to oil the social wheels and get the group to gel. However, native speakers who are not competent language learners themselves are likely to be unaware of the unnecessary complexities of the language they are using and its effect on non-native speakers. If accompanied by a strong regional accent, the difficulties are compounded. But it is not always simply a question of asking the speakers to tone down his/her accent. Accent, certainly in English, conveys identity and often a pride in identity – and to ask someone to speak in a more 'standard' way could be seen as an affront or as a source of discomfort in that they are betraying their roots. This issue requires sensitivity and language awareness training for native speakers may be an important and effective method of raising such issues. The results of even minimal training, in my experience can produce great improvements in communications.

The Kværner project: a case study

In 1996, trade union organisers in the Norwegian-owned oil, gas, construction and engineering multinational Kværner ASA were becoming increasingly aware of the need for their trade union, and EWC representatives, to build up a communication network in their rapidly expanding company. They had recently signed an Article 13 agreement establishing their EWC, and trade union convenors felt that it was important to establish cross-border corporate trade union networks. But with a largely blue-collar workforce amongst which language and ICT skills were poor, the project had to develop a method for implementing such worker networks within the company which would convince these blue-collar workers that training in these skills would be beneficial in developing the power and role of the EWC. The aim of the project therefore, was to build a communication network around which language training was firmly linked to access and training in the use of ICTs.

After initiating a successful bid for European funding, a project was set up by the Kværner unions in Norway and Sweden along with partners from Northumbria University UK, and De Facto, an Independent Norwegian Research Institute (Tully *et al.* 2000).

History and background

At the start of the project (September 1996), the company had developed rapidly over ten years from a Norwegian mechanical and engineering company with 10,000 employees into a major multinational company with 80,000 employees. The company had recently acquired a UK conglomerate, Trafalgar House and moved its company headquarters to London with the resultant decision that English was to become the official company language. During the course of the project, the Group ran into a financial crisis which led to a change in senior management and a dramatic restructuring of the company, allowing a concentration on the core business and resulting in a dramatic reduction in the workforce to 30,000 by the year 2000.

Therefore, in this climate of rapid change it was possible to see how internationalisation would influence the company and the ability of the EWC to play an active role.

Objectives

The project itself had three phases:

- The organisation phase – which involved the participating representatives in the design and development of the network.
- The skills development phase – which involved the participants in acquiring the necessary technical skills to participate in the network.
- The training phase – which consisted of language training via residential courses and distance training using the Internet. This would allow participants to practice their newly acquired technology skills. The training was tested, delivered, evaluated and revised throughout the course of the project.

Getting started

As confirmed by our subsequent interviews with a wide range of EWC representatives, access to technology was the initial challenge faced by the project team. Norwegian and Swedish trade unions faced negative attitudes from local management. Even when unions themselves agreed to purchase equipment, local management refused to provide telephones lines with the excuse that lines were not available. However, the greatest challenge was faced in the UK. The project team, with support from the GMB union and the then AEEU (AMICUS), organised a meeting of EWC representatives and trade unionists from Kværner-owned sites in the UK. This was the first time that they had met and access to the company Intranet was almost non-existent for many.

Despite support for the project from central management, in many cases only after great pressure did local management agree to provide computers for representatives. There was, however, a gradual change in attitude throughout the project as local management began to find that they could use the EWC representative as a source of information for themselves. Project leaders were also able to get support from local IT managers who were keen to promote the use of technology and often came up against reluctant IT users in local management.

Attitudes to training

An important issue that the project team was aware of from the outset was that there would be some resistance to the training. Many of the largely blue-collar workers had left school with negative learning experiences and/or felt anxious and lacking in confidence about their own abilities to learn a language or to use a computer. Training approaches were required which placed much more emphasis on fluency rather than accuracy of language and which shifted the focus away from grammar to a communicative approach geared towards responding to the real language needs of the representatives. Confidence building was seen as paramount and the materials were designed after a careful needs analysis and delivered by trainers who were specialists in English for trade union and EWC purposes. The content and focus of the training was continually negotiated, with participants providing regular feedback and evaluation.

Between the residential courses, participants were expected to carry out tasks using their newly acquired computer skills, first to network with each other (Norwegian and Swedish representatives) then later to extend the network into Finland and then to native English speakers in the UK. These tasks were designed to practice their newly acquired skills and were short and easy to execute. The networking tasks focused on the following main areas:

- Discussing key issues and policy within the company.
- Developing an understanding and information exchange on different trade union systems and terminology.
- Developing an understanding of the broader trade union and political context in other countries.
- Raising awareness of cultural differences and in doing so, examining ones own cultural perceptions.

There was also a degree of personal information exchanged. At the same time, the non-native speakers of English were being provided with feedback on their language skills by a tutor who was copied into their e-mails. Despite the difficulties, a considerable amount of networking took place between representatives. This was mainly conducted by e-mail but also involved the distribution of a newsletter and in a few cases, the cementing of social relations when some Norwegian delegates took holidays in the UK and contacted EWC representatives before, during and after their stay on a more social level. By the end of the project there had been a noticeable change in the mindset of a number of representatives from that of maintaining a local perspective to that of developing a more transnational one. As one EWC representative commented, 'I feel I am part of an international company instead of a small plant in a little Norwegian town.'

Key to the success of the training was the Select Committee's commitment to maintaining a close link between the objectives of the training and the objectives of the EWC/trade union network itself. To quote the convenor, 'if the participants in the courses felt that they did not have ownership of the project, the project would fail to achieve and maintain the commitment of participants for such a long period of time'.

This was in itself one of the major factors in the lack of motivation shown by the UK representatives. The experience of the non-native English speakers was that whilst they were communicating with other non-native speakers and receiving feedback from their tutor on the development of their language skills things worked. However, when it came to getting responses from native English speaking representatives, there was a lack of commitment. Many of them failed to reply and networking opportunities were missed. One possible reason for this was that the native English speakers were not involved in the language-training phase of the project and hence did not feel part of the overall objectives of the training. It could also have been a lack of awareness about the difficulties of operating in another language, which native speakers of English usually do not have experience of in a transnational context.

This observation was reinforced when EWC representatives met at their annual meetings. Written communication had the benefit of allowing time to decipher the language and a certain standardisation of delivery so that intelligibility was less of a problem. However, in the spoken form, accents, local dialect, colloquialisms and idiomatic English left the non-natives speakers with a sense of despair at how little they seemed to have improved their English and how far they still had to go. It was at this point that it became clear that language awareness training should have been part of the project, so that native speakers were also involved in some sort of language training task.

Supporting a network: leadership, co-ordination and local networks

During the interviews with a range of EWC representatives, several of them commented that it was important, particularly for the Select Committee, to have people who would drive the networking, keep things moving and encourage others to communicate.

One Danish representative stated, 'if you have patience, work hard and are positive, it [the EWC networking] will work but you have to keep in contact'. Whilst an Austrian representative added, 'it is very important point, to have regular contact with other EWC representatives. What is happening at their site? Which problems are there and where can we help? We take these points on the agenda'.

It also seems crucial that the Select Committee is constantly disseminating information back to the EWC forum representatives. In some cases this would be via an EWC website, newsletter, e-mail or phone-call but it means that they keep in touch, that the network is connected. It may be that there are working groups on specific issues but it would appear that everyone needs to be linked in at some point and feel part of the group.

As a UK representative commented, 'there seems to be an absence of a proper communication infrastructure, for example, there are still representatives [after four years] who do not have e-mail. It is difficult if it is only left to the individual representative'.

In the Kværner project, the Union Convenor was the driver behind the project. He was also one of three union members on the Board of Directors (Norwegian employment law) and was the chair of the Select Committee. His vision and motivation kept the project on track. As he commented:

> If trade unions have a common interest in exerting influence at company and at European level, they have to take the necessary steps to make this technical and communication network possible. The (Kværner) project and the ambitions on an EWC level are closely linked together. If we continue with the traditional way of working on a local level, the EWC will be a head with no body, fingers or fist. The employer would realise this and the EWC will have no influence.

Communication is also important with representatives constituencies so that information can be disseminated. For those representatives who belonged to trade unions, a communication route to members and each other was through the established union network. This was true also of those representatives whose national structures have works councils in place. For those representatives outside of these networks there seem to be two problems: how to disseminate their information but often more importantly, to whom. It became clear in interviews and in observations of EWCs in action that there are some representatives who are still not clear about who they are actually representing.

A Swedish representative stated, 'earlier we had a problem with UK representatives. They didn't represent anyone except themselves. I asked them if they thought it was wrong not to be elected so they went back and had an election'.

The support of the union was also acknowledged as being very important, particularly as a possible source of funding for equipment, training and networking visits to meet representatives from other EWCs in order to broaden perspectives and disseminate best practice. In the words of a Belgian representative, 'if we are going to do a good job we need the support from unions. It's so good [*sic*] experience to talk to my colleagues in Europe [i.e. representatives from other EWCs]. It gives me so much more experience'.

Conclusion

Kværner project outcomes

When the Kværner project started in early spring 1997, very few representatives were connected to the Internet and e-mail system. None were connected to the

Kværner Intranet. By the end of the project in 2000, the situation was quite different. All Norwegian and Swedish local union offices (25 offices, ranging from 15 to 900 members) had more than one 'skilled' person (often three, four or all shop stewards) connected. Some local unions were developing an IT-strategy for their union, connecting members to home-based networks. Letters of information had increased enormously. One union was even sending out a weekly newsletter by e-mail. Communication modes that had seemed impossible before were being regularly used. Requests had been raised that Intranet-computers be installed in company canteens or other appropriate places so that employees might have access to the same information as the office workers.

All EWC members had access to e-mail and representatives kept in touch on a regular weekly basis, if only to exchange pleasantries. Daily amounts of e-mails to the two Group Convenors on the Select Committee were on average about 10–20. Some were responses to reports and messages they had generated and some were initiated locally. The Group Convenors had also established contacts outside Europe, mainly in China and the US.

During the radical restructuring of the company towards the end of the project, much networking took place and the communication infrastructure seemed to support this. EWC representatives were able to function at a heightened transnational level than previously. Two particularly positive outcomes emerged. One was that the language learning skills and ensuing confidence that had been acquired by those representatives who participated in the project were transferable and indeed an asset. An example of this was that a representative who had been sceptical about his own abilities to improve his language and technology skills 'at his age', was instrumental in developing Internet contact with shop stewards in two other companies that had been targeted for acquisition by several companies.

Some companies were bought-out by American and UK multinationals or by other enterprises, which used English as the company language. Representatives who had been part of the project and were now in another company felt that they could begin to set-up networks in their new companies and even lobby for technical hardware and language training. At the very least, participants felt they would try to carry on the spirit of the project by being more proactive in contacting other representatives within their new company. Representatives commented that they felt a sense of empowerment through growing feelings of solidarity, confidence and organisation that the project had engendered.

The second positive outcome was that it was generally agreed that the networking skills developed during the project had made it much easier for members of the EWC to keep each other informed and had led to a change in mindset of many of those who participated. EWC representatives were beginning to view issues in a broader and less parochial way and were looking much more at the 'bigger picture', having developed feelings of trust and mutual support. It showed that building a good communication network amongst EWC representatives in a global company was possible and desirable. Such a network would seem to build a sense of corporate solidarity and most definitely allows workers increased access to vital information. Within and beyond the company it deepened understanding of other workers in different systems and cultures.

The way ahead

It would seem from my experience as a partner in this project and from interviews and observations of EWC representatives in action that a much more strategic approach to language is needed if EWCs are to truly break down national borders across a multinational company and operate as an effective transnational body. The key issue to address would seem to be providing more opportunities for specific and targeted group training. Much more time is needed to exchange information and raise awareness of different social, cultural and political attitudes in order that a strong sense of group identity can be achieved and representatives can operate in an atmosphere of mutual trust, understanding and co-operation. This training, however, must be 'owned' by EWC members themselves if it is to be effective. Time is also needed to allow the EWC to develop its own identity, to be open and honest about the challenges it must face and open debate should be encouraged. Particularly discussion of cultural, social and political differences, in an environment of linguistic tolerance and awareness. Currently, because of the short time that EWC representatives spend as a group, such discussion, which would ultimately strengthen the group, is often not prioritised as more pressing company policy is discussed. This will be to the detriment of building a strong and united transnational forum.

If training is prioritised it should be defined by clear objectives and be delivered in a way which constructs a strong communication infrastructure. By developing a strategy for networking, by extending the network in targeted stages and capitalising on opportunities to expand it, such a strong infrastructure will be established.

These objectives can only be achieved by a strong commitment from central management to take their EWC seriously and to develop central policy to reasonably support its needs. It would seem that in many companies the issue of language should be addressed centrally in order to be beneficial to all employees who have language learning needs. It should also be learner-centred, using a needs-based syllabus and exploiting authentic opportunities to exchange information across the group on personal, social, cultural and company issues, thereby developing the communication network. It therefore would ideally be delivered by experts in the field of language for EWCs and trade unions.

Commitment is also needed from policy-makers to prioritise support for language and language-awareness training, particularly for workers from countries on the periphery of Europe and for those who have had negative learning experiences at school or few opportunities to learn another language. Trade unions also have a part to play in not only providing expertise but also by providing financial support to allow representatives more extended training opportunities. These provide the opportunity for networking with EWC representatives from other companies in order to spread best practice in organising across borders.

Finally, enthusiasm, commitment and vision are required to build-up and maintain the communication network and build a sense of corporate solidarity. Cross-border organising is possible and desirable, but to under-estimate the issues of language and culture may result in poor intercultural communication and a focus on diversity. In order to develop a truly strong body, EWCs need both time to explore diversity and support to help them develop ways of creating a sense of united transnational representation which can only be in the long-term interests of the workforce as a whole. It will also require the political will of all those concerned, policy-makers, trade unions, management and representatives, to recognise such issues as central to the EWC agenda and to devise a communications development strategy which is realistic, supportive, fair and which recognises that if training is required it must be specific, inclusive and above all, trainee directed and needs based.

References

Blommaert, J. (1997) 'Introduction: Language and Politics, Language Politics and Political Linguistics', *Belgian Journal of Linguistics*, 11: 1–10.

Blommaert, J. and Verschueren, J. (1998) *Debating Diversity. Analysing the Discourse of Tolerance*, London: Routledge.

Crystal, D. (1997) *English as a Global Language*, Cambridge: Cambridge University Press.

ECOTEC (1999) *Cost and Benefits of European Works Councils*, London: Department of Trade and Industry.

Hymes, D. (1974) 'The Ethnography of Speaking', in B. Blount (ed.) *Language, Culture and Society*, Cambridge, MA: Winthrop Publishers.

Marshan-Piekkarri, R., Welch, D. and Welch, L. (1999) 'Adopting a Common Corporate Language: IHRM Implications', *International Journal of Human Resource Management*, 10(3): 377–90.

Miller, D., Tully, B. and Fitzgerald, I. (2000) 'The Politics of Language and European Works Councils: Towards a Research Agenda', *European Journal of Industrial Relations*, 6(3): 307–23.

Pennycock, A. (1994) *The Cultural Politics of English as an International Language*, London: Longman.

Rampton, B. (1999) 'Sociolinguistics and Cultural Studies: New Ethnicities', Liminality and Interaction', *Social Semiotics*, 9(3): 355–74.

Tully, B., Porter, E., Eilertsen, R., Hansen, T., Myhre, E. and Utgaard, R. (2000) *How to Establish Trade Union Communication Across Borders in a Multinational Company: A Handbook*, Oslo: De Facto.

Part IV

The future of European Works Councils

The concluding chapters in this part return to the underlying theme of the book in assessing the limits and possibilities of European Works Councils (EWCs) in the context of the general development of the international labour movement. Such a focus reflects both the origins of EWCs and the area for which they have the most potential significance. As we have seen, it has been the persistent and continuing pressure of the institutions of European labour and social democracy that created the legal framework for EWCs. Employers were, in general, consistently opposed to the development and only a tiny number had taken any initiative before the Directive was in place and many have shown a marked reluctance to take action since. Employers have adopted one of three approaches. First, there are those that have been proactive and worked with their employee representatives in implementing structures that offer them some 'added value' in worker commitment through information and participation. This has involved the sharing and reinforcing of company values in a competitive global marketplace and employee support (or at least understanding) for restructuring where it has been necessary. Second, there are employers who have 'reluctantly acquiesced' to the Directive and sought to implement structures and processes that fit the EWC into the business and make it work for them. The approach may range from a recalcitrant minimalism to a more responsive marginalism with, in both cases, EWCs having limited impact on the organisation or its employees. Third, there remain the intransigent oppositionists who have not yet signed agreements or, where they have, they have done their best to make them inoperable and ineffectual. The approach of employers is critical if EWCs are to become genuine foci for consultation within companies but this is not to suggest that they make such decisions as if their trade unions were in absentia or that EWCs are divorced from wider developments in the global labour movement. It is to these issues that these final chapters turn and in doing so they highlight both the potential for EWCs within broader trade union strategies and the contradictions within them that restrict their role.

The chapters in this final part focus on the inter-related issues of structure, function and potential outcomes and the significance of training for EWC development. Structures provide a form or framework that supports or inhibits action and is, itself, a dynamic shaped by the actions of those that create the structures (see Chapter 3 by Miguel Martinez Lucio and Syd Weston).

Without the EWC Directive, few trans-company employee organisations would exist, but the Directive itself poses constraints and, potentially, even inhibits more dynamic developments outside of formal structures. In effect, the Directive creates contradictory opportunities for structures to develop that reinforce a Euro-centric, company focused, labour elitism or that extends the boundaries of organised trade unionism to provide global networks of support for organising and bargaining. Chapter 12 by John Stirling begins by reviewing how EWCs fit into national and global structures and looks at the limits and potentialities for their development as trade union based organisations. The chapter then reviews the significance of training for underpinning the development of effective communications within an EWC.

EWCs sit between national and global structures and our expectations of them are partly dependent on how effective these are. National works council systems may be structurally advanced (as in Germany) or virtually absent (as in the UK) and they may have a close or distant relationship to national trade union organisations. The new European Directive on national works councils will provide for some uniformity in national legislation although the differences in systems are likely to remain strong at least into the foreseeable future. Nevertheless, the Directive and its implementation provides a significant opportunity, particularly in the UK, to tie in European and national works councils that has the potential to increase their representativeness and responsiveness to workplace trade union organisation.

On the other hand, the institutional and legislative framework beyond Europe is weak and marginal for labour and tied to entrenched neo-liberal economics (see Chapter 14 by Jane Wills). The International Confederation of Free Trade Unions now dominates global trade union organisation following the effective collapse of the former Soviet Union-led World Federation of Trade Unions. However, labour remains a minor player in organisations such as the WTO (World Trade Organisation) and, where it does have a role, such as in the ILO (International Labour Organisation), the outcomes are often weak, difficult to implement and near impossible to effectively monitor. The initiative taken by the ETUC and the AFL-CIO to use the institutional framework provided by the Transatlantic Labour Dialogue (described in Stirling's chapter) has been described as offering 'minimal action in a weak structure' (Knauss and Trubek 2001). Although the authors were writing before the first transatlantic training programmes for EWC delegates and trade unionists in the US had taken place. Few EWCs have gone global, however this has not inhibited some from taking actions that have global implications, although not necessarily global support.

Jane Wills and Doug Miller in Chapters 14 and 13, respectively, take the argument beyond structures into analysis of action. In doing so, they are inevitably drawn to the work of the Global Union Federations (GUFs) and their role in providing frameworks for that action. If they are to take such a role then there are major implications for national union movements in terms of ceding decision-making powers and providing resources. At the moment grand sounding names and the membership numbers of affiliates conceal the often heroic efforts of tiny numbers of staff with minimal budgets to provide an effective role for the GUFs. That they do so is argued by one insider (Doug Miller's chapter) and through the strength of the case-study evidence offered by Wills, but both chapters also reflect on the contradictions and limitations of action.

Miller takes us closer to the relationship between EWCs and developments in global relationships between employers and trade unions. He focuses on the complexities of the global textile, clothing and footwear sector and the potential role of EWCs in the development of International Framework Agreements (IFAs). The international companies that Miller cites have adopted the differing employer strategies that we identified above and he concludes that some EWCs have been reduced to meaningless 'rump forums' that can only be revitalised through the admission of new delegates from the central and eastern European countries (CEEC) where the multinationals have transferred production. This, Miller argues, offers the hazardous potential for EWCs concluding IFAs negotiated with no representation from production workers at facilities located outside the European Economic Area (EEA). More positively, he cites the Code of Conduct agreement at Triumph International that involved national trade unions in Germany, the EWC and the European representative of the GUF. In offering these contrasting examples, Miller's chapter raises critical questions about the relationships between a variety of different codes and agreements, the NGOs and the trade unions and the key issue of 'who is representing who' and 'who has the authority to sign what'? These are not simply questions of rhetoric as agreements signed 'on behalf' of workers with no role in their formulation leaves them at best ineffectual and, at worst, counterproductive.

Jane Wills' chapter takes us beyond the negotiation through to the use and implementation of the Union Rights Agreement at the Accor hotel group. In her brief review of twelve agreements we can see that the complexities identified by Miller are illustrated in reality. One of the agreements is signed by the national trade unions alone, two by EWCs alone, six solely by GUFs and three by the federations in explicit association with the trade unions of a single country. The formal signatures on agreements do not necessarily reflect more broad-ranging trade union and worker involvement, but the agreements reflect the continuing difficulties in this area. Wills takes one of the agreements signed by the GUF as the starting point for her case study analysis with its particular focus on organising in a sector where trade union membership levels are often low. In doing so, she brings the book to a point that takes us beyond the European context and locates local organising in an international context and seeks to draw the connections between the two. This raises key questions for the future of EWCs and their role beyond Europe in a global economy and an internationalising trade union movement.

Reference

Knauss, J. and Trubek, D. (2001) 'The Transatlantic Labor Dialogue: Minimal Action in a Weak Structure', in Pollack and Schaffer (eds) *Transatlantic Governance in the Global Economy*, Lanham, MD: Rowman & Littlefield.

12 Connecting and communicating

European Works Council training for global labour networks

John Stirling

Introduction

There has been a consistent dichotomy in the analysis of European Works Councils (EWCs) that has developed into broadly optimistic and pessimistic traditions and these have been reflected in the other chapters in this book and in earlier arguments from ourselves (Miller and Stirling 1999; Stirling and Fitzgerald 2001). This is not the place to rehearse them again but rather I argue here for an optimistic view of EWCs as an important agency of trade union organisation and strategy that must ultimately break from their European constraints.

The significance of the establishment and development of EWCs can easily be overlooked as they become a recognised part of the institutional framework of European employee relations (see the Introduction by Ian Fitzgerald). Their small and insecure foundations in forerunners such as the first two founded by formal agreement at Thomson (France) in 1985 up to the forty-nine established before the introduction of the Directive in 1994 became the base for 739 EWCs in 1,865 multinationals (Kerckhofs 2002: 33). At marginally more than a third of multinationals identified as covered, in nearly a decade, there is more than room for a pessimistic assessment of the success rate. However, of the potential 17.1 million workers covered by companies subject to the Directive, 11.2 million (66 per cent) are in those with an agreement. Moreover, they are in the larger companies with operations in the greater number of EEA Member States (ibid.: 36). The enlargement of the European Union (EU) will expand the number of companies covered by the Directive and offer the opportunity for the inclusion of Eastern European representatives where they are not currently represented. It is already clear that there is a significant need for expansion in this respect. Kerckhofs' (ibid.: 65) analysis suggests that 41 per cent of companies with subsidiaries in EU applicant countries are without EWCs and only 15 per cent of those with EWCs already have representatives from them.

There clearly remains much to be done in formal terms through agreements and the establishment of effective institutional arrangements for representation and communication. However, taking a rough average of 20 members of each EWC (Kirckhofs estimates that 73 per cent have between 10 and 30 members, ibid.: 55) there is a minimum of 13,000 representatives meeting at least once a year across European boundaries in a way that was hardly happening a decade before. This is, however, well short of the sort of optimistic figures of up to 40,000 suggested by some early commentators (Miller 1999). There also remain key problems in relation to the terms of reference of EWCs and whether they are broad and inclusive or narrow and constrained as well as ever-present problems of communication (see Chapter 11 by Barbara Tully for example as well as the discussion here) and effective networking (see Chapter 3 by Miguel Martinez Lucio and Syd Weston). Training is a key factor in overcoming such problems and the Directive itself missed a key opportunity to regulate and support works councillors in this respect (Miller and Stirling 1998). Nevertheless, as was argued then (ibid.), the founding of the European Trade Union College (ETUCO) in 1991 and the subsequent development of the European budget line for training were critical for the success of EWCs. In spite of some employer hostility, training has continued to expand exponentially since 1998. It was suggested by Miller and Stirling (1998) (drawing on a 1996 analysis of Article 13 agreements by Carley *et al.*) that 23 per cent of agreements referred specifically to training provision, whereas a later analysis of a larger number of Article 13 agreements provides a figure of 35 per cent (calculated from the European Foundation database 2003). Moreover, two analyses of the later, Article 6, agreements suggest a reference to training in 31 per cent of cases (Platzer *et al.* 2001) and over 56 per cent in another (European Foundation database 2003). A survey of UK companies by Incomes Data Services suggests that:

> It is increasingly being recognised that representatives, especially employee ones, require a number of new skills if they are to perform effectively in their role. In the early days of EWCs, this was often not seen as a high priority, but there are signs that this may be changing. Originally, training was often limited to an initial familiarisation session, with little or no follow-up, but it is now becoming more widespread as the needs are more clearly recognised.
>
> (IDS 2002: 8)

Training materials are now available on-line through ETUCO in cases where representatives are denied the opportunity to work with colleagues face to face. It is also the case that, some employers have taken an opposite view to training where they see EWCs as integral to their business and have developed programmes that are funded by themselves and not reliant on EU budgets (Stirling and Tully 2002) and may not even have been referred to directly in agreements. Training not only provides the opportunity to develop skills and knowledge but is also an important factor in building the network of internal relations critical to the effectiveness of the EWC (see Chapter 11 by Barbara Tully).

The rest of this chapter places EWCs in the context of international trade union organisation and discuss the key question of communications. It is argued that training programmes are central to the development of effectively functioning EWCs and existing provision is explored as well as the potential for future developments that go beyond European boundaries.

Fitting in between the workplace and the world

It is not the intention of the Directive to provide the basis for EWCs to fit into a global network of trade union communications and there is, of course, no reference to trade unions themselves in the Directive. It is difficult to analyse membership or non-membership of trade unions as a characteristic of EWC representatives given the changing composition of EWCs and the neglect of non-union members in much research. An analysis of agreements (calculated from the European Foundation database 2003) suggests that less than 20 per cent of agreements use nomination by trade unions as a method for electing EWC representatives and less than 5 per cent use this as the sole method. Although, this is not, of course, an indicator of the lack of a trade union presence the extent of non-union employee involvement should not be ignored as it is likely to represent a significant role in EWCs in terms of numbers and influence. Moreover, trade union members have to develop a working relationship with non-unionists who might represent major sections of the company's employees. However, it is the trade unions and their members that have been the key instigators of EWC development and in many cases they are likely to provide a majority of EWC representatives. It follows from this and other factors that trade unions will seek to incorporate EWCs into their existing organisational structures and provide mechanisms of support as well as guidance on best practice. This is not a simple process as there is a range of potential players with the possibility of conflict between them.

In general terms, EWCs are company-based organisations whilst trade unions also have an organisational basis across companies in economic sectors and occupations. This can lead to dual organisational forms. For example, in the UK a complex structure of workplace representation via shop stewards and branches does not necessarily fit neatly into trade union formal structures focusing on a series of elected or appointed positions in local, regional and national committees. In Germany, the dual structure of its industrial relations is well established with formal and legal differences between workplace organisations based on works councils and trade union functions in areas such as collective bargaining. In other countries, for example in Scandinavia, these structures may be more integrated although workplace representatives may also guard their autonomy. Whatever the particular national situation it is the trade union structure that forms the basis for international trade union organisations and the workplace structure that is the basis for EWC representation. Such differences are blurred and coexist in national practice following longstanding traditions, agreements or legislation that have clearly defined roles even where the same individuals may occupy them. Thus, for example, the phenomenon of trade union dominance of employee-based works councils is commonplace in those countries where they exist. However, this raises complex issues for EWCs as new company-based organisations where trade unions seek to be the dominant influence.

The EWC sits between national workplace systems of representation, national trade union organisation and confederations at one level and the organisations of global labour – the European Industry Federations (EIFs), the ETUC and the GUFs – at another. Each of these might seek to develop policy options for 'their' European Works Councillors or offer advice, guidance or even instructions on whose status is dependent on an interplay of more or less agreed hierarchies and relationships. Moreover, the response to EWCs as new institutions was a steep learning curve for trade union organisations that might have had little meaning-ful advice to give in the early years of development. Finally, there might be an equal reluctance from EWC representatives to accept such policy guidelines. Inevitably, such arguments are resolved in practice as different organisations take the initiative or are ceded the initiative in particular areas and, consequently, develop an expertise that reinforces their acquired status. This is perhaps understandable in terms of the negotiation of formal agreements where external expertise and comparative information can form an important source of information and support. EIFs have played a key role in the development of EWCs and were signatories to almost a third of all EWC agreements and to 39 per cent of agreements in companies with more than 10,000 workers (Kirckhofs 2002: 53). The European Trade Union Institute (ETUI) has also had a critical role in the development and dissemination of information and research in relation to EWCs (Danis 1996). Elsewhere, however, the formation of networks and the agreement on policy and strategy might be less easily developed, particularly where communication barriers lead to misunderstandings of roles or where there is not established practice. (For the latter see, for example, the Chapters 14 and 13 by Jane Wills and Doug Miller, respectively, on the relationship between EWCs and the work of the GUFs. In relation to the former, training again becomes a critical issue and is discussed further in the next section.)

Communicating with each other

Tully's chapter develops an analysis of language and cultural awareness as a key factor in the development of effective communications and offers a case study account of the creation of a communications framework in one multinational company. Her argument can be further developed through a more detailed analysis of the potential communication links existing within EWCs and in relation to their external context. Stirling and Tully (2002) suggest that there are dynamic and flexible groupings internal to EWCs that are based on both the organisational and representational role of delegates. For example, a delegate might represent white-collar union members in a specific part of the business at a particular workplace. Groupings might fragment and reform to coalesce around particular issues and be further disrupted by organisational restructuring that sees delegates come and go. Informal communications often reinforced through training programmes that develop group cohesion become central to the maintenance of internal networking.

However, this focus on the internal dimension neglects the external framework provided for trade union representatives through their own organisations. These operate in terms of national unions and confederations and in relation to the international organisations already discussed. However, each of these organisations will have developed their own policy and practice in relation to EWCs and there is at least the potential for conflict between them. This might reinforce different approaches to the role of EWCs adopted by delegates with, for example, some delegates regarding them as a vehicle for raising terms and conditions of employment in their national branch of the company and others as an opportunity to influence central management decision making in relation to company structure.

The potential for simple confusion or genuine clashes of interest can be illustrated through a discussion of the role of experts on the EWC. The subsidiary requirements of the Directive allow for the EWC and its Select Committee to be assisted by experts of their choice and this has also been incorporated widely into voluntary agreements. For example, calculations from the European Foundation's database show that 197 Article 13 agreements (over half of all agreements in the database) allow for the attendance of experts at meetings by invitation. This can be increased if we include trade union officials as 'experts', or if there was data available for the consultation of experts by EWC representatives even when they are not in attendance at meetings. However, the Directive does not define experts, simply referring to representatives being assisted by 'experts of their choice' and leaving the interpretation very open although not in the sense that this must be agreed with management. It might be anticipated that experts would advise in relation to particular issues, for example, financial experts in relation to company restructuring or legal experts in relation to national laws in respect of redundancies. In a number of European countries it is common practice for national and local works councils to consult their own experts in response to company information. However, the Scottish and Newcastle case study (described in detail in Chapter 8 by Antonia S. McAlindin) offers an illustration of the potential difficulties that might arise in defining experts in the absence of guidance in the Directive. These difficulties relate both to communications problems and differences in national employee relations systems. The Scottish and Newcastle European Forum has strong roots in the UK and has a powerful presence from UK trade unionists. They are supported by 'experts' who are 'generalist' full-time officials from the unions represented by EWC delegates. Their expertise, as is typical in the UK, is in relation to the negotiation of collective agreements and the representation of the interests of 'their' members. They will also be gatekeepers that offer access to the specialist resources of the union such as the research department and they will be expected to have some general familiarity with the organisation and strategy of the companies with which they negotiate. They will not generally be expected to have financial expertise or a broader knowledge of company strategy in relation to Europe or beyond. The UK full-time officers' dominance of the 'expert' places on the European Forum was a source of concern to UK EWC delegates as it seemed to reflect an unfair weighting of the membership. They were particularly concerned to extend membership to 'full-time officials' of the French unions. This was already complicated by the membership of two different confederations: CGT and CFDT and the French labour code (supplemented by collective agreements) allowing for full-time union posts to be established within an organisation (Kerckhofs 2002). The French reps were not seeking 'generalists' to balance the UK presence but rather the support of 'experts' who might assist them with their understanding of the presentations on the company's accounts as they might use within their own national industrial relations system.

The confusion illustrated by this example is not simply a language or cultural one but derives from significant differences in industrial relations systems and trade union traditions. UK workplace representatives have little experience of information and consultation or the use of experts whilst it is common practice for their French counterparts. However, whilst this particular issue might be resolved through more effective communication there is the possibility of more challenging issues arising. For example, in the case of restructuring proposals that involve potential plant closures, then the selection of an expert from a particular country might be greeted with suspicion. In this context there is clearly a role for the EIFs and it is one that they are taking some steps to fill. Equally, the ETUC has a more general role to play in offering expert advice or research and information through the ETUI or training via ETUCO. This will require a shift in both authority and resources from national unions and confederations if it is to be successful in the long term and their willingness to meet that requirement remains an open question. Whatever developments take place in providing expertise externally it can only be supportive and complementary to the work of European Works Councillors themselves and in the development of their own expertise in which training has a crucial role to play.

Developing training

Until very recently the training of European trade unionists was a national undertaking and one that had come under considerable resource pressure after a period of rapid expansion in the 1970s (Bridgford and Stirling 2000a; Stirling 2002). As such, their were major potential difficulties in addressing the training requirements following the rapid expansion of EWCs in the immediate post-Directive period and, as Gohde suggested, at this early stage there were 'hardly any empirical results . . . from which a sound analysis of the objectives of training members of European Works Councils could be systematically derived' (1995: 261). As well as the immediate problems there were further issues in relation to long-term training developments that would also need to be confronted. The trade unions and their EWC members were challenged by a series of problems that had to be urgently addressed. These problems were related to resources, organisation and delivery; content; and pedagogy.

Resources, organisation and delivery

The first issue in relation to resources was and remains relatively straightforward: they are few and far between. Some finance was available from European budget lines although it was limited and on a reducing scale with restrictions on how it might be spent (Miller and Stirling 1998). Some employers were opposed to even this funding being available (see Chapter 6 by Richard Hume-Rothery) although others were willing to discuss training programmes with their works councils and provide resources and support. However, the money could only buy what was available and the dominance of national-based training and the relatively recent establishment of ETUCO meant that an organisational infrastructure for provision had yet to be established. Moreover, there was a mixed development of a European dimension to national trade union training programmes and, even where it had emerged strongly, the focus was not necessarily on EWCs which were a minority pursuit for most trade unionists (see the country contributions to Bridgford and Stirling 2000a). The delivery of EWC programmes could be met by a variety of agencies at national and European levels encompassing trade union-based organisations as well as public sector educational institutions, independent consultancies and employers. This has significant implications that are discussed in more detail later in relation to pedagogy and joint training

Alongside the key issues of resources were the usual practical issues facing those delivering training, although in a pan-European context they are compounded by costs, travel, location and language interpretation. In relation to each of these the commonest objective is, unsurprisingly, to minimise them. Thus, questions of where and when are normally dealt with by linking training with the regular meetings with the EWC. As well as the cost advantage in that only extra night's accommodation is required, there are pedagogical advantages in running training into meetings and offering the opportunity for the immediate translation of knowledge and skills into action. There is a timely relevance to the programme and the opportunity for social interaction. However, this 'relevance' can over-whelm a programme as participants are strongly focused on immediate problems and the exchange of current information so that programmes leave little time for reflection or exploring less 'topical' areas. Taking training out of this context but retaining a residential element offers the opportunity to develop responsive and reflective programmes that are less dominated by pressing problems.

Another problem with this mode of delivery is that training becomes confined to a short period (one or two days at the most) once a year. The Directive is unhelp-ful in supporting time off work in this area and needs strengthening through revision (see Chapter 5 by Willy Bushak). What is necessary is a longer term train-ing strategy based on a training needs analysis of the EWC and programmed development over a number of years. This will invariably be disrupted by company reorganisations and delegate changes but a core group of EWC members would gain considerably more benefit from this than a series of *ad hoc* responses.

Content

The next question was what precisely needed delivering in terms of content (Müller and Hoffmann 2001). First, there were clearly issue-based areas of knowledge development that were important in relation to the company itself, the Directive and the company's agreement and a comparative awareness of differences in industrial relations systems. Second, there were questions of personal and collective skills developments in relation to language, culture, teamworking and communications.

It was apparent that these led to immediate short-term needs that related particularly to understanding the Directive (and its national transpositions) and the development of best practice in agreements. The medium-term training issues for works councillors can be loosely grouped around the key issue of 'working together'. This category captures the diversity that is suggested above and characteristic of the loose groupings within an EWC and emphasises the centrality of communications and the development of mutual trust as the crucial issue for training.

These issues have coalesced around four main areas for the ETUC, which is a major training provider in this area:

- Helping participants to become more familiar with the different national bargaining systems of workers represented by the council, their possible impact on the expectations of representatives from other countries and the functioning of EWCs themselves.
- Various ways of overcoming the language and cultural barriers between representatives from different countries...
- Examining the problems that the workers' representatives encounter in working together on councils, and differing examples of representation in different countries.
- Compiling topics for potential co-operation and a comparison of best practices and solutions.

(LeDouaron 2001: 3)

There is a strong emphasis here on understanding industrial relations systems and building co-operation which are discussed later, but there are also issue-based knowledge questions in relation to the company itself that are part of the functioning of the EWC but often an integral part of training as well. The two key issues are in relation to dealing with the information that is provided and establishing an effective dialogue that leads from information to consultation. There appear to be continuing problems with information provision. Once it arrives it needs to be understood and management can, for different reasons, opt for opaqueness or transparency. Even in the latter case, there may be need for a specifically trade union analysis that can give a broader picture of the company's strategy in relation to competitors or a more focused review of, for example, a particular product division. The objective of training in the area of management financial data cannot be to turn individual works councillors into accountants. What it can do is help them to identify alternative sources of information – including themselves – and ask pertinent questions in response to the clues about company strategy embedded in financial data.

The dialogue with management around these issues can only develop within a context of trust that may be lacking where an adversarial relationship with management already exists. This may be more characteristic of US- and UK-based multinationals that lack a tradition of social partnership and information sharing more commonplace particularly in Northern European-based companies. In such cases data may be opaque or management revert to issues of confidentiality and market sensitive information. In this context in the UK there is often reference to 'Stock Exchange rules' not allowing for the disclosure of price sensitive information. However, in its consultation on national systems of information and consultation the UK government made it clear that the 'listings rules' in relation to company restructuring '...do not create an obstacle to... consultation because they allow companies to inform employee representatives in confidence about the proposals during the preparatory stage before they are announced' (Department of Trade and Industry 2002).

This example of an issue-based element in training programmes returns us to the key questions of communication and the establishment of mutual trust. As Stirling and Tully (2002: 2) have argued 'communications reflect and shape power relations and carry with them cultural identities that inhibit or enhance solidarities between European Works Council members'.

The issue of power relations is central here as individual EWCs may be structurally unbalanced with the opportunity for particular groups to be exclusive and dominant leaving smaller countries or occupational groupings isolated and disaffected. This may be reinforced by language and cultural differences that extend beyond formal meetings into the social relationships that provide the binding agency for effective EWCs. In such circumstances it is difficult to build the mutual trust between employee delegates that is critical to the Europeanising of the works council and developing a solidaristic identity (Lecher *et al.* 1999).

Furthermore, I share Gohde's early argument in his discussion of the content of EWC training programmes that 'direct, non-bureaucratic contacts between delegates from EWCs are an essential prerequisite for ensuring effective representation of trade unionists' interests' (1995: 267).

Clearly there are different communications networks, different modes of communications and a range of barriers to be overcome and only key issues are focussed on here (language is dealt with in Tully's chapter). Communications need to take place between delegates, between delegates and management and within and between meetings and effective strategies have to be developed in each of these areas. A particular barrier cutting across each of them relates to the understanding of different cultures in a general sense and, more specifically, in relation to industrial relations systems. Examples of misunderstandings are commonplace in respect of the different understanding of, for example, 'collective bargaining', 'shop steward' or 'works council' when removed from their particular cultural context. This can have considerable importance in communications when it is considered that the chair of a French works council will be an employer and that their German equivalent will be a worker. Training programmes have acquired a particular focus on this area, given its importance in underpinning effective communications.

Another key issue for communication within the EWC is the vexed question of team building which Miller has argued has 'tended to remain on the margins of trade union education in Europe' (1999: 356). Whilst there has been some avoidance of what might be seen as fashionable management-orientated training strategies there have been developments in team-building programmes for officers and officials in the UK and other trade union movements have been less averse to developing training in group dynamics and leadership skills. However, this inevitably raises questions of pedagogy in delivering training that might involve participation from union members and non-members as well as managers and shop floor workers.

Pedagogy

As well as the question of who might deliver the training, there were related questions of who they might deliver it to. As argued, EWCs are collections of interest groups that, more specifically, includes union and non-union members. In some countries and traditions there is a strong divorce between trade union education for trade unionists and joint programmes with employers. Elsewhere, for example, in those countries such as Germany, with works council systems, this distinction is less clear cut and trade unions may compete with public agencies and even employers for the provision of training (Stirling and Miller 1998). One outcome of this is that training programmes covering more than one EWC might be more likely to retain a trade union focus (although EU funding would preclude exclusivity) whilst training directly with individual EWCs would invariably include non-union members (particularly if employers were paying) and trainers and training materials had to adapt learning strategies to those circumstances. One example that illustrates this point is the development of team building.

Whilst team building is not specifically built into programmes it underpins the whole pedagogy of trade union education. In the case of the EWC, Miller argues that EWCs be viewed as 'learning organisations' and that the training agenda 'be approached in a collective sense *by and for the whole EWC*' (ibid., emphasis added). In one sense this is unavoidable, particularly where training is resourced in financial or personnel terms by the employers. However, the 'whole EWC' encompasses non-unionists and, very often, managers who might be mistrusted by union representatives. Team building training needs to recognise these tensions and the accommodations that will need to be made if the outcome is to conform to the inclusive model that Miller suggests offers the best opportunity for EWC development.

In this respect, the generation of trust is a two-sided process that raises a further question for the provision of training in relation to the involvement of managers. If the training is to be for the whole of the employee side of the EWC then it is likely that supervisors and middle managers will already be delegates and their inclusion in programmes is inevitable. In some cases these staff may be union members (although this might be in separate white-collar confederations) but they may equally be non-union or anti-union and even the direct managers of other participants. Senior managers who represent the employers' side of the EWC may or may not participate in all or part of the training either as 'experts' making presentations or as 'team members'. This may also change over time as in the case of Sharp which provided 'an initial three-day joint training session for both employee representatives and management...subsequent training has been mainly for employee representatives, with only the final day including management' (Incomes Data Services 2002).

This leaves trainers with potentially contradictory scenarios in which they may be seeking to build trust between employee delegates or develop skills that are challenging to management but with individual managers taking part in the programme. There will be different responses to this that are dependant on national industrial relations systems and traditions with delegates from countries characterised by social partnership having contrasting attitudes to those where adversarial workplace relations continue to prevail.

Finally, there are questions related to the delivery of programmes in a multilingual multicultural environment where tutors as well as participants may come from different traditions and have different expectations. Participative learning methods are now well embedded in trade union education programmes at the European level (Bridgford and Stirling 2000b) but the assumption cannot be made that they are widely accepted by EWC delegates. There is often a presumption of, and a preference for, expert-led and knowledge-based presentations and these are certainly easier to deliver where trainers are working with interpreters. There are also cultural norms in relation to participation that can generate misunderstandings and resentments if they are not understood. For example, questions of the appropriateness of making interruptions or a preference for presenting and defending a policy position rather than engage in open discussion. Inevitably, these cultural differences are added to if the tutor is unaware of them and when the whole process is slowed down by the need for interpretation.

In spite of the difficulties in development, the lack of resources and the problems of delivery, effective training remains central to the development of works councils at the European level and, if this is the case, then it is even more so if EWCs develop beyond Europe.

Beyond the boundaries

To paraphrase a commentator from a very different context 'what do they know of Europe who only Europe know?' Such is the subject of the following chapters by Miller and Wills but it is also central to the argument here. EWCs have a number of potential opportunities for development beyond the scope of their current activities although these may be restricted by both structural constraints and the motivations and actions of EWC participants. They may develop simply by doing the same but with more participant countries or they may seek to develop their activities into areas such as organising (Chapter 14 by Jane Wills) or negotiating global agreements (Chapter 13 by Doug Miller). These two are not necessarily mutually exclusive as the introduction of new country participants into an EWC offers the potential for developing other activities.

The key structural constraints on the development of EWCs beyond their European boundaries are fourfold. First, the Directive is confined to EEA member countries and there are no rights to the extension of its remit beyond that, although this may be agreed at an individual company level on a voluntary basis. However, there is also a limited opportunity here in that enlargement of the EU brings within the scope of the Directive many of the countries that multinationals have been extending into. The second structural issue relates to the company itself. If it operates within a narrow range of European countries then there is no opportunity for expansion and little point in doing so and, although trade unionists might seek links with other companies within a sector, this is clearly beyond the scope of any likely European legislation. The third structural issue relates to the interpretation of the Directive and consequent agreements in relation to the terms of reference of the EWC. Miller discusses this complex issue in more detail but it is clear that individual EWCs operate on a range that has been usefully classified by Lecher (2001) and his colleagues from 'symbolic' through 'service provider' and 'project-oriented' to 'participatory'. Each category offers broader scope for the development of action within EWCs and, potentially, for the involvement of actors beyond Europe. Finally, there are constraints imposed by the 'competition' in the sense that other trade union-based organisations such as EIFs and GUFs, might seek to fulfil the same role as EWCs.

Alongside these structural constraints are the potential limitations imposed by the EWC participants themselves. For employee representatives there may be a tendency to maintain existing (power) relationships that are exclusive and excluding and preserve a 'Euro-elitism' at the expense of other countries. They may also regard other countries as hostile competitors for jobs and wish to maintain their own access to management decision making and exclude those others from such influence. Less categorically, EWC representatives might seek a 'step-by-step' approach in which they view their own EWC as a relatively new institution in which they are still learning and developing policies and strategies. The introduction of other country's representatives might be regarded as a step too far at this stage of development although not for the future. That future might be regarded as a 'staged process' in which membership of the EWC could be extended by 'observer' status or through invitations to selected countries. In the latter case EWC growth may be more likely in connection with other developed countries with stable trade union movements and financial resources rather than with developing countries where there may be further issues of language and culture. Management will also have a strategy for the EWC that may be 'minimalist' in terms of its response to the Directive and reluctant to go beyond the legally established boundaries. There might still be perceived advantages in a divided workforce not being given the opportunity to meet and develop strategies of co-operation.

In spite of the potential difficulties there have been developments some of which extend back as far as the trade union world councils (see Chapter 2 by Paul Knutsen) of which the first, O'Kelly (1995) argues, was established at the then Danone in 1987 (following European developments in the 1970s) and at which Latin American delegates had observer status. Others which have grown out of

EWC developments and have been inspired by management as well as in response to trade union pressure. However, numbers are small and difficult to assess accurately. Moreover, there are differences between global groupings that have been established and resourced through the trade unions and those that have developed organically with management support via the company EWC. Indeed, there is the possibility (and some anecdotal evidence) that these organisations might clash with employers using their 'official' EWC to challenge solidarity action organised through trade union-based world councils.

The globalisation of EWCs in whatever way it might happen will pose even further problems for the development of appropriate training programmes. This is illustrated by the training programme developed by the ETUCO and the AFL-CIO as part of the transatlantic labour dialogue (see Knauss and Trubek 2001 for a discussion). The same problems of resourcing, organisation, delivery, content and pedagogy that was identified earlier in relation to EWCs were simply multiplied in seeking to deliver a programme involving trade unionists from the US and European Works Councillors. There is a further constraint in that there is no legal framework with global applicability giving workers rights to participate in training programmes.

Financial resources for the programme derived from State agencies in Europe and the US, trade unions and, indirectly, from employers in terms of time off work without loss of pay. These were, inevitably, restricted given that they needed to be extended to cover costs such as tutor support, materials preparation, administration, accommodation and transatlantic travel. Organisation was highly complex and demanding of time and resources given the desire to cover different sectors, match companies and work with and through trade union agencies and employers. Delivery was restricted to a four-day programme plus additional time for a site visit to workplaces owned by the companies involved. These issues were demanding enough but there were even further challenges in relation to planning programme content between tutors from Europe and the US with significant differences in priorities and pedagogies.

Programme content was eventually finalised around the key areas of comparative industrial relations systems and trade union organisation; company organisation and strategy; developing effective and sustainable communications and designing an action plan. Pedagogy was rooted in a shared assumption about practice being student-centred although working this through in delivery posed practical problems demanding pragmatic solutions. This partly resided in the differing approaches deriving from national industrial relations systems and cultures in general and attitudes towards company management in particular. Attitudes could not be assumed to be shared but had to be worked out in practice. Nevertheless, the training provided a catalyst for the development of continuing dialogue, information exchange and the potential for solidaristic action.

Conclusion

This chapter has been concerned with the future development of EWCs and the critical role of training not only in developing skills and knowledge but also in providing a space for the development of dialogue and the overcoming of cultural differences. There has been a major expansion since the inception of EWCs when there was virtually no training infrastructure and limited awareness of precisely what training was required. What has developed has had to cope with delivering programmes to trade unionists, non-unionists and managers and developing pedagogical practice that underpins the emergence of trust between participants. It is clear that independent trade union programmes remain an important priority but there remains little funding or resourcing and an ultimate dependency for much of the delivery on institutional finance from the European State. Nevertheless, clear training strategies have emerged and there is a widely accepted curriculum in terms of key course content issues. There is also some limited growth in extending programmes beyond Europe and involving cross-national and cross-cultural participation that will develop new learning strategies (see, for example, the comparative studies in Spencer 2002). Without training programmes as active agencies for development and action EWCs will be significantly weaker and less sustainable. It cannot resolve structural and organisational problems nor be a panacea for difficulties in building cross-cultural relationships but it offers the opportunity for developing the skills and knowledge to build a strong and effective EWC.

Acknowledgements

John Stirling would like to thank fellow trainers whose practice and argument has directly contributed to this chapter. In particular thanks to Barbara Tully and Sjef Stoop for our joint work with European Works Councils and to Andy Banks, Jean-Claude LeDuron and Teresa Conrow in relation to the transatlantic dialogue training. None of this would be possible without Jeff Bridgford's infinite patience, organisational skills and personal friendship.

References

Bridgford, J. and Stirling, J. (2000a) 'European Systems of Trade Union Education', in J. Bridgford and J. Stirling (eds) *Trade Union Education in Europe*, Brussels: European Trade Union College.

Bridgford, J. and Stirling, J. (2000b) (eds) *Trade Union Education in Europe*, Brussels: European Trade Union College.

Carley, M., Geissler, S. and Krieger, H. (1996) *European Works Councils in Focus*, Working Paper EF/96/65/EN, Dublin: European Foundation for the Improvement of Living and Working Conditions.

Danis, J.-J. (1996) 'European Works Councils', in E. Gabaglio and R. Hoffmann (eds) *European Trade Union Yearbook 1995*, Brussels: European Trade Union Institute.

Department of Trade and Industry (2002) *High Performance Workplaces: The Role of Employee Involvement in a Modern Economy*, Discussion Paper, London: Department of Trade and Industry.

European Foundation (2003) *EWC Database*, Dublin: European Foundation for the Improvement of Living and Working Conditions.

Gohde, H. (1995) 'Training European Works Councils', *Transfer*, 1(2): 258–72.

Incomes Data Services (2002) 'European Works Councils', *IDS Study* 722, London: Incomes Data Services.

Kerckhofs, P. (2002) *European Works Councils in Facts and Figures*, Brussels: European Trade Union Institute.

Knauss, J. and Trubek, D. (2001) 'The Transatlantic Labor Dialogue: Minimal Action in a Weak Structure', in Mark Pollack and Gregory C. Schaffer (eds) *Transatlantic Governance in the Global Economy*, Lanham, MD: Rowman and Littlefied.

Lecher, W., Nagel, B. and Platzer, H.-W. (1999) *The Establishment of European Works Councils: From Information Committee to Social Actor*, Aldershot: Ashgate.

Lecher, W., Platzer, H.-W., Rub, S. and Weiner, K.-P. (2001) *European Works Councils: Developments, Types and Networking*, Aldershot: Ashgate.

LeDouaron, J.-C. (2001) 'European Works Councils: Training for Unity between Representatives and Workers', Agora, July, Brussels: European Trade Union College.

Miller, D. (1999) 'Towards a "European" Works Council', *Transfer*, 5(3): 344–65.

Miller, D. and Stirling, J. (1998) 'European Works Council Training: An Opportunity Missed?', *European Journal of Industrial Relations*, 4(1): 35–56.

Müller, T. and Hoffmann, A. (2001) *EWC Research: A Review of the Literature*, Warwick Papers in Industrial Relations 65, Industrial Relations Research Unit, University of Warwick.

O'Kelly, K.P. (1995) 'The Future of Employee Relations within European Enterprises', in P. Cressy and B. Jones (eds) *Work and Employment in Europe*, London: Routledge.

Platzer, H.-W., Rub, S. and Weiner, K.-P. (2001) 'European Works Councils – Article 6 Agreements: Quantitative and Qualitative Developments', *Transfer*, 7(1): 90–113.

Spencer, B. (ed.) (2002) *Unions and Learning in a Global Economy*, Toronto: Thompson Educational Publishing.

Stirling, J. (2002) 'Trade Union Education in Europe: Emerging from the Gloom', in B. Spencer (ed.) *Unions and Learning in a Global Economy*, Toronto: Thompson Educational Publishing.

Stirling, J. and Fitzgerald, I. (2001) 'European Works Councils: Representing Workers on the Periphery', *Employee Relations*, 23(1): 13–25.

Stirling, J. and Miller, D. (1998) 'Training European Trade Unionists, International', *Journal of Training and Development*, 2(2): 108–18.

Stirling, J. and Tully, B. (2002) *Policies, Process and Practice: Communications in European Works Councils*, paper presented to the BUIRA conference, University of Stirling.

13 The limits and possibilities of European Works Councils in the context of globalisation

Experience in the textile, clothing and footwear sector

Doug Miller[1]

Introduction

In dealing with European Works Council (EWC) developments within a particular industry, there is a strong tendency to engage in an institutional analysis of the number, content and status of agreements in the sector. However, in considering the emergence and development of EWCs in the manufacture, distribution and retailing of textiles, clothing and footwear (TCF), such an approach would be both anodyne and apolitical. As Martinez Lucio and Weston (2000) have argued:

> Methodologically, the study of EWCs needs to go beyond the content of agreements, their structure or their pattern of bargaining, no matter how important these issues. The reality is that EWCs are shaped by the environing political and social context. The interconnections between different types of regulation, state support, political action and ideological projects will be crucial for the development of this new form of regulation. A broader remit in EWC research is not solely an academic issue but also a political one.
>
> (ibid.: 212–3)

For any conceptual framework to be useful in understanding the environing social and political context within TCF, both a macro- and micro-level approach is necessary. At a macro level at least three interrelated perspectives are relevant. First, in perhaps no other manufacturing sector has the process of globalisation been so far reaching and profound in effect and this can most certainly be said in relation to the European TCF industries (European Commission 2001: 366; Stengg 2001). Rapid advances in transport and communications technology in the 1990s have significantly paved the way for brand owners to outsource their production, whilst retaining marketing and design functions in-house. This process has been greatly assisted by an increasing mobility of international capital and the free trade policy of the World Trade Organisation (WTO). As developing countries have sought to attract foreign direct investment (McMillan *et al.* 1999), numerous export processing zones (EPZs) have been set up throughout the world offering generous incentives to, amongst others, European headquartered multinationals. Such incentives have included a relaxation of local labour laws. The outcome in TCF has been the emergence of a highly complex buyer-driven supply chain networks (Gerrefi and Korzeniewicz 1994; Dicken and Hassler 2000), which have resulted in a major increase in sub-contracting, particularly in the global markets for garments and footwear.

Second, it is precisely in these parts of the sector – particularly sportswear – that the employment relationship must be viewed from a gender perspective (Hurley 2000). Some 74 per cent of the global garment workforce is female (ILO 2000: 25). In many cases these women are 'lost' in a sub-contracting chain which, upstream, can become increasingly informal, resulting in extensive home-working (Gallin 2001: 225–7; Hale and Shaw 2001: 215; McCormick and Schmitz 2001; Balakrishnan 2002).

Third, in such a context of internationally competitive sub-contracting, the downward pressure on labour conditions is intense, leading to job insecurity, poverty wages, long hours, unhealthy working conditions, abusive management regimes, child labour and the suppression of trade union rights (for a general summary see ILO 2000). Against such a backdrop, industrial relations merits consideration from the perspective of mobilisation theory, which places emphasis on the relevance of *injustice* in the employment relationship (Kelly 1998: 64–5). Advances in information technology and the emergence of global campaigning networks (Waterman 2001) ensure that the major injustices which daily occur in the supply chains of the major multinationals are brought to the attention of those companies, their governments and their customers.

This chapter attempts to examine the extent to which EWCs can become sites of social unionism capable of mobilising either downstream and/or upstream in the supply chain to improve the situation of specifically female and child workers beyond the boundaries of the EEA. In order to address this question, it will be necessary first to consider, the particular strategies of EU and non-EU head-quartered multinationals operating both within and from the European Economic Area (EEA) at a micro level. The impact of such repositioning on the composition of EWCs will then be considered before finally discussing the limits and possibilities for EWCs to bring about changes in the way that their companies manage their supply chains.

The repositioning of multinationals in textiles, clothing and footwear in the European Economic Area

Europe is the world's largest importer of textiles with 40 per cent and clothing with 45 per cent of world imports. However, it has also been increasing textile exports as a share of world exports from 14.5 per cent in 1990 to 15.2 per cent in 1998, although clothing exports for the same period have declined from 10.5 per cent to 8.8 per cent (European Commission 2001: 20). It can be assumed that this trend of rising imports is likely to be sustained with the gradual elimination of import quotas under the WTO Agreement on Textiles and Clothing (ATC), which replaced the Multi Fibre Agreement in 1995. Between 1990 and 1995, Europe saw a fall in employment in textiles by 31 per cent and a further fall of 15 per cent between 1995 and 1998. In clothing, it fell by 35 per cent between 1990 and 1995 and a further 12 per cent between 1995 and 1998 (ILO 2000: 14–5). Employment in the European footwear industry has also fallen steeply in recent years. In 1994, it accounted for 325,436 direct jobs in the 15 member European Union (EU); since then it has fallen steadily, and in 1999, the total was under 300,000, 4 per cent down on 1998 (European Commission 2001). In summary, the TCF sector in Europe is characterized by a significant and continued decline in jobs and global market share, offset only by the marginal increase in textile exports (but not employment) in the 1990s. These job losses can only be understood in terms of the ongoing repositioning of multinationals within complex supply chains, forged on the anvil of increasingly liberalised and globalised market conditions.

Upstream in these chains are those MNCs specialising in the manufacture of yarn and components such as zips, for example, Coats plc now incorporating DMC (UK), and fabrics, Sara Lee/Courtauld (UK), Miroglio (Italy) and Chargeurs International (France). Downstream are the principal contractors, including multinational retailers, with markets predominantly in Europe such as H&M (Sweden), Marks and Spencer (UK), and European headquartered merchandisers with global brands such as Gucci (Italy), Triumph (Germany), Ecco (Denmark), Adidas (Germany) and Zara/Inditex (Spain). Other principal contractors operating in Europe are US-owned brands such as Lee and Wrangler belonging to the Vanity Fair Corporation (VF Europe), as well as, Levi Strauss and Nike.

These companies source their products in a range of ways. They may predominantly use their own production facilities as in the case of Coats plc, Vanity Fair and Levi Strauss. They may outsource their production and/or use cut, make and trim (CMT) facilities owned by sub-contractors that are, in some cases, multinationals themselves. With straight outsourcing, companies may go to multinational supply chain managers and logistics companies such as the Tibbet and Britten Group (e.g. Mothercare and Levi Strauss). A third form of supply management is known as co-sourcing. Here the sub-contractor buys the fabric and sells a finished product but the model/design is that of the prime contractor. Examples here would be Marks and Spencer, Adidas, Ecco and H&M. With co-sourcing, greater control is exercised by the retailer/merchandiser over fabric type, yarn, components and quality etc. Fourth, there is 'trade', where the model is owned and mass-produced by the manufacturer, and reworked by the prime contractor before delivery to market.

According to a study by IFM – the French Fashion Institute (De Coster 2002) – choice of sourcing by major MNCs reveals a distinct difference between north and south Europe. In the north, prime contractors in Belgium, Denmark, Germany, the Netherlands, Sweden and the UK appear to be largely drawn to

Asia and other global regions. In the south, contractors in France, Italy, Portugal and Spain mostly source still in Europe and the 'Euromed' zone. There is also a difference between the sourcing radius of European garment manufacturers and that of the brands and distributors. Garment manufacturers are largely 'proximity sourcers', with UK distributors in particular sourcing mainly from Asian suppliers, whereas global brands are likely to take an intermediate position. For example, Nike, Adidas and Reebok source their garments from countries in Central and Eastern Europe (CEEC) but sub-contract their athletic footwear principally from the Far East.

As the market for TCF is subjected to an ever-increasing liberalisation and globalisation, multinationals have restructured and rationalised in recent years. Clothing and distribution have been the subject of increased horizontal merger activity in medium-sized enterprises, while the larger firms have shed production capacity and in some cases whole divisions in a bid to systematically move production to low-cost locations. The tendency to restructure has been ever present in the sector since the 1960s and 1970s with shifts in production from the centre to the periphery of Europe. Greece, Portugal and Spain were all targets for investment prior to entry into the then EEC. In 1970, German shoe contractors such as Ara-Elefanten, Adidas and Schuh already sub-contracted work to Portugal. As the Community widened during the 1970s and 1980s to include Portugal, Spain and Greece, companies then began to relocate their production to CEEC countries and the Maghreb. Benetton and Miroglio, for example, sought out Egypt as a new source of supply. In the CEEC, there was the emergence of the 'Lohn' system where pre-designed and cut garments are sent to a garment assembler for outward processing before tariff free re-importation into the EU. This Outward Processing Trade (OPT) accounted for 11.3 billion Euros, which amounted to more than one-quarter of total clothing imports into the EU in 1999 (OETH 2000). However, MNCs have kept shifting the boundaries within the CEEC area and switched their sourcing from countries such as Turkey to Romania and Bulgaria. Whilst those European and US headquartered MNCs with owned production, such as Levi Strauss, VF and Coats plc, have engaged in major restructuring initiatives within the EEA/CEEC. For example, both of these companies have shifted jeans manufacture to the periphery – VF jeans wear now operates from Malta, Poland and Turkey whilst Levi Strauss has closed down its Belgian, French and UK operations to shift production to Hungary, Poland and Turkey.

European headquartered MNCs with a global market share have been involved in a process of 'de-verticalisation', which is effectively a decision to make no further investment in machines, factories and buildings and instead to focus solely on design, marketing and distribution functions within the EEA. MNCs such as Adidas, Benetton, Gucci and Triumph have pared down European manufacturing to a minimum, outsourcing much of their supply to the Far East, CEEC and in some cases Central America. This has had a major impact on upstream multinationals such as Coats plc. Originally straddling contract clothing, fashion retail, home furnishings and yarn and industrial products (yarn and zips) Coats

Viyella, as it was originally called, was forced by the decision of Marks and Spencer – a major client – to no longer source its product from the UK, to restructure its operations and concentrate on industrial and craft products. This means that Coats plc – the first company in the sector to set up an EWC in 1996 – must constantly chase the manufacturers and strategically locate bulk production of yarn where fabric and garment assembly is concentrated in the world. This has had a crippling impact on EEA jobs within the company and pressures continue to exist even on those production units in the company's core business within Europe.

These shifts of production from Europe to downstream garment assembly factories – which are generally clustered in EPZs in the Mahgreb or in the Far East, or low cost OPT locations in Central and Eastern Europe – has raised major questions about social responsibility, a point to which we return later.

The impact on European Works Council composition

Such repositioning has been accelerating during much of the period of gestation of the EWC Directive and has had a crucial bearing on the composition and activities of transnational worker representation within those EWC eligible companies in the sector. The European Trade Union Institute (ETUI) identified some ninety-two multinationals in the European TCF sector, which qualify under the terms of the EWC Directive (Kerckhofs and Pas 2000). Some of the companies identified in the ETUI database are conglomerates with substantial interests in other sectors. Taking those conglomerates with information and consultation forums out of the equation, there are currently some twenty-seven EWCs in the sector (see Table 13.1), which is approximately one-third of all eligible companies.

Some EWCs have since disappeared due to merger activity in the sector such as the acquisition of DMC by Coats plc, and Courtaulds by Sara Lee. Generally, EWCs have been set up in those companies with a strong trade union presence. However, in other cases, particularly US-owned multinationals questionable developments have occurred. In the case of Nike Europe, an Informative Forum for the Nike Europe Team (IFNET) is a company-driven initiative. In the case of the European jeans wear operations of the US merchandiser/manufacturers Vanity Fair (Wrangler and Lee) and Levi Strauss (Levis and Dockers), their process of restructuring has rendered their respective EWCs into 'rump' forums.[2] Reebok International has not yet established an EWC, although the deadline for the subsidiary requirements has clearly elapsed. In the case of Adidas-Salomon, which is headquartered in Germany, an EWC was negotiated in June 2002 to provide a European forum for those workers in the remaining administration and distribution functions within the company. In the case of both Adidas and Nike, the European Trade Union Federation for Textile, Clothing and Leather (ETUF-TCL) was not informed or involved in the negotiation of the EWCs.[3]

Where EWCs have been reduced to a rump only the process of assimilation of CEEC candidate countries can potentially redress this problem. To some extent

Table 13.1 Companies with principal activities in TCF, which have EWCs (March 2002)

Name of company	Country of HQ	Principal activity
ADIDAS-SALOMON	Germany	Sportswear
BERRY	Belgium	Carpets
CHARGEURS INTERNATIONAL	France	Wool based fabrics
CLARKS	United Kingdom	Footwear
COATS (inc DMC) PLC	United Kingdom	Thread and zips
ECCOLET SKO A/S	Denmark	Footwear
DOMO	Belgium	Floor coverings, fibres and yarns
ERICH ROHDE KG, SCHUHFABRIKEN	Germany	Footwear
FRANZ FALKE-ROHEN STRUMPFFABRIKEN	Germany	Hosiery, fashion wear under licence
GAMMA HOLDING NV	The Netherlands	Engineered and exotic textiles
GRUPPO TESSILE MIROGLIO SPA	Italy	Textiles and apparel
GUCCI	Italy	Fashion wear
IPT	United Kingdom	Textiles
KANSAS WENAAS	Denmark	Work wear, clothing
ROYAL TEN CATE	The Netherlands	Technical textiles
LEVI STRAUSS	United States of America	Jeans wear
LOHMANN GMBH	Germany	Adhesive, tapes medical textiles
NIKE	Belgium	Sportswear
ONTEX	Germany	Sanitary and Baby products
PAUL HARTMANN AG	Germany	Medical textiles
SALAMANDER	Germany	Footwear
SARA LEE	United States of America	Garments
SARA LEE COURTAULDS	United States of America/ United Kingdom	Textiles
SCHIESSER-EMINENCE-GRUPPE	Switzerland	Lingerie, Clothing
TRIUMPH INTERNATIONAL	Germany	Lingerie
VF	United States of America	Jeans wear
VINCENZO ZUCCHI SPA	Italy	Household fabrics, clothing

this latter process is underway in other EWCs, where the increase in OPT and the debate concerning CEEC applicant countries has been reflected in the efforts of the ETUF-TCL to negotiate seats for CEEC delegates to EWCs. Prior to 1996 non-EU delegates already attended proto-EWC meetings in some companies and Hartmann, Schiesser-Eminence Group and Coats plc each has CEEC representation on their respective EWCs.

A further issue relating to EWC composition concerns the question of gender. Although the gender composition of EWCs in the sector is approximately 50/50 the 'disappearing woman syndrome' still prevails in the select committees of existing EWCs in the sector. This is an issue, which the European regional organisation is keen to address in the future.[4]

European Works Councils and mobilisation at the micro level

As the process of restructuring within the European TCF sector continues unabated, the challenge for organised labour is first and foremost to intensify the internal social dialogue (Hyman 1997) within the labour movement on a number of inter-related fronts. First, there is the need for dialogue about the issue of EWC composition. Given the movement of production from core to periphery of the EEA, it is vital that existing EWCs, which have suffered as a result, are reconstituted and repositioned. This will not be an easy process given the state of trade union organisation in the sector in some of the candidate countries. Hopefully the 'acqui communitaire' status of the EWC Directive will facilitate this process as applicant countries acquire full membership of the EU. In this context the Maghreb must not be ignored as North Africa continues to play an important role in the OPT of the EU and key multinationals continue to source product from here. EWCs could at the very least move to establish observer status for representatives from those countries of source in this region, as in the case of the Sara Lee/Courtaulds EWC Agreement amended to include Moroccan colleagues.[5]

Second, internal dialogue needs to be further developed between the regional organisations of the Global Union Federations (GUFs) – specifically between the ETUF-TCL and UNI-EUROPA (the regional organisation of the GUF for workers in the service and commerce industry). Since there has also been merger activity in both distribution and textile services (work wear hire and laundry) within the industry, for example, the take over of Berendsen by the Davis Group of Companies. Furthermore, the 'capture' of transnational worker representation in the distribution sector is critical, since this is a key link within multinational supply chains in the sector.

Third, and related to this latter point, there is potential for extending social dialogue within an EWC on the issue of corporate social responsibility (CSR). This may be lent some weight by the European Parliament Resolution to proceed with a White Paper on the issue (Commission of the European Communities 2002) but most pressure has been exerted by the vigilance of the international trade union movement and non-governmental organisations (NGOs) which have successfully brought abuses of labour and trade union rights to the attention of the world's media and damaged the reputations of the global brands by direct consumer action in the high street and on the university campuses, where particularly in the US major global merchandisers are licensed to manufacture college apparel (Klein 2000). Most certainly, multinationals in clothing and footwear merchandising, manufacture, and retail in particular, now ignore CSR at their peril and have responded by issuing and attempting to implement corporate codes of conduct and have been forced in Europe to participate in multi-stakeholder initiatives such as the Ethical Trading Initiative (ETI) in the UK (e.g. Levi Strauss, Pentland, Marks & Spencer, Monsoon and Littlewoods) (ETI 2002); joint monitoring arrangements with national members of the European networked NGO the Clean Clothes Campaign (CCC) (e.g. C&A (Netherlands) H&M, Kapp-Ahl (Sweden) Auchan, Carrefour (France) Migros (Switzerland) (Ascoly *et al.* 2001). In Germany, the *Kampagne für saubere Kleidung* has taken a more independent stance in direct campaigns against Otto Versand, Triumph and Adidas.

Beyond unilateral corporate and joint company/NGO initiatives, the European regional Federation of textile unions ETUF-TCL has been active since the mid-1990s in addressing the problem of the maintenance of globally recognised employment standards in the supply chains of European headquartered MNCs. Regional framework agreements known as Charters (codes of conduct) have been negotiated with the respective European employers' organisations for CTF.[6] Significantly, the strategy for implementing the sectoral framework agreement between the European Apparel and Textile Organisation (EURATEX) and the ETUF-TCL involves specific promotion at those meetings of EWCs in multinationals covered by the terms of the agreement (ILO 2002). This has led to the negotiation of a small number of company codes with varying levels of involvement of the EWC, as at Hartmann,[7] Freudenberg[8] and Triumph International.[9] Beyond this the International Textile Garment and Leather Workers' Federation has been pursuing an explicit policy of negotiating international framework agreements (IFAs) on global employment standards with a number of targeted European headquartered multinationals (Miller 2002), and other GUFs notably UNI has an agreement with Carrefour.[10]

Looked at both from a European and global perspective, this plethora of existing regulatory initiatives presents a somewhat confusing picture and has not yet succeeded in instilling any credibility in the industry where CSR is concerned (Kearney 2002; Miller 2002). Furthermore the multitude of new actors in the field of CSR, corporate monitoring teams, NGOs (some involved in outright campaigning, others involved in monitoring) 'independent' auditing/verification agencies presents at times a confusing picture which detracts from traditionally desired methods of regulating the employment relationship (Justice 2001). Consequently the demarcation of roles between trade unions and NGOs, for example, has become blurred, often because some NGOs are broad coalitions of actors, some of whom consider themselves more effective advocates of worker interests than trade unions and some who are hostile to trade unions *per se*. Part of this reaction can be explained by an inability on the part of the trade union movement in the sector to accelerate its efforts to address the problem of women's under-representation within its structures given the feminisation of labour in major parts of the global clothing and footwear sector.

One company where the collaboration between NGOs and organised labour and the involvement of the EWC appears to have worked well is Triumph. Arguably it presents a case study of the way in which an EWC can play a part in linking with broader campaigns to pressure multinationals to face up to their corporate responsibility. The company had set up a manufacturing location in Myanmar (Burma), thus attracting the opprobrium of organised labour and numerous NGOs since the country had been cited by the ILO in relation to its failure to implement Conventions 87 and 98 on freedom of association and collective bargaining, and Convention 29 on forced labour. Following sustained and widespread global pressure for a boycott, the company finally ceased production in December 2001 and subsequently entered into an agreement with the IG Metall – the national union covering textiles and clothing (also a member of the German section of the NGO-based CCC), a representative of the European Organisation of the International, Textile, Garment and Leather Workers' Federation and the EWC.[11] This agreement, although termed somewhat confusingly a code of conduct, specifically refers to the EURA-TEX/ETUF-TCL Charter but is explicit on the duties of suppliers and licensees, as well as, an implementation mechanism. Carrefour, a French retail multinational, with its own private label clothing brand, presents a contrasting example of a company with an agreement which does not even cover the core ILO conventions and fails to include duties to disclose supplier locations, and implement and review the terms of the agreement.

This involvement of EWCs in codes of conduct negotiation constitutes a new dynamic of transnational worker representation at work and an example of a mechanism whereby the workplace activities of European trade unionists can be articulated with those of trade unionists and workers elsewhere in the world (Waddington 2000: 328). The IG Metall has even concluded that currently EWCs are the only international trade union structures capable of implementing the International Metalworkers' Federation resolution on codes of conduct[12] (although the situation regarding International Textile Garment and Leather Workers Federation (ITGLWF) resolutions is less clear). However, this is not an unproblematic development for the trade union movement. First, in the case of merchandiser and retailer MNCs, where, arguably the scope for negotiated approaches to the regulation of labour standards in the supply chain is greatest, opportunities to engage in social dialogue at this level may be limited. On the one hand, EWCs, if they exist at all, are either poorly organised in such merchandiser MNCs, or are removed from the interests of workers involved directly in production because only marketing, design and distribution functions tend to remain in Europe. On the other hand, because these companies have a global market and manufacturing presence, any attempt to regulate the issue of labour standards needs to be made at this global level. In this context, one may even question whether the concept of the Euro-company in industrial relations terms (Marginson 2000) is of any analytical or practical benefit at all in TCF. Second, there is the question of the legitimacy of an EWC to negotiate on behalf of workers in regions outside of Europe. In circumstances such as this, it may be more appropriate for those unions with representation on EWCs with a global reach to seek to work with the ITGLWF. In the case of one supplier MNC targeted by the ITGLWF for this purpose, a member of the select committee of the EWC is also a member of the global co-ordinating committee set-up to assist the process of information gathering and consultation in advance of negotiating an IFA with the company. In two other cases involving merchandisers with their headquarters based in Europe, preliminary talks about an IFA with the company have been brokered by the national affiliates.

Inevitably, such developments are beginning to throw up further questions. Specifically, what is the difference between a framework agreement negotiated between a GUF and a multinational and a code of conduct negotiated between an EWC and the European headquarters of an MNC? When and where is each relevant? What should be the role for trade unions in the promotion of each? And at what level should relevant negotiations be undertaken? What should be the appropriate procedures for initiating, negotiating and ratifying agreements with multinational enterprises? Moreover, how can the internal organisational dialogue be improved, specifically between GUFs with membership in the same multinational company? Finally, the ability of the emerging transnational social dialogue between companies and international trade union organisations to deliver on global employment standards will depend very much on the commitment of the central management of the company in question and its authority over its owned production facilities and sub-contractors along its supply chain. As the social dialogue inevitably develops on this issue, EWCs in retailer and merchandiser multinationals will have to take a global perspective and work through and with the relevant GUF. It is likely also that the relationship and demarcation between GUFs and NGOs will need to be clarified since those MNCs, which enter into agreements with EWCs and GUFs are likely to pressurise them into jointly denouncing some of the campaign activities of the NGOs.

Conclusions

This chapter has concerned itself with an examination of the limits and possibilities for EWCs, as emerging transnational worker organisations, to be an effective part in the regulation of abuses of labour rights within the global supply chains of the TCF sector. In a sector driven by the imperatives of globalisation, EWCs are limited by constant restructuring which impacts on both composition and the ability to develop a social agenda. Furthermore, merchandiser and retailer multinationals will be resistant to CSR initiatives, which seek to fundamentally address the issues of a living wage and excessive overtime in supplier firms, since improvements in these items will impact inevitably on profit margins somewhere along the chain. Multinationals in the sector are likely therefore to concede on these issues only if the debate on corporate social responsibility is taken to the multinationals as part of a co-ordinated campaign. There are signs that EWCs can play a *part* in this type of mobilisation. However, for this to be effective, the *internal social dialogue* between the main protagonists needs to be developed and intensified. This will mean greater collaboration between the GUFs with interests in the same multinational, more effective co-ordination between EWC co-ordinators, select committee members and European regional secretaries of the GUFs and a deepening of the relationship between all these parties and those NGOs, which patrol the sub-contracting chains of the multinationals in the sector.

Notes

1 The views expressed in this chapter are those of the author and do not reflect those of the ITGLWF.
2 Correspondence with ETUF-TCL regional secretary Patrick Itschert.
3 Telephone interview with Patrick Itschert, ERO regional secretary 12 September 2002.
4 Telephone interview with Patrick Itschert, ERO regional secretary 12 September 2002.
5 Report of ERO regional secretary to the Presidium of the ITGLWF Brussels 24 April 2001.
6 ETUF-TCL and Euratex Charter by social partners in the European Textile/clothing sector 1997 and ETUF-TCL and CEC (European Confederation of the Footwear Industry). Charter by European social partners in the footwear sector 1995, updated 1997 and 2000. European Framework Agreement with Cotance – the Employers' Association in the Leather sector regulating global tanneries 10 July 2000.
7 IGMetall (2001) Weltweit gegen Sozialdumping – Fur Verhaltenskodizes, Frankfurt: IGMetall: 4.
8 Interview with chair of the Freudenberg EWC.
9 DGB Bildungswerk (2002) Kampagne fur saubere Kleidung Rundbrief 1: 1.
10 Agreement between the retail multinational Carrefour and UNI signed at the European Committee on Information and Consultation 27–28 November 2000. Carrefour has a private label clothing range hence its relevance for the sector.
11 Verhaltesnkodex Triumph International 12 December 2001.
12 Bertold Baur (2002) Umsetzung von Verhaltenskodizes den gebotenen Schub verleihen in IG Metall/Hans Boeckler Stiftung/DGB Bildungswerk (2002) Verhaltenskodizes in multinationalen Unternehmen, Frankfurt am Main, IGM/HBS/DGB: 14.

References

Ascoly, N., Oldenziel, J.and Zeldenrust, I. (2001) *Overview of Recent Developments on Monitoring and Verification in the Garment and Sportswear Industry in Europe*, Amsterdam: SOMO.

Balakrishnan, R. (ed.) (2002) *The Hidden Assembly Line: Gender Dynamics of Subcontracted Work in the Global Economy*, Bloomfield, CT: Kumarian Press, Inc.

Commission of the European Communities (2002) 'European Parliament Resolution on the Commission Green Paper on Promoting a European framework for Corporate Social Responsibility', (COM (2001) 366 – C5-0161/2002 – 2002/2069 (COS)) Brussels: European Commission.

DeCoster, J. (2002) Trends in European Garment Sourcing, online. Available HTTP: http://just-style.com/features_detail.asp?art=528&app=1&fotw=sct (accessed 30 December 2002).

DGB Bildungswerk (2002) *Kampagne für saubere Kleidung Rundbrief 1*, Düsseldorf: DGB Bildungswerk.

Dicken, P. and Hassler, M. (2000) 'Organising the Indonesian Clothing Industry in the Global Economy: The Role of Business Networks', *Environment and Planning*, 32: 263–80.

Ethical Trading Initiative (2002) *Learning our Trade Annual Report 2000–2001*, London: Ethical Trading Initiative.

European Commission (2001) *Report on the Promotion of Competitiveness and Employment in the European Footwear Industry*, Commission Staff Working Document SEC (2001) 366: Brussels: Commission of the European Communities.

Gallin, D. (2001) 'Propositions on Trade Unions and Informal Employment in Times of Globalisation', in P. Waterman and J. Wills (eds) *Place, Space and the New Labour Internationalism*, Oxford: Blackwell.

Gerrefi, G. and Korzeniewicz, M. (1994) *Commodity Chains and Global Capitalism*, Westport, CT: Greenwood Press.

Hale, A. and Shaw, L. (2001) 'Women Workers and the Promise of Ethical Trade in the Globalised Garment Industry: A Serious Beginning?', in P. Waterman and J. Wills (eds) *Place, Space and the New Labour Internationalism*, Oxford: Blackwell.

Hurley, J. (2000) 'Global Supply Chains, Gender and the Challenges to the Labour Movement', *Proceedings of the Women Working Worldwide Seminar*, Manchester Metropolitan University Research Unit on Global Studies.

Hyman, R. (1997) 'Trade Unions and Interest Representation in the Context of Globalisation', *Transfer*, 3(3): 515–33.

IG Metall (2001) *Weltweit gegen Sozialdumping – Für Verhaltenskodizes*, Frankfurt: IGMetall.

IG Metall/Hans Böckler Stiftung/DGB Bildungswerk (2002) *Verhaltenskodizes in multinationalen Unternehmen*, Frankfurt am Main: IGM/HBS/DGB.

International Labour Office (ILO) (2000) *Labour Practices in the Footwear, Textiles, Leather and Clothing Industries*, Geneva: International Labour Office.

International Labour Office (ILO) (2002) *Codes of Conduct and Multinational Enterprises*, Geneva: International Labour Office.

International Textile Garment and Leather Workers' Federation (2002) *Draft International Framework Agreement*, Brussels: ITGLWF, online. Available HTTP: http://www.itglwf. org/displaydocument.asp?DocType=Links&Index=63&Language=EN (accessed 30 December 2002).

Justice, D. (2001) The International Trade Union Movement and the New Codes of Conduct, Brussels: International Confederation of Free Trade Unions, online. Available HTTP: http://www.icftu.org/displaydocument.asp?Index=991215157&Language= EN (accessed 30 December 2002).

Kearney, N. (2002) Interview, in *Trade Union World*, 5 May, Brussels: International Confederation of Free Trade Unions: 8–9.

Kelly, J. (1998) *Rethinking Industrial Relations*, London: Routledge.

Kerckhofs, P. and Pas, I. (2000) *Multinationals Database – Inventory of Companies affected by the EWC Directive*, Brussels: European Trade Union Institute.

Klein N. (2000) *No Logo*, London: Flamingo.

McCormick, D. and Schmitz, H. (2001) *Manual for Value Chain Research on Homeworkers in the Garment Industry*, Brighton, Sussex: Institute of Development Studies.

McMillan, M., Pandofi, S. and Salinger, B.L. (1999) *Promoting Foreign Direct Investment in Labour Intensive Manufacturing Exports in Developing Countries*, Consulting Assistance on Economic Reform II Research Report, Cambridge MA: Harvard Institute for International Development.

Marginson, P. (2000) 'The Euro Company and Euro Industrial Relations', *European Journal of Industrial Relations*, 6(2): 9–34.

Martinez Lucio, M. and Weston, S. (2000) 'European Works Councils and 'Flexible Regulation': The Politics of Intervention', *European Journal of Industrial relations*, 6(2): 203–16.

Miller, D. (2002) *International Framework Agreements in the Global Textile, Garment and Footwear Sector: Ongoing Action Research*, paper given at the British Universities Industrial Relations Association Annual Conference: University of Stirling, 4–6 July 2002.

OETH (L'Observatoire Européen du Textile et de l'Habillement) (2000) OETH report on the Textile and clothing sector, Brussels: L'Observatoire Européen du Textile et de l'Habillement.

Stengg, W. (2001) 'The Textile and Clothing Industry in the EU – A Survey', Enterprise Papers No2–2001, Luxembourg: Office for Official Publications of the European Communities.

Waddington, J. (2000) 'European Trade Unions Search for a New Agenda', *Industrial Relations Journal*, 31(4): 317–30.

Waterman, P. (2001) 'Trade Union Internationalism in the Age of Seattle', in P. Waterman and J. Wills (eds) *Place, Space and the New Labour Internationalism*, Oxford: Blackwell.

14 Organising in the global economy

The Accor–IUF trade union rights agreement[1]

Jane Wills

Introduction

Just ten years after the neo-liberal euphoria that accompanied the fall of the Berlin Wall in 1989, street protests in Seattle, US bore testament to an emerging current of international dissent. National governments, international regulatory bodies and global corporations have been quick to respond to this new mood of popular hostility and concern. The UN Global Compact was established by Secretary General, Kofi Annan, at the Davos World Economic Forum in February 1999 'to develop and promote the principles of human rights, labour standards and respect for the environment' (*Financial Times* 2000). This Compact has brought 12 Non-Governmental Organisations (NGOs) into direct contact with 50 leading multinationals, including such popular targets as Shell, Rio Tinto and Nike. The corporations involved have pledged themselves to nine principles that include support for human rights, trade unionism, anti-discriminatory practice and protection of the environment. In this regard, many transnational corporations (TNCs) have published codes of conduct committing themselves to responsible practice in employment, community and the environment (Diller 1999; Hale 2000; European Works Councils Bulletin 2000a; Hughes 2001; Pearson and Seyfang 2001). Yet, as Hale (2000) suggests, with particular reference to the garment industry, these efforts to promote labour standards are constantly undermined by the downward pressure on costs associated with global competition, led by the very same companies that sign up to corporate codes.

In the contemporary context, trade unions should be well placed to intervene in these developments and debates. New social movements are coalescing around questions of workers' rights and employment conditions in the global economy, many employers appear defensive about these concerns and many millions of workers recognise the need for self-organisation. By focusing on the importance of workers' rights at all levels of the global economy, trade unions can play a critical role in the emerging networks of global protest to insist that union organising is essential to the defence of working conditions. The fact that trade unions represent workers at a variety of scales, from the workplace to the national and international, means that they can contribute in at least four different ways.

First, rather than allowing companies to adopt codes of conduct that are simply statements of good intent regarding corporate responsibility, the Global

Union Federations (GUFs) are in a position to monitor the implementation of such agreements. Using their own networks of internal communication, and links to NGOs at the various sites of corporate activity, GUFs can ensure that particular codes of conduct are respected. Violations can then be used as leverage and campaigning issues to secure improved rights for workers along corporate chains. Moreover, the same networks can also be used to ensure that workers are consulted about, and involved in, the development of codes of conduct and any subsequent campaigns that take place (see Hale 2000; Hale and Shaw 2001).

Second, where global federations of trade unions have sufficient strength and the necessary channels of communication to senior management in any TNC, they can negotiate agreements that go beyond codes of conduct. Rather than statements of good intent, International Framework Agreements (IFAs – see Chapter 13 by Doug Miller) allow the unions a role in establishing the terms of good conduct and in monitoring developments on the ground. In this way, the IFA can endorse workers' rights and then act as a support to union organising efforts in different parts of the world. GUFs can ensure that workers' rights are respected, that information is shared, and when necessary, build alliances to force the company to respect its agreements.

Third, when many campaigns in the North are being fought *on behalf of* workers in the South, there is a danger that assumptions are made about the best interests of workers in different parts of the world (see Kabeer 2000). Campaigns about child labour or working conditions in the abstract can prompt companies to relocate or change their sub-contractor and so loose workers their much-needed employment. Global federations of trade unions are well placed to provide a bridge across geographical difference, between campaigners in one part of the world (often consumer activists in the main markets) with workers producing the goods in another. Dialogue can ensure that campaigns are built around the interests of those doing the work and in this way, the voices of workers in the free trade zones of the world can be heard alongside those of concerned Western consumers. By getting involved, the trade unions can ensure that the needs of workers themselves are the key determinant of any campaign. Moreover, in this context, the focus on workers' rights is critical as the freedom to organise allows workers to decide what is in their best interests.

Finally, by focusing on workers' rights, GUFs can also provide invaluable service in highlighting the violation of those rights in *all* parts of the global economy, not simply the South (see Human Rights Watch 2000). In this way, arguments about globalisation and working conditions can be 'brought home' to activists in the North. Whereas labour internationalism has often been viewed as an issue of aid and development, whereby rich workers in the North 'help' trade unions develop in the South, ongoing processes of globalisation are helping to break down these preconceptions (Waterman 1998). In the past, job losses in the North have all too often been blamed on so-called 'cheap' workers in the developing world and there has been no effort to build solidarity between workers in the two spheres of the world (Kabeer 2000). By highlighting the violations of human rights at both the centre *and* the developing periphery of the capitalist system, however, GUFs can begin to break down the notion that jobs are good when they are in the North and bad when they move to the South.

Moreover, genuine solidarity might involve unions in the North actually sanctioning the relocation of jobs to the South after negotiating agreements about the conditions of work and union involvement at the new site. In the wake of such relocation, a union could then ensure high levels of support for the workers being made redundant. Demands might be made for workers' education and training, business support and investment in the social economy. Such solidarity is hard to imagine, but when so much new investment is taking place in the South *regardless* of union protests, genuine solidarity might prove a means to improve the lot of workers, both in the North and South. Moreover, in forming such alliances, workers could find common cause for the long term. In every location employers and governments are generally hostile to trade unionism; manufacturing workers are threatened with the relocation of investment if they organise; workers are often on short-term or part-time contracts and have little job security; the time involved in meeting work and family responsibilities erodes the free time and energy for organising activity; migrant workers may not have the status they need to live without fear of deportation; and unions themselves have few resources devoted to organising new workers. By developing new strategies focused on workers' rights, trade unions might find ways to foster alliances and shared understanding between workers in different circumstances in different parts of the global economy (see also Ewing 2000).

This chapter seeks to contribute to ongoing debate about the ways in which unions can intervene to secure workers rights in the global economy. The first section briefly reviews the impact of globalisation on labour and a number of responses adopted by the international trade union movement. The chapter then looks at the implementation of IFAs by focusing on the agreement between the International Union of Food (IUF), Agricultural, Hotel, Restaurant, Catering, Tobacco and Allied Workers' Associations and Accor, the French-owned hotel chain. The chapter outlines the terms of the Accor–IUF trade union rights agreement (TURA) and then explores its impact through snap-shots of union activity in different parts of the world. The chapter concludes with some speculation about the future development of IFAs in the context of globalisation and new patterns of labour internationalism.

Trade unions and globalisation

As is well documented, globalisation has intensified spatial competition to attract capital. Sites of manufacturing production are often advertised on the basis of cheap, malleable and unorganised labour. Sites of potential service employment are increasingly marketed in the same way, most notably in the scramble to attract call centres and administrative operations in old rust-belt regions. In this context, workers' organisation is often viewed as an expensive luxury in the cut-throat battle to secure jobs and investment. In their efforts to organise, workers might be threatened by the possibility of capital relocation or victimisation, and workers are genuinely scared about losing their jobs. Moreover, large companies are increasingly sub-contracting most of their production activities, making it more complicated for unions to organise the workers deployed by any large company.

The international labour movement has taken a number of initiatives to respond to the challenge of globalisation. At the highest level, the International Confederation of Free Trade Unions (ICFTU) has led a campaign to get labour standards onto the agenda of the World Trade Organisation (WTO), arguing that trade should only be conducted with companies that abide by minimum social and environmental standards. These standards are to include workers' right to organise and secure collective bargaining, the elimination of forced and child labour, and the elimination of discrimination in occupation and employment (the International Labour Organisation (ILO) core conventions on workers' rights). The ICFTU has long sought to make compliance with these standards a condition of participating in world trade, governed by the rules of the WTO, with a role for the ILO in implementation.

There are, however, trade unionists and social movement activists on both sides of this debate (see Hoogvelt *et al.* 1996; Breitenfellner 1997; Hughes and Wilkinson 1998; Hensman 2001; Waterman 2001). While the majority would agree that there is a real need to regulate the actions of corporations and stop the 'race to the bottom', opinion is divided as to whether lobbying the WTO and using the ILO are the best way to achieve it. Indeed, as the WTO has led the process of neo-liberal globalisation it has little credibility as far as social and environmental standards are concerned. In practice, as illustrated by the limited social clause attached to the North American Free Trade Area (NAFTA), organising workers to exercise their rights at work, or to gain rights to organise if they do not currently have them, remains critical to the impact of any social clause on the ground (see Compa 2001).

At the corporate level, the GUFs have concentrated their efforts on building networks of workers within particular TNCs. A recent review has identified forty-seven such initiatives which represent 'the first steps, on the trade union side, towards the creation of structures within multinational companies for the conduct of industrial relations at world level' (European Works Councils Bulletin 2000b: 7, 2001). Concentrated in the metalworking, transport, utilities, telecoms and food industry, these corporate networks are focused on exchanging information, spreading organisation and monitoring codes of conduct. A number have also arisen through particular campaigns, such as the networks of unions challenging Rio Tinto; that built around a strike at Bridgestone-Firestone tires in the US; the solidarity network fostered in support of the Tate and Lyle workers at Staley in the US; and the response to Coca-Cola's actions in Guatemala in the 1980s.

This practice of labour networking in TNCs goes back as far as the 1960s but the ease of communication and travel, coupled with the new corporate environment, now makes it much easier to bring workers together. A number of these networks have also been strengthened by the 1994 European Works Councils (EWC) Directive that requires all TNCs operating in the European Union (EU) to establish new procedures for transnational information sharing and consultation with workers (see Wills 1998, 2000, 2001). EWCs allow workers to meet the senior managers of their companies, and as we will see, some unions are beginning to use the EWC as a means to raise issues of corporate responsibility in and beyond the EU. In the context of popular anxiety about globalisation, on the back of global union networks and the development of EWCs, unions are finding new space to bargain with TNCs about transnational concerns. This has led to the signing of IFAs such as the one between Accor and the IUF.

The Accor–IUF trade union rights agreement

The IUF has prioritised the development of IFAs and has signed agreements with the French-owned food producer, Danone and the French-owned hotel and associated services company Accor. Both are companies with strong traditions of social partnership and both have long-standing relationships with the IUF. While the Danone agreement is more comprehensive in scope, it is the Accor agreement that provides a better case for examining the potential of IFAs to improve workers' organising activity world-wide. Accor is one of the largest groups in the hotel, catering and tourism industry and it is best known for its Sofitel, Novotel, Mercure, Ibis, Motel 6, Red Roof Inns, Etap and Formula 1 chains of hotels. Accor is also active in the travel agency sector (and owns Carlson Wagon-lit), in casinos and in corporate services. The company employs more than 120,000 people in 142 countries, in at least 3,000 medium-sized and small hotels.

The hotel sector has traditionally proved very difficult to organise for unions in the North; jobs are often short term or part time, labour turnover is high, wages and conditions are poor and management is largely hostile to union organisation (see Piso 1999). In contrast, hotels have provided good jobs in some parts of the developing world and workers are well organised in countries like Barbados, the Philippines and Malaysia (personal interview with Ron Oswald, General Secretary of the IUF, 15 September 2000). The IUF does not have strong union membership in Accor and explains the TURA as a product of particular relationships with the Human Resources Department and the corporate image of the company. Signed in June 1995, the TURA endorses workers' rights to join trade unions and the company states that it will not 'oppose efforts to unionise its employees' (for the full text of the TURA, see Box 14.1). As such, local IUF affiliates can use the TURA to reinforce their organizing efforts and to challenge any managers who violate this agreement.

These agreements do not seek to substitute in any way for local or national collective bargaining. IUF agreements are, in essence, about organising and bargaining for 'space'. Once space for local trade unionism is secured through the TURA in this way, the IUF rely on 'active and energetic and militant local organizing to fill that space. If they don't we've done it for nothing' (personal interview, Ron Oswald, IUF, 15 September 2000).

The TURA is reviewed in a formal way at every annual meeting of the Accor EWC and this allows non-European concerns to find their way onto the agenda of the EWC. The EWC has delegates from IUF affiliates in Belgium, Germany,

Box 14.1 The Accor–IUF TURA

The Accor Group and the IUF noting that, in the global economy, all social and economic progress is contingent upon the maintaining of a society based on democratic values and respect for human rights; further noting that the hotel industry needs peace and social consensus in order to grow; being committed, therefore, to work in this direction, above all by the example they set; recalling the basic right of each employee to be represented and defended by a union of his or her choice; recognising the reciprocal legitimacy of the other party and its right to intervene in both social and economic affairs, while both retain their own responsibilities, to the extent that they comply with applicable laws, contracts or collective agreements; are therefore convinced that reinforcing democracy in the Group is the duty of both parties and that this implies both the recognition of differences over ways and means as well as the search for solutions through collective bargaining; further note that this goal requires, for its achievement, an effort at educating and informing the employees concerned and their representatives, so that they can better understand the problems, constraints and challenges faced by the company.

In this spirit, the Accor Group and the IUF shall undertake to:

1   Verify the faithful application by all Accor establishments of ILO Conventions 87, 98 and 135, pertaining respectively to:

- the rights of employees to affiliate to the union of their choice;
- the protection of employees against all acts of discrimination that tend to violate freedom of association;
- the protection of employee representatives against any measures that could harm them, including discharge, motivated by their status or activities as employee representatives, insofar as they act in compliance with applicable laws, contracts or collective agreements.

The Accor Group therefore undertakes not to oppose efforts to unionise its employees.

The Accor Group considers respect for union rights to be part of the good reputation of its brand names:

2   Encourage the management of subsidiaries and entities to allow union representatives to carry out their mandates and to have access to the same opportunities for training, pay increases and advancement as all other equally qualified employees.

Both parties agree that any differences arising from the interpretation or implementation of this agreement will be examined jointly, for the purpose of making recommendations to the parties concerned. The French version of this agreement shall be the point of reference.

the Netherlands, Spain, Portugal, France, Switzerland and Italy. This forum has been in place since 1994 and it was only formally turned into an EWC in June 1996. By integrating the EWC into the TURA, the IUF is successfully using the EWC as part of its weaponry for promoting union organisation across the group. In many cases, EWCs have remained focused on a managerial and solely European agenda and the IUF has identified a way to use the TURA to counter these trends.

In the following text, four key impacts of the TURA are explored in turn, drawing upon the experiences of affiliates in different parts of the world.

Opening doors for union organising

Wherever possible the IUF has used the TURA to try and secure access for their local affiliates to organise workers in Accor hotels. In the UK for example, the IUF held a number of meetings with their affiliates who organise workers in this sector, the General and Municipal Workers Union (GMB) and the Transport and General Workers' Union (T&G) and Accor managers, to discuss union access to workers in the hotels. A large number of the workers were found to be on short-term placements from Continental Europe, with little interest in union organisation. Others were found to be working for agencies, making it difficult to organise them for the long term. As a consequence, the unions have done very little to try and build organisation in the Accor chains and without such efforts, the TURA cannot come into play.

Likewise, in New Zealand, the Accor hotel chain is now very poorly unionised. The Service and Food Workers Union of Aotearoa (SFWA) has one collective agreement at the Novotel hotel in Auckland that has been in place for more than ten years. In Africa the IUF has raised awareness of the TURA with its affiliates and held seminars for Accor unions in 1997 and 2000. These seminars allowed union delegates to compare conditions and identify best practices across the region while also discussing ways in which the TURA might be put to best use. Likewise, the first ever meeting for IUF affiliates in Asia and the Pacific was held in 1998. The IUF sought to inform delegates of the existence and purposes of the TURA with a view to encouraging new efforts at organisation. It is clear from these examples that while the TURA might stimulate activity or reinforce new campaigns, union success lies in the strength of local organisation.

Developing the international dimension of everyday trade union practice

When a local or national union is planning to organise a hotel in the Accor chain the IUF now likes to be notified and involved in developments as they unfold on the ground. In May 2000, Local 274 of the North American Hotel and Restaurant Employees Union (HERE) targeted the Sofitel in Philadelphia for a union organising campaign. However, workers were frightened off by management actions and the union has not been able to sustain the campaign alongside others ongoing in Philadelphia. Without ongoing activity by Local 274 at the Sofitel in Philadelphia, the IUF is relatively powerless to force the company to concede recognition.

In a different way, the TURA has also been invoked in battles between the Australian Liquor, Hospitality and Miscellaneous Workers Union (LHMU) and Accor. Despite there being a national agreement between the union and employers covering the hotel sector in Australia, the 1996 Conservative Government introduced the means for employers to make non-union collective agreements with existing employees and to introduce Australian Workplace Agreements – which can violate nationally negotiated standards – at any new operations. The Accor management (assisted by Andersen Consulting) saw this as an opportunity to undermine the national award and did so by setting up staff consultative committees to discuss new terms and conditions.

As part of its campaign to resist this the LHMU was able to bring the TURA into play. The union accused the company of breaking the terms of the TURA by violating nationally negotiated agreements and by undermining the LHMU in the process. The union involved both the national trade union federation (the Australian Council of Trade Unions, ACTU) and the IUF in writing to the company to protest about the violation of nationally and internationally negotiated agreements. In addition, however, the LHMU was also able to develop a very positive relationship with the Construction, Forestry, Mining and Energy Union (CFMEU) that was being denied access to Accor construction sites for the purposes of union organisation. As a result of their actions the Accor management signed up to a *Memorandum of understanding regarding industrial relations between Accor Asia Pacific, the ACTU, the LHMU and the CFMEU* in October 1999. This Memorandum ensures compliance with the TURA and formally recognises the role played by the LHMU in representing Accor employees in Australia.

In recent years, the LHMU has also moved additional resources and personnel into organising and it aims to foster activism in each Accor hotel. While the national award has helped to protect terms and conditions in the industry, unionisation has traditionally been low, labour turnover is high, casual employment often reaches 50 per cent of all staff and many of the workers are from immigrant groups. As far as Tim Ferrari (Assistant National Secretary) is concerned, the existence of the TURA and the IUF 'helps to support activism and organising work, but in and of itself, it is no substitute for it. We see it as one element in a range of tools that can be useful' (telephone interview, January 2001). A new agreement at the Sydney Airport Ibis hotel seeks to develop a workplace culture that fosters employee involvement, excellent training, improved pay and conditions, union recognition and facilities for trade union duties. As this chain of hotels is further developed across the country, the LHMU will seek to replicate this agreement. By informing – and where necessary involving – the IUF in such developments, the union will also seek to spread best practice to other parts of the world.

Intervening to support union organising on the ground

As has been discussed, the TURA allows the IUF to get involved in local trade unionism, and when necessary, to intervene more directly. However, in at least two cases in Canada and the US, the TURA has also made a real difference to the outcome of union organising campaigns.

In the campaign in the US, the New York Hotel and Motel Trades Council (which includes a number of different unions in the sector) had a long-running organising campaign, including Court battles, at Novotel until the IUF eventually became involved, invoking the provisions of the TURA. To explore the possibilities of action, two union representatives attended the Accor EWC meeting in Geneva during May 1997 with a view to raising the case with the management and EWC delegates from Accor. This visit gave the union the opportunity to shatter the negative picture being presented by the managers in New York and to convince the European managers that the North American strategy was a disaster. In response, Accor's management appointed three new people to lead their operations in North America, and they promptly declared their intention to start negotiating with the Union. Moreover, as part of their negotiations with the company, the union pushed to include the new New York Sofitel in the discussions. The plans to build this hotel had been announced at the EWC meeting and the union sought to sign an agreement *before* the hotel had even been built. A dispute that stretched back to the mid-1980s was thus successfully resolved with the intervention of the IUF and senior management, and a union contract was agreed with the Sofitel as well as the Novotel, covering at least 400 workers in the two hotels.

The TURA has become an important organising tool in giving confidence to workers involved in campaigns that have been strongly resisted by management.

Fostering internationalism amongst the workforce

In many parts of the world, the hotel sector is staffed by immigrants, many of whom have traditions and experiences of union organisation that move with them as they travel to a new home. By integrating the international dimension into everyday union organising and practice in the Accor chain, the TURA is helping to awaken the latent cosmopolitanism of staff in the sector. Rather than assuming that the international dimension is too far away and remote from the everyday detail of trade unionism, it can be argued that it is the international scale that can help ignite interest in the very act of organising and participating in the union. The TURA can act as a bridge from workers in one place to those in another and thus help to reinforce the message of organisation.

Moreover, for workers who have already travelled across the world to end up working in a hotel, servicing other workers who come from different locations, the idea of internationalism is not an alien concept. Just as the hotel industry has to be open to other cultures, so too, the unions involved can embrace a progressive cosmopolitanism as a critical part of their strategy. The TURA can reinforce a celebration of the cultural diversity and rich geographical heritage of hotel workers, igniting the internationalism of their experience. Indeed, the Canadian hotel workers' union in Toronto has made much of this cultural heritage in their interventions around Toronto's bid for the 2008 Summer Olympics, using it as an opportunity to increase the profile of hotel workers and push for improved wages and conditions (Tufts 2001). The TURA is thus assisting this recognition of the power of cosmopolitanism by embracing labour internationalism in very practical ways.

Concluding remarks

The TURA between Accor and the IUF demonstrates the importance of bargaining for space for workers to organise in the global economy. Although many workers already have the right to join unions on paper, in practice, there are many obstacles put in the way of such organisation. Reaffirming and extending the right to organise through a union-negotiated international framework agreement provides a mechanism to support local organisation and prevent the violation of workers rights (see also Chapter 13 by Doug Miller). The Accor–IUF agreement has allowed the IUF to open doors for local affiliates to try and extend trade union organisation and has helped to reinforce trade union organising efforts in Accor hotels.

In this regard, IFAs between trade unions and TNCs are a robust way of enforcing corporate responsibility in the global economy. Most codes of conduct endorse the right of workers to join unions, but in practice, the code does nothing to actively support unionisation. If violations are identified they can be used in corporate campaigns, but the trade unions have to act from the outside to defend and extend workers' rights. In contrast, an IFA like the Accor–IUF TURA, gives trade unions the power to monitor corporate behaviour and act upon any violation of workers' rights *during* organising campaigns. As such, IFAs are a much more powerful way to reinforce economic justice alongside processes of globalisation.

However, the examples outlined in this chapter demonstrate that the TURA is only a small part of a bigger equation. Without active local trade union organisation, the TURA has made no difference to the exercise of trade union rights in the Accor hotels. In the UK and New Zealand, for example, the trade unions responsible for organising workers in the hotel sector have not targeted Accor chains and without such efforts, the TURA is largely cosmetic. In contrast, unions in Australia, Indonesia and North America have been able to integrate the TURA into their organising activities in Accor hotels. Indeed, the TURA has allowed the unions to develop a *multi-scalar* approach to organising, combining a focus on local hotel workers – and in the case of Australia, on preserving a nationally negotiated agreement – with the active support of the IUF. In instances where local managers have violated the spirit of the TURA, as in North America by hiring anti-union consultants and refusing to respect ballot results, in Indonesia by sacking strike leaders and in Australia by seeking to undermine nationally negotiated agreements, the IUF has intervened directly by contacting the group human resources department in Paris. The IUF has thus been able to offer concrete support to those organising on the ground. Moreover, in the case of New York and Toronto, this intervention has been decisive in shaping the outcome of local disputes.

In this context, the Accor–IUF TURA allows trade union affiliates to develop a spatially sophisticated approach to organising; developing specific activities and interventions at a variety of scales. As is illustrated by developments in Australia, a union might be fostering local organisation alongside efforts to defend national agreements that might involve alliances with other national unions, the national confederation of trade unions and a global trade union body. As such, this type of intervention echoes much recent academic literature about the scalar implications of economic change for people and place (see Dicken *et al.* 2001: 95):

> (A) distinctive feature of contemporary capitalism is its ability to operate on multiple scales, but none of these scales should, in themselves, be considered a privileged level of analysis ... Scales – including the body, neighbourhood, nation-state, region and globe – are mutually constitutive parts of a globalising economy.

Rather than assume that the international level becomes more important than the local and national in a global economy, it is argued that social actors have to develop a multi-scalar approach in order to tackle the challenges of globalisation. In organising workers in the hotel sector, for example, there is no substitute for local organising and if possible, for defending such activity with national agreements. However, should those workers be part of a TNC, there is also scope for using an IFA as an extra lever in supporting such activity and even in ensuring the activity is a success (for the scalar politics of trade union activity in relation to the Liverpool Dockers dispute see Castree 2000; and for the GM–UAW strike, see Herod 2000, 2001).

Whereas trade union internationalism has traditionally involved appealing for financial, emotional and industrial support for workers in a dispute, an IFA allows GUFs to get much more involved in active negotiations with corporate managers on workers' behalf. This approach allows the federations to develop a bargaining relationship with managers at the head office of a TNC, rather than having to respond indirectly through local affiliates and international campaigns. In the case of the Accor–IUF TURA, the IUF has access to the group human resources department and it can intervene in cases where workers' rights are not being respected. In this way, the IUF has greater practical significance to workers on the ground.

There is the potential to build on existing relationships between union members within TNCs which have often built up since the 1970s, to develop a more concrete and meaningful form of trade union internationalism through IFAs. Such activity will only benefit those workers employed directly (or indirectly if the IFA extends to sub-contractors) by TNCs but it also illustrates the importance of a rights-based approach to the struggle for economic justice in the global economy (see also Ewing 2000). Whatever rhetoric is adopted by corporations in their codes of conduct, or by campaigners in their battle against capitalist globalisation, it is critically important that workers have the right to organise on the ground. The endorsement and extension of workers' rights to organise can ensure that globalisation is humanised in ways that empower, rather than further disempower, those working at the most exploitative end of the global economy. Moreover, rather than building campaigns around what Northern activists *assume* is best for workers in the South, the IFA approach allows workers everywhere to decide what is best for themselves. The principle of self-organisation underlies these agreements, and although GUFs can encourage and support local organising efforts, the implementation of an international agreement depends upon unions and workers deciding to act. When they do so, an IFA can play a pivotal role in ensuring success. Moreover, it can provide a platform from which to build alliances with other social movements to fight for workers rights in a global economy.

Note

1 The research presented in this chapter is part of a larger project exploring the future of the trade union movement in the UK, funded by the *Economic and Social Research Council* (grant number R000271020).

References

Breitenfellner, A. (1997) 'Global Unionism: A Potential Player', *International Labour Review*, 136: 531–55.

Castree, N. (2000) 'Geographic Scale and Grassroots Internationalism: The Liverpool Dock Dispute 1995–8', *Economic Geography*, 76: 272–92.

Compa, L. (2001) 'NATFA's Labour Side Agreement and International Labour Solidarity', *Antipode*, 33: 451–67.

Dicken, P., Kelly, P.F., Olds, K. and Yeung, H.-C. (2001) 'Chains and Networks, Territories and Scales: Towards a Relational Framework for Analysing the Global Economy', *Global Networks*, 1: 89–112.

Diller, J. (1999) 'A Social Conscience in the Global Marketplace? Labour Dimensions of Codes of Conduct, Social Labelling and Investor Initiatives', *International Labour Review*, 138: 99–129.

European Works Councils Bulletin (2000a) 'Codes of Conduct and Industrial Relations, Part One', *European Works Councils Bulletin*, 27, May/June: 11–16.

European Works Councils Bulletin (2000b) 'Trade Union Councils and Networks in Multinationals, Part One', *European Works Councils Bulletin*, 30, November/December: 7–10.

European Works Councils Bulletin (2001) 'Trade Union Councils and Networks in Multinationals, Part Two', *European Works Councils Bulletin*, 32, March/April: 12–15.

Ewing, K.D. (2000) *International Trade Union Rights for the New Millennium*, London: The Institute of Employment Rights.

Financial Times (2000) 'Responsible Business', a collection of articles available at ft.com/responsible business, first published 14 November 2000.

Hale, A. (2000) 'What Hope for "Ethical" Trade Union the Globalised Garment Industry?', *Antipode*, 32: 349–56.

Hale, A. and Shaw, L. (2001) 'Women Workers and the Promise of Ethical Trade in the Globalised Garment Industry: A Serious Beginning?', *Antipode*, 33: 510–30.

Hensmann, R. (2001) 'World Trade and Workers' Rights: In Search of an Internationalist Position', *Antipode*, 33: 427–50.

Herod, A. (2000) 'Implications of Just-in-time Production for Union Strategy: Lessons from the 1998 General Motors United Auto Workers Dispute', *Annals of the Association of American Geographers*, 90: 521–47.

Herod, A. (2001) 'Labour Internationalism and the Contradictions of Globalisation: Or, Why the Local is Sometimes Still Important in a Global Economy', *Antipode*, 33: 407–26.

Hoogvelt, A., Cadland, C., MacShane, D., Ali, K., Barrientos, S. and Sum, N.-L. (1996) 'Debate: International Labour Standards and Human Rights', *New Political Economy*, 1: 259–82.

Hughes, A. (2001) 'Global Commodity Networks and the Organization of Business Responsibility: Insights from the Kenyan Cut Flower Industry', unpublished paper available from the author.

Hughes, S. and Wilkinson, R. (1998) 'International Labour Standards and World Trade: No Role for the WTO?', *New Political Economy*, 3: 375–89.

Human Rights Watch (2000) *Unfair Advantage: Workers' Freedom of Association in the United States under International Human Rights Standards*, online. Available HTTP: http:www.hrw.org/reports/2000/uslabor/ (accessed 30 December 2002).

Kabeer, N. (2000) *The Power to Choose: Bangladeshi Women and Labour Market Decisions in London and Dhaka*, London: Verso.

IUF (1997) IUF Seminar for Accor Trade Unions in Africa, Minutes, Geneva: IUF.

Pearson, R. and Seyfang, G. (2001) 'New Hope or False Dawn? Voluntary Codes of Conduct, Labour Regulation and Social Policy in a Globalizing World', *Global Social Policy*, 1: 49–78.

Piso, A.-M. (1999) 'Hotel and Catering Workers: Class and Unionisation', *Employee Relations*, 21: 176–88.

Tufts, S. (2001) 'Placing Workers in Urban Tourism Development: Boosters, Activists or Somewhere In-between', paper presented at *the Association of American Geographers Annual Conference*, New York, March.

Waterman, P. (1998) *Globalization, Social Movements and the New Internationalisms*, London: Cassell.

Waterman, P. (2001) 'Capitalist Trade Privileges and Social Labour Rights in the Light of a Global Solidarity Unionism', unpublished paper available from the author.

Wills, J. (1998) 'Taking on the Cosmocorps: Experiments in Transnational Labor Organization', *Economic Geography*, 74: 111–30.

Wills, J. (2000) 'Great Expectations: Three Years in the Life of a European Works Council', *European Journal of Industrial Relations*, 6: 85–108.

Wills, J. (2001) 'Uneven Geographies of Capital and Labour: The Lessons of European Works Councils', *Antipode*, 33: 484–509.

Index

For Product Safety Concerns and Information please contact our EU
representative GPSR@taylorandfrancis.com Taylor & Francis Verlag GmbH,
Kaufingerstraße 24, 80331 München, Germany

Printed and bound by CPI Group (UK) Ltd, Croydon, CR0 4YY
01/05/2025
01858362-0001